ONE PEOPLE

The Story of the Eastern Jews

ONE PEOPLE

The Story of the Eastern Jews

Dr. Dvora and Rabbi Menachem Hacohen

Revised Edition

with an Introduction by Abba Eban

Adama Books, New York

Translated by Israel I Taslitt ■ Designed by TUT ■ Photographs by Yaacov
Aviel, Anna Riwkin Brick, B. Carmi, Erde, P.J. Gross, David Harris, Z.
Kluger, H. Sadeh, Aron Zuckerman

The publishers and authors acknowledge their indebtedness to, The Israel
Museum, Jerusalem ■ The Museum of Anthropology and Folklore, Tel
Aviv ■ Heichal Shlomo, Jerusalem ■ (especially its curator J.B.
Bialer;) ■ Mahanayim (periodical) ■ Ariel (periodical) ■ The Government
Press Office ■ Reuben Kashani, Israel Yeshayahu, David Barzilai, for their
kind permission to reproduce photographs from their collections ■ and to
Beth Hatefutsoth, The Nahum Goldmann Museum of the Jewish Diaspora,
for permission to reproduce photographs in the chapters "Georgia"
(Museum's Archive) and "Ethiopia" (Doron Bacher, photographer).

Library of Congress Cataloging-In-Publication Data
Hacohen, Dvorah.
One People.
Bibliography: p.
1. Jews — Islamic Countries. 2. Jews — Balkan Peninsula. 3. Jews — India.
4. Islamic Countries — Ethnic Relations. 5. Balkan Peninsula — Ethnic
Relations. 6. India — Ethnic Relations.
I. Hacohen, Menachem, 1933 — . II. Title.
DS135.L4H3 1985 909'.04924 85-13531.
ISBN p-915361-18-3

Adama Books, 306 West 38 Street, New York, N.Y. 10018
Printed in Israel

5

CONTENTS

Introduction

Diaspora has been a central reality in Jewish history since the destruction of the First Temple in 586 B.C.E. Jewish communities were scattered across Babylonia and the Greek and Roman worlds while Judea remained the center of Jewish faith and worship. After the destruction of the Second Jewish Commonwealth by the Roman legions of Titus in the year 70, diaspora became the majority condition of Jews. They might sit by the waters of Babylon and weep when they remembered Zion, but they had become a part of universal history even if their original homeland stirred their deepest sentiments and their most poignant recollections.

The wonder of it all lies in the capacity of Jews to maintain a sense of common identity and kinship when all the circumstances of their history seemed to favor fragmentation. They had no territorial base, no unifying political institutions, no common vernacular, none of the cohesive factors that arise in human relations through the simple experience of living together day by day. All that they had in common was their devotion to an ancient faith and the experience of sufferings to which their very Jewishness appeared to commit them for all time. But they also carried their own memories, most of them tragic beyond compare, but lit up here and there by recollection of past glory. Their condition might be poor to the point of squalor, but in their own consciousness they were the descendants of kings and prophets who had once ruled and preached in Israel and made their nation an eternal influence in human destiny.

At the beginning of this century Jewish history was enacted mainly in Europe. Between the 1880's and the 1920's the immigration of two million Jews from Europe to America transformed the demographic pattern. Never had so large a proportion of the Jewish world lived under a single jurisdiction; and never had a Jewish community had so large an influence within an arena of world power. If we add Soviet Jewry and the communities of Western Europe to the great homeland concentration in Israel we find a tendency of Jews to live in large communities. Since the Roman period Jews have nearly always found themselves, whether by fortune or design, in Christian or Muslim environments, with little relationship to the faiths and cultures of the Far East.

There is therefore an exotic quality in the few Jewish communities that have maintained their identity on the outer margins of the Jewish world. In parts of India and the Chinese mainland Jews have tenaciously withstood the corrosive effects of their collective smallness and their isolation in order to bear witness to their legacy in distant lands. In doing this they have given eastern peoples a glimpse of Jewish faith and ritual. The general result is an assertion of Jewish universalism and the communication of a dignified picture of Jewish pieties to peoples who would otherwise have no idea of what Jewishness means. In Africa the genius of Jews in self-preservation is exemplified by the Jews of Ethiopia who cultivated their identity for centuries until the wheel of Jewish history brought them back to Israel — to the original source of Jewish creativity.

The central theme is the extraordinary paradox of unity in alliance with diversity. Different from each other in speech and ways of thought, in dress and manners, in color and in cultural habits, Jews nevertheless retain a transcendent

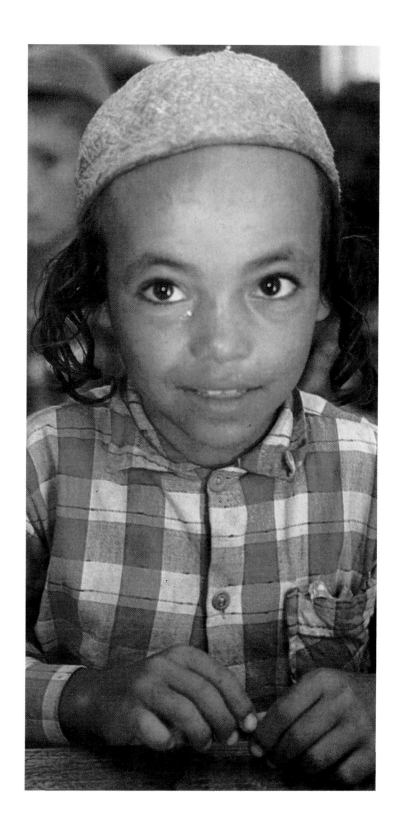

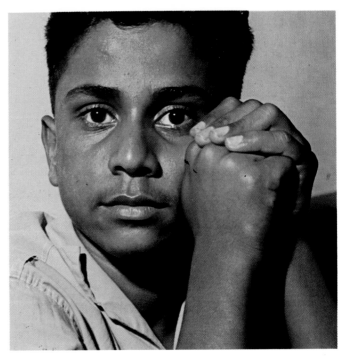

9

unity of devotion and of mutual responsibility. Israel, in which most of Eastern Jewry is now assembled, is a tapestry rich in the diversity of its component parts. In the constitutive moments of Israel's modern history the mass immigration from Yemen and Iraq gave its society a character that it had never known in modern times. Large currents flowed to Israel from North Africa. Egyptian and Syrian Jews found Israel to be a haven and shelter from the sad results of regional hostilities and tensions. From Salonika and Bulgaria Jews escaped the haunting memories of Nazi occupation and persecution. Each of these tribes of Israel faces a daunting challenge: how to preserve its own cultural individuality within the integrative process of Israeli nationhood. For they are now homeward bound: ''I will bring your seed from the east and gather you from the west. I will say to the north 'give up' and to the south 'keep not back'. Bring my sons from afar and my daughters from the ends of the earth . . . . ''

Jerusalem, May 28, 1986   Abba Eban

Iraq and Kurdistan

In the intricate tapestry of Jewish diasporas that span the past two and a half millennia, Iraq, the Babylonia of ancient days, is a golden thread. Shining brightly at times, invisible at others, it is a community with a poignant,unparalleled history unique in the annals of even such a people as Israel.

The history of this community dates from the latter part of the eighth century B.C.E., with the arrival of the exiles deported from the Kingdom of Israel by the Assyrians. The community grew substantially following the destruction of the First Temple when most of Judah's population was exiled to Babylonia. Ever since then, the sojourn of Jews in the country now called Iraq has been uninterrupted.

Even after Ezra and Nehemiah called on the exiles to join in the return to the ancestral homeland, most of them remained in Babylonia. Their numbers swelled following the period of Roman rule in the Land of Israel, when Jewish scholars moved en mass to Babylonia.

Through the years the community weathered the various vicissitudes that shook the Babylonian Empire: the Persian conquest, the sweeping victories of Alexander the Great, the threat of Greece and the removal of the threat by the Parthians, the fanatic rule of the fire-worshippers, the incursion of Islam and the establishment of the Baghdad Caliphate. Through it all they fashioned an impressive and imperishable legacy of scholarship to ensuing generations. In Nehardea, Sura, Pumbeditha and Mehoza they established *yeshivot*, academies of learning which produced great scholars who enriched the general Babylonian scene and enabled the Jewish community to influence the intellectual level of the entire country.

At the helm of the community stood the *Resh Galuta,* the Head of the Exile, a title and position reserved for members of the Davidic line and passed on from father to son. The responsibilities of the *Resh Galuta* ranged from judiciary powers to representing the community in the royal court. The backbone of the community was its rich complement of scholars and sages who made Babylonia a confluence of wisdom and erudition, both for its own sake and as a means of strengthening the community. Hebrew early gave way to the Aramaic vernacular, although it continued to be the language of documents and served as the language of letters with the sages in the Land of Israel until the failure of the Bar-Kochba revolt brought most of them to Babylonia.

Learning and diligence in worldly matters went hand in hand in this community. Jews engaged in all productive occupations, from farming and wood-cutting to seafaring, fishing and weaving. The more affluent were involved in trade and manufacturing, in pharmacology and medicine.

Throughout the Diaspora, Jews always fared well when their rulers were genuinely interested in the welfare of all their constituents. Such was the case with the last caliphs of the Eabas dynasty, who, in the twelfth and thirteenth centuries, integrated the Jews into the economic fabric of the land. The Jews who grew affluent, however, were perhaps foolishly ostentatious in their dress and mode of living, and attracted the enmity of the Moslem population. Fortunately, the invading Mongols look possession of the country in the thirteenth century and pursued the same policies towards the Jewish community as the Eabas Caliphs. A Jew, Sa'ad ad-Dawleh, served under the Mongols as Grand Vizier of the Mongol

Empire and contributed enormously to its economic growth. He brought so many of his coreligionists into the administration that the country became known as "the Jewish State." Ad-Dawleh's rise to power, however, aroused the envy and hostility of not only the Moslems but the Mongols, as well. When his patron died, Ad-Dawleh's enemies accused him of killing his patron. He was convicted and executed with barbaric cruelty. From that period until the conquest of the area by the Turks towards the middle of the seventeenth century, the lot of the Jews was generally very poor; entire communities fell prey to the insatiable sword of Islam.

Led by the Baghdadians, the Jewish communities strengthened their institutions. They established contact with the rabbis of Safed, and generated scholarship within their own confines. In time, Iraqi Jewry became the spiritual center for the Jewish communities of Persia and Kurdistan, who drew on Baghdad for matters concerning Jewish lore, litigation and liturgy. The truly Golden Age of Iraqi Jewry came in the century immediately preceding World War I, when the liberal government policy (in contrast to the general feeling of the Moslem populace) opened to the Jews major avenues to affluence and power; following the Revolt of the Young Turks, several Jews were elected to the Iraqi parliament.

The community was headed by the president, who dealt with secular administrative tasks, and the chief rabbi, known as the *Hacham Bashi*. In the nineteenth century, the community leaders established a social service association called *Shomrei Hahomot* (Guardians of the Ramparts), which organized free loan agencies, built hospitals, provided medicine for the needy and made Jewish schooling possible. Separate schools were established for girls, and attendance was in the thousands.

Kurdish Jews in agricultural settlements in Israel.

In contrast to this well-developed community structure, the Kurdish Jewish community, subject as it was to the whims and moods of the *aga,* the local ruler, was entirely unstructured. The Jews were his serfs and servants. All marriages had to receive the *aga*'s approval. Whenever he needed money, he merely sold some of his Jews into slavery. Needless to say, the insecurity of this life-style was not conducive to intellectual growth. Geographically, too, the Kurdish Jews were at a disadvantage. Long intervals would pass between the visits of a *mohel* or a *shochet* to a village. It was all they could do to get to the nearest town for High Holy Day services. In the towns, the rabbi was also the *mohel,* the *shochet* and the teacher. Schooling consisted at least in part of the older boys teaching the younger ones. Synagogues were usually built near a stream. Each worshipper had a pew assigned to him (in reality this was no more than a place on the mat-covered floor, located in accordance with his position in the community); the pew was handed down from father to son. At the entrance, part of the yard was roofed and fenced in with stone, and services were held here during the hot summer days.

Synagogues in Baghdad, on the other hand, were far more elaborate. They consisted of a roofless square courtyard and a pulpit in the center for the cantor. Around the pulpit, which was elevated by seven steps and covered, were benches for the sages, the legal authorities and the heads of the community; other dignitaries sat on rugs spread over stone benches built into the walls surrounding the courtyard. Off to one side was the ark, usually overflowing with Torah scrolls; Iraqi Jews considered it a great *mitzvah* to contribute a scroll to the synagogue. The scrolls were encased in wood that was either carved or adorned with gold.

The homes of Iraq's Jews reflected their economic and social standing. The homes of the wealthy, built in the Oriental Damascus style, were set amidst flowers and fruit trees; the rooms were ornate, the floors covered with rugs. Each home had one or two rooms for receiving guests. The women's quarters were in a separate wing. The flat roofs, made secure with railings, were used for sleeping on hot nights, and the houses were built so close together that it was possible to climb from one roof to the next. If the heat became too oppressive, the family could go down to the cellar, which housed, among other facilities, the private *mikve* of the head of the household.

A *Hanukat Bayit,* or housewarming, was an important and often flamboyant event. Sages and dignitaries were greeted at the entrance by the mistress of the house, who sprinkled them with water and kernels of wheat, for good fortune and prosperity. Once the house was dedicated — by the study of selections from the *Mishnah* and the affixing of the *mezuzot* to the doorposts — a meal followed and only at the very end of the festivities were the furnishings brought in. For added security against demons and spirits, some Jews affixed deer antlers and a horseshoe above the entrance.

The homes of the Kurdish Jews were far less pretentious. Furnisings consisted of mats, mattresses and a low dining table.

Food, on the other hand, was quite plentiful in Kurdish households, with lamb, vegetables and dairy products predominating. Burgul was very popular, and supplies to last as long as a year would be stored away in lambskin sacks. Vegetables stuffed with rice or meat and grain dumplings were the standard delicacies. The bread, baked by the women, resembled a large *pita;* in the hilly regions bread was

hardly eaten at all. Though meat was in abundance, fowl was a delicacy reserved for Sabbaths, holidays, and other festivities. A popular delicacy was cold chicken served with mushrooms and nuts. The men, unlike the women, generally abstained from sweets. They preferred *arak*, the milky-white liquer. For less potent beverages, they drank grape juice and sour milk. Tea and bitter coffee were reserved for guests.

Opposite: the traditional dress of Jewesses from Iraq was retained only by the older generation.

Both Iraqi and Kurdish Jews dressed like their Moslem neighbors. In Iraq, Jews followed the lead of the enlightened Moslem classes and adopted European dress; in Kurdistan, both Moslems and Jews retained the traditional attire — tall headgear brimmed with colorful scarfs, shirts with long, flapping sleeves, pleated pants, wide at the waist and tapering at the ankle, wide linen waistbands and a large scarf at the neck. Shoes were worn only by the more affluent; all others either wore sandals or went barefoot. The women dressed in wide-skirted dresses over striped pantaloons. The girls and young women, particularly in the provinces adjacent to Turkey, wore tight-fitting, embroidered blouses of black wool. Hair was usually worn in thin braids tied with ribbons or strips of linen. The wealthier women wore a multitude of pins and brooches that at times weighed as much as eight to ten pounds. In public, the women wore an inexpensive black cloak. Shoes and sandals became popular among the ordinary people only in recent times, as did the more modest versions of European dress.

Marriage was one of the major focuses of life. For centuries, girls had been married off at the age of eight or nine; the minimum age was then raised by the rabbis to thirteen. Because long engagements might lead to a change of heart on the part of the parents — and a broken engagement, like marriage, called for a formal divorce — engagement periods were limited to a maximum of one year. In Kurdistan, this period was extended for fathers of a groom who needed more time to raise money for the dowry. During the engagement period the groom was permitted to drop in to see his in-laws, but he had to send word ahead, so as to allow the young bride time to hide.

The rabbis limited the amount of the dowry which the father of the bride could demand. This did away with the practice of using the bride as a means of building up the family fortune. Restrictions were also placed on the value of the gifts that tradition bade the bride and groom to exchange. In more recent times, other changes came about as well. Arranged marriages became less prominent and parental consent became less important. When the parents of the bride objected to a groom, he simply "kidnapped" his beloved and the consent usually followed.

The Kurdish Jews, hungry for bright spots in their lives, made the most of wedding festivities. The preferred day for the ceremony was Wednesday, the fourth day of Creation, when the celestial luminaries were fashioned. The exact date was selected by lot. The ceremony took place in the home of the bride, to which the groom was led with much pomp. The bride, her fingernails painted with henna and adorned with jewelled ornaments from head to foot, sat in a separate room. Although she was not seen, her presence was made known by the tinkling of little silver bells set into her hair. A golden nose ring completed her attire.

The two were led forth from their respective homes, and as the two contingents met, a loaf of bread, brought by the bride's entourage, was broken above their heads. In some districts of Kurdistan, the bride was led astride a beribboned horse, preceded by a band of musicians and a torch parade. Friends and relatives of the

Kurdistani mountain Jews began immigrating to the Land of Israel about a century and a half ago. Below: this woman and her husband settled in an agricultural settlement, soon changing their traditional life-styles and dress. Right: a Kurdistani Jewess in traditional attire.

bride gathered on the rooftops along the route and pelted her with nuts and kernels of wheat, symbols of fertility. The ceremony consisted of the accepted ritual although in Baghdad, a piece of linen listing the items taken to the husband's home was held up while the *ketuba* was being read. When the whole party reached the home of the couple, a sheep was slaughtered as "atonement for groom and bride." The bride's family then returned home, while the groom's relatives sat down for the wedding meal. These festivities were always enhanced by the performance of the musicians, since it was considered a bad omen for the young couple if no musicians were present.

The splendor of the wedding was in sharp contrast to the drab life the young wife led afterwards. Her entire existence was subordinated to her husband's will. She ate separately, usually after her husband had finished his meal. Feasting, for her, meant eating whatever delicacies her husband chose to leave over. When the couple went out, the wife walked a few steps behind her husband. The husband never tarnished his dignity by helping his wife in her household duties.

A husband whose wife ceased to please him could pay her the amount written in the *ketuba* and divorce her. A wife saddled with a difficult husband could not as easily be rid of him. Kurdish men practiced polygamy, sometimes adding a wealthy widow to their household as a means of relieving economic pressures. In Iraq, a family with more than one wife was a rarity.

Rarely, if ever, did the woman venture beyond the confines of the Jewish Quarter. She spent most of her days knitting, weaving rugs and embroidering. The sole exception in a woman's humdrum existence came when she was pregnant. Although she continued doing her chores, she became the center of attention. The older women plied her with advice. She abstained from spicy food and consumed generous quantities of wine and honey, as a means of lending "character" to the life beginning within her. She was careful not to spill water on the ground — a precaution designed to ward off demons and spirits.

The birth of her child was attended by midwives, whose skill was so well-established that they were called in by Moslem women as well. If the new arrival was a girl, the news was broken gently to the father. A boy, on the other hand, was announced with shouts that would warm the cockles of the father's heart. The mother's bed and room were studded with amulets to ward off various demons and the evil eye. In Kurdistan, mother and child were also daubed with blue or yellow. No two new mothers were visited on the same day, and when paying the visit, the visitor always stopped off at his own home first. The third day after a birth was an occasion for a festive meal. The sixth night was considered the most crucial; it was then that the evil spirits were supposed to launch a major assault on the new-born babe. That night the child was put not in his crib but in bed with his mother. Neighborhood children gathered at the house with earthenware and watermelon rind that had been immersed in special water. They cast these on the floor, crying "*shasha*," after which they were given sweets and sent home. If the newborn baby was a girl, she was given a name on *shasha* night.

The circumcision rite was performed in the synagogue. The father was the first to

A young salesman of Iraqi pitot (left); this Kurdistani mountain Jewess and her children were part of the mass immigration of Iraqi Jewry to Israel in 1950 (right).

17

arrive, followed by the mother carrying the infant in embroidered dress. Musicians played and sang. The ceremony took place after the morning service. "Elijah's Chair," on which the ceremony was performed, was decorated with expensive silks, flowers, myrtle branches and a pair of Torah crowns.

In Kurdish villages, the crib was made of strong, rough linen and suspended from the ceiling. The child was breast-fed for two years and this was his sole nourishment. The appearance of the first tooth was a special occasion, marked with a festive gathering of the family, sweets for the children and portions of porridge for the poor.

The death of any individual Jew cast a pall on the entire community. In Iraq, the family of the deceased immediately sent word to the synagogue, where the news would be announced. In Kurdistan, a herald with an armband marked "Mourning" was dispatched through the streets. With a black flag in one hand, he announced the sad news, at which the friends and relatives immediately went to the deceased's home. The women lamented shrilly, cast mud on their heads and shoulders and scratched their faces. If the deceased was a young man engaged to be married, the women sang wedding songs, broken by wailing and keening.

In Baghdad it was customary to recite *kaddish* as the deceased was carried from the house, rather than after interment. The bier was circled seven times and *kaddish* recited each time. Eulogies were made only if the departed was a rabbi or a dignitary. Women were not allowed to participate in funerals.

In Kurdistan, cemeteries were on a hillock outside the walls of the town. The more important members of the community were buried higher up on the slope. The graves had no tombstones, but each was surrounded with four low stone enclosures. In Iraq, a tombstone was set on the eighth day; the name and merits of the departed were inscribed on a sheet of paper which was then imbedded, under glass, in the brick-and-mortar stone.

All through the *shiva* period, the house of the departed was full of people who came to console the bereaved. Iraqi Jews donned black the entire year of mourning, until the rabbis forbade it about a century ago. Nevertheless, the expressions of grief were obvious in many ways: the members of the family abstained not only from happy occasions but also from the purchase of new clothing, food delicacies, the use of ornaments and — quarreling.

In Baghdad, relatives of the deceased and the poor were given certain kinds of cookies during the first eight days of the month of Av, in atonement for the sins of the departed. On Hanukah, a pastry of flour and sugar was eaten by anyone to whom the deceased had owed a debt of any kind. At the end of the year, the name of the deceased was enshrined on a Torah scroll. Memorial synagogues were built by the wealthy in memory of departed family members.

Sabbaths and holidays regularly sustained the community. In Kurdistan, the advent of the Sabbath was announced with the blowing of the *shofar*, at which the women hastened to light the Sabbath lamps (wicks dipped in oil-filled vases of earthenware or glass). On Saturday, services and meals were similar to those of Jews the world over, centering on the *chamin*. Sabbath afternoon was set aside for visiting the homes of newborn infants, brides, grooms, and mourners. The women, dressed in their finery, gathered in the courtyards for lively chats. The men came together for a sip of *arak*, a bit of cold food, and tales of courage and valor.

A Kurdistani Jewess in traditional garb.

Passover was the high point of the year's festivities. Preparations for the holiday were so difficult for the women that they called it *az frihli,* "the festival of falling apart." But the results were worth the effort. In Kurdistan, Jews who lived in the villages went to the large towns to celebrate the *Seder,* and it was not unusual for as many as forty families to gather at one *Seder.* The host — the *mori psacha* — did his best to surpass other hosts in the number of guests at his table. Passover was also an occasion for acquiring new clothes — to the point that the Great Sabbath, just before Passover, when these clothes were first paraded about, was called "Fashion Show Sabbath."

Matza shmura, unleavened bread prepared from special wheat, was baked by the men; fuel for the oven consisted of myrtle branches and palm fronds saved from the previous Sukkot. In preparing for the *Seder,* the host covered the *Seder* plate with fine silk, on top of which he placed a copy of the Zohar, the ancient treatise on Jewish mysticism. The *Seder* table resembled others throughout the Jewish world, except that there was no "Cup of Elijah." On returning from the synagogue, the men kissed the Zohar before sitting down to the *Seder,* the host being the last to do so.

Baghdad Jews used to recite the opening lines of the *Hagadah,* the *Ha lachma,* six times — three in Hebrew and three in Arabic. The young children then lined up in front of the host, and he asked them: "From where are you coming?" and they replied: "From Egypt." "And where are you going?" he continued. "To Jerusalem." "And what food do you have for your way?" At this, the children returned to their seats and recited the traditional four questions, *Ma Nishtana.* In Kurdistan, the men raised the *Seder* plate and moved about in the form of dance; at the recital of the words "free men," the entire assemblage broke out into cheers. When singing the traditional *Seder* song, *Dayenu,* it was customary for everyone present to pelt each other with green onions.

The focal point of the Shavuot celebration was a visit to the tombs of holy men, which also gave the festival its local name, *zeira,* or "pilgrimage." Iraqi Jews visited the tomb of Ezekiel, reputedly located at Kiffil, and the tomb of Ezra. Kurdish Jews visited the alleged tomb of Jonah, in Mossul. The town of Alkosh was the purported burial place of the prophet Nahum. Crowds also visited Elijah's Cave at Bet-Tanura and Daniel's tomb in Kirkuk. The Jewish communities in those places provided food and shelter for the pilgrims.

One unusual Shavuot custom was to spray water from the roof tops on passersby below.

On Sukkot, Kurdish Jews built communal *sukkot,* with several families sharing one. In Baghdad, every household had its own. Owning a splendid *etrog* was a matter of status and involved a large expenditure. The poor, therefore, paid early-morning visits to the homes of the more affluent in order to pronounce the benediction over the *etrog* and *lulav.* Simhat Torah brought to all the Jews their highest moments of ecstasy. As the men went around and around in the *hakafot,* the women sprayed them with fragrant water. The small children, prayer book in hand, were carried aloft on their fathers' shoulders.

The month of Elul, preceding the High Holy Days, cast a pall on the community, but the *Shofar* was not blown then, as it is in other Jewish communities, so as not to diminish its impact on Rosh Hashanah. On Rosh Hashanah eve, it was customary to eat fruits and vegetables with some relevance to the Day of Judgment. For Yom Kippur, *kaparot* consisted of a hen for each individual; the wealthy made use of sheep. Preceding the service, in Kurdistan, the cantor applied a penitential lash to all who wished to be cleansed of their transgressions. *Kol Nidre* was recited three times in Hebrew and three times in Arabic, so that everyone would understand its meaning. Women who could find no room in their gallery in the synagogue gathered on the rooftops of the adjacent houses.

For the ninth of Ab, Baghdad's Jews recited, "By the waters of Babylon" and other laments peculiar to Iraqi Jewry. In the synagogue, the cantor described the fall of Jerusalem and the desolation of Judea in moving tones. In Kurdistan, it was customary to slaughter a cow, as a sign of penitence, and distribute the meat among the poor.

Hanukah received little attention, except for the prescribed liturgy and ritual. The *menorah* was made of plain metal or clay. Hanukah candles were given out by teachers to their pupils to mark the occasion.

Tu Bishevat in Baghdad was an occasion for eating the fruits grown in the Land of Israel. In Kurdistan, however, it was also celebrated as the festival of fertile crops. In exchanging good wishes for bountiful harvests, the Jews sent each other bowls of fruit containing as many as thirty varieties.

Purim was the holiday of the *majala,* i.e., the *megillah* (scroll) of Esther (the Arabs called it the "holiday of playing cards," since card playing was once used as a camouflage for clandestine study of the Torah). Haman was beaten and burned in effigy.

In addition to the traditional Purim, Iraqi Jews also celebrated local "Purim" days on the eleventh of Av and the sixteenth of Tevet, to commemorate events which brought their ancestors respite and salvation from evil decrees.

About one hundred and fifty years ago a wave of Jews from Kurdistan settled in Jerusalem. They also founded the Jewish Quarter in Bet-She'an, which was then a completely Arab town, and joined in the settlement of Sejera in Lower Galilee. Near Haifa, they founded the village of Alroy, in commemoration of their hero, David Alroy.

In 1932, a new wave arrived and founded new settlements near Jerusalem and in the north of Israel, on the fringe of the Hula Valley and near the borders of Syria and Lebanon. At the same time, a wave of Iraqi Jews made their way to Palestine, and settled in the Old City of Jerusalem, near the Ozer Dalim Synagogue.

Iraq came under British Mandate rule in 1917. As the Jews were better educated than the Arabs, they soon achieved prominence in commerce, finance, and governmental institutions, as well as in the free professions. Increasing affluence also enabled their community life to flourish and to expand in several directions. A Zionist organization was founded in Baghdad, and Hebrew culture — even to the publishing of a Hebrew newspaper — spread on a large scale.

The idyll lasted only 15 years. In 1932 Iraq became independent, and the whip of Arab nationalism drove the Jews from all influential positions. Zionism was outlawed and Jewish education came under strict surveillance. Inflamed mobs were given free rein to loot, burn, and kill at will. The unbridled venom of the masses

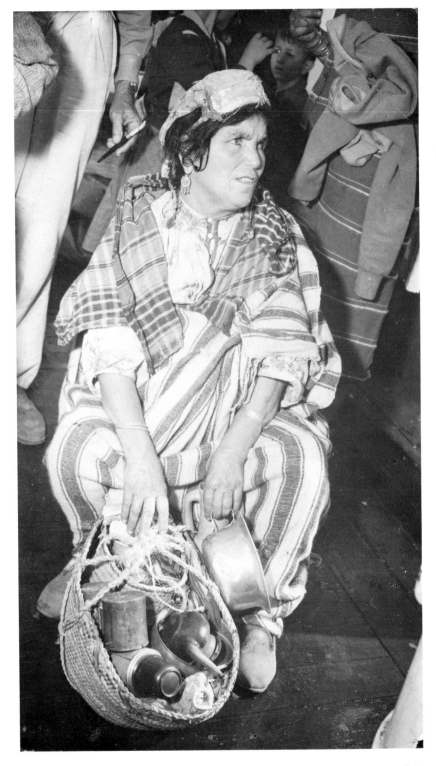

reached its peak on Shavuot of 1941 (Iraq had already allied itself with the Nazis); hundreds of Jews were massacred and many more put to torture.

When the state of Israel was proclaimed, 20,000 Iraqi Jews managed to get to Basra, on the Persian Gulf, and from there to Israel. In 1950 the Iraqi legislature passed a law allowing Jews to emigrate, without their possessions. In all the synagogues the call was sounded: "Jews, out of Babylonia!" On Shavuot of that year "Operation Ezra-Nehemiah" was launched and within 18 months, more than 120,000 Jews left the Babylonian exile.

Persia

Since the Persian Jewish community is the only Diaspora community mentioned in the Bible itself, it can trace its history farther back than any other Jewish community in the world.

According to the Book of Esther, Jews came to Persia during the reign of King Jeconiah (Jehoiachin), during the Babylonian exile. But Persian Jews claim even earlier residence, maintaining that the Jews exiled a century and a quarter earlier by the Assyrians were deported to "cities of the Medes," among others, and that these cities were part of the Persian Empire.

Legend has it that the exiles settled at Benihana in Esfahan because its soil and water corresponded to the soil and water of Jerusalem, some of which they had brought with them. The community grew to such proportions that the name of the locality was changed to "Alyahudiya." Still, the Jews regarded their presence in Persia as a temporary phase, pending the return to Zion. Their leaders — Daniel, Zerubabel, Ezra, and Nehemia — gained positions of influence in the Persian court, where they exerted pressure on behalf of the return to Zion and the construction of the Second Temple. But significant numbers remained in Persia even after the Jews were allowed to return to their homeland.

The community maintained close contact with the reestablished community in the Land of Israel. The Persian Jews derived spiritual sustenance from this contact, especially when liberal rule in Persia gave way to a regime which oppressed the Jews, and rescinded all the rights and privileges they had once enjoyed. The

A Persian Jew, in his new occupation as a farmer.

persecutions lasted throughout the rule of the Ahmgush and Sassenid dynasties and until the conquest of the land by the Saracens, in the seventh century. But even this relief did not last long, since the refusal of the Jews to adopt Islam militated against them in Persia, as it did elsewhere.

The sad state of Persian Jewry gave rise, in the eighth century, to a spurious messianic movement, centered about the self-styled prophet, Abu-Issah Alispahani, who claimed he had been sent to announce the advent of the Messiah. An uneducated tailor, Alispahani was credited with writing divinely-inspired books, and when he called for an armed uprising against the Moslems, thousands of his coreligionists joined him in battle. Although he was killed in the fighting, his followers insisted that he was still alive, hiding in a secret cave. They continued to observe his customs, abstaining from wine, women, and meat, and praying seven times a day. The messianic spirit was still alive when Eldad Hadani arrived on the scene towards the end of the ninth century, with tales about learned and sovereign Jews living beyond the legendary Sambatyon River. His accounts kindled the hopes of Persian Jewry for generations.

Another messianic furor was raised in the twelfth century with the appearance of David Alroy. The emotional surge grew into resistance, which the Persian authorities forcefully put down. The entire Jewish community was saved from annihilation only as a result of paying an enormous bribe. Nevertheless, the community's fate was sealed. When Rabbi Benjamin of Tudela visited the region, he found 15,000 Jews in Esfahan, 7,000 Jews and fourteen synagogues in Shushan, and 50,000 Jews in Hamdan, and all were doing well. Only a few years later, when Rabbi Petachya visited Persia, he found only two Jews in Shushan; the Jewish communities, he was told, had been destroyed. Community life as such was not reestablished even when the Safoyad dynasty, at the close of the sixteenth century, replaced the rule of the Caliphate and the Mongols.

The Safoyads succeeded in removing foreign rule and influence from the country, and Persia became a sovereign state, after an interruption of almost a millenium. The new regime consisted of Moslem Shiites. The ousted Turks had been Sunnites. The fanaticism of the Shiites expressed itself in the persecution of the minority religions — Christianity, Zoroastrianism, and Judaism — whose members were regarded as *najas* — "unclean." Conversion by coercion was standard practice.

The economic status of the Jews was understandably poor. Most of the ten thousand Jewish families in the realm, both in large cities and small villages, subsisted from peddling. A few were engaged in the manufacture of fine silks, in tailoring, milling, silver-working, and dealing in precious stones, antiques, and incense. Some may have engaged in foreign trade with India, across the Persian Gulf. Jews held a monopoly on the distillation of intoxicants, forbidden to the Moslems. This occupation frequently boomeranged, since trangressing Moslems often repented by attacking the distillers.

The most prestigious profession among the Jews was medicine, including medicinal magic. Jewish women were midwives and also engaged in telling fortunes from cards. According to Charadin, a traveller in the mid-seventeenth century, these women found ready clients in the harems for their potions of love and hate, pregnancy and anti-pregnancy, and similar inducements "which fetched

high prices and achieved nothing." Describing the Jewish community in general, Charadin wrote that the Jews were poor, without influence, and with no one to speak or intercede for them.

A bright spot in this period was the rule of Shah Ebas I (1588 –1621), an energetic sovereign who was prepared to forgo the traditional Safoyad aversion to other faiths in order to raise his country out of its economic stagnation. His policies brought to Persia masses of traders from neighboring lands, from the Ottoman Empire and especially from Armenia and Georgia. In 1613 he wrested Georgia from the Turks and according to Babi ben-Lutaf, a Persian Jew of that period, the Jews of Georgia welcomed the shah and helped him. He, in turn, promised them eternal friendship, took them back to Persia, and built for them a brand-new city, Farah-Abad, "city of joy," which he took under his wing. He also appointed Hanuka, brother of the head of the Jewish community, to be tax-collector of the Glan Province — after his conversion to Islam.

Prosperity was, however, according to ben-Lutaf, too much for the Jews of Persia, and internal strife put an end to their happy state. It seems that a member of the community, an acknowledged scholar named Laar, did not satisfy the community in his capacity as *shohet* and butcher. One Yom Kippur eve he slaughtered a large number of sheep for the pre- and post-fast meats. But the suspicious Jews refused to buy the meat. The staggering loss drove him mad and in reprisal, he and his family converted to Islam, and he changed his name to Khuda abu El-Hassan Lari. He convinced the shah to decree that all Jews be compelled to wear a tall, ludicrous hat and the shah appointed the apostate to supervise the implementation of the decree throughout the kingdom. Lari fulfilled his task with great diligence, enriching himself in the process by exempting from the decree those Jews who bribed him generously. In Shiraz, the Jews prevailed on the local Khan to substitute a small round patch for the tall hat. Lari met his end in Farah-Abad, where he had come to enforce the decree. He was invited by the Jews to a beach party on the shore of the Caspian Sea where he drowned.

The "Decree of the Hat" was the first in a long series of decrees. Another apostate, Siman-tov Mumin, took vengeance on his former coreligionists by convincing the shah that the Jews were using black magic found in their holy books to plot against his welfare. The angry shah ordered all the Jews of Esfahan to convert to Islam. Mumin was assigned the task of burning all the Jews' books including Torah scrolls, prayer books, and the Talmud. Several Jewish sages were put to death. The community outwardly accepted Islam, although they continued to observe the Jewish faith in secret. After the death of the shah, in 1627, they returned to Judaism openly. The shah's son Shah Safi protected the Jewish community and forbade others to take a hand in the affairs of the Jewish community: the date of this event was subsequently observed by the Jews as a holiday.

The wheel of Jewish fortune turned to disaster once again in the reign of Ebas II. According to ben-Lutaf, the new misfortune began when the shah's gardener stole a gem-studded dagger from the monarch's collection and sold it to two Jews. The two were apprehended with the dagger in their possession and were forced to convert in order to escape death. Ebas II then reinstated the decree that the Jews convert, with even greater rigor than his predecessor.

Three generations of Persian Jewish immigrants in Israel: the grandfather was a peddler in Esfahan; his son is a farmer in the Negev.

The new Moslems *(jadeed al-Islam)* were exempted from paying the Jewish per capita tax and wearing the badge of shame. Instead they were given a 'conversion grant,'' intended to lend an economic aura to the act of faith. Most of the Jews, however, continued to practice their faith in secret, buying non-kosher meat publicly, then disposing of it and eating meat clandestinely prepared in accordance with Jewish law.

The conversion of so many Jews was gratifying to the rulers, but it played havoc with the royal coffers. The next course was obvious: the Jews were allowed to "reconvert." To do this, they had to return the "conversion grant" and pay back per capita taxes for all the years they had lived as Moslems. They once again had to don the cloth badge of shame. Jews who could not pay the accumulated taxes were turtured. In 1661 the shah wearied of this policy and permitted the Jews to return to their faith without further ado. The Jewish community was able to breathe again.

The Jews of Persia felt that much of their trouble stemmed from the absence of communal authority. "In the days of the flood," wrote a seventeenth-century Persian Jew, "there was Noah, and in other days there was Ezra, but in our days we have no man of spiritual stature." Continuous hardship bred apathy toward religious observance, and communal morality was at a low ebb. The advent of Shabtai Zvi aroused the Jews of Persia to feverish excitement. Entire families donned sackcloth and ashes, left their homes, and went out to the fields to await the coming of the Messiah. There they were set upon by the Moslems and subjected to further humiliation.

By 1720, the Safoyad dynasty had disintegrated sufficiently for the Afghans to take over Persia, but the change of rulers brought little improvement to the lives of the Jews. There was some improvement in their status during the rule of Bedir Shah (1736 –1747), who annulled Shiism as the state religion. But Bedir was assassinated by the deposed Shiites, and matters reverted to their former state.

On a day the Moslems were mourning one of their holy men, a youngster fell into a quarrel with a Jewish woman who wanted him to kill a dog because a doctor had told her that canine blood would heal leprosy. The youngster ran through the streets of Meshed screaming: "The Jews are desecrating and disgracing the holy ones of the city." Others took up the cry, and soon a howling mob broke into the Jewish Quarter and kiled scores of its inhabitants. Those who remained alive were forced to convert; any Jew caught practicing his faith in secret was summarily put to death. This did not deter the Jews. Couples who were married by the Moslem court were also married secretly in accordance with the "law of Moses and Israel."

Many Jews succeeded in escaping. Some, ostensibly on a pilgrimate to Mecca, "defected" and found their way to Jerusalem. Others, in the guise of merchants engaged in foreign trade, reached France, England, India, and Afghanistan. Other Jews, wearied by the incessant struggle, joined a new religion, the Baha'i, which

Many immigrants from Persia continued working at their former crafts. Above: a bead threader.

Opposite: adjusting to a new life.

called for equality, brotherhood, and peace among all peoples. These people ceased to be members of the Jewish community, but they were not regarded with the same animosity reserved for the Jews who became Moslems in order to improve their material status.

The disciplined, tightly-knit family structure of Persian Jewry considerably eased the hardships of existence. The father was the undisputed head of the family. The mother's role was to bear and raise children, with barrenness considered a curse caused by demons or the "evil eye".

Once a wife conceived, everyone in the household was "mobilized" to protect her against evil; she wore amulets around her neck, prepared by "certified mystics." Additional protection was supplied by armbands and anklets engraved with combinations of potent names. When she visited friends, they had to feed her whatever she fancied, otherwise, they felt, she was likely to miscarry. This might also happen if she were to tread on fingernail parings, or drop things or pour water on Saturday nights when evil spirits that had been restrained by the Sabbath would be out in force. The final months of pregnancy were spent preparing the cradle and diapers and in prayer for a son; a daughter would only bring on a husband's ire.

If the new child was a son, the strict guard over the mother increased. The mother now slept with a knife and an assortment of amulets under her pillow. Special incantations were recited by experts, who accompanied their vocal efforts with the waving of fistfuls of salt above the heads of mother and babe; the salt was then thrown into the fire. The mother spent the eight pre-circumcision days in bed with the infant at her side; the two were not left alone for an instant.

In the synagogue, on the Sabbath prior to the circumcision ceremony, the father would be called to the Torah and showered with seeds and sweets. Friends and relatives brought their Sabbath meals to the home of the proud father and ate at his table, amidst appropriate singing. The night before the *brit* was spent in the recitation of Psalms. All participants in the ceremony, other than the hero of the occasion, immersed themselves in a ritual bath prior to the occasion.

After his Bar Mitzvah at the age of thirteen, the young lad was considered a man — ready to help his father earn the family bread and to become the object of matrimonial negotiations. His bride was, in all likelihood, nine or ten years old. The engagement was marked by a handshake between the fathers of the bride and groom, and usually lasted a year or two, during which the couple exchanged gifts on holidays. A special reception was given for the groom by the parents of the bride, to which he would arrive carrying a large wooden or copper tray laden with sweets and flowers artistically arranged. The bride, veiled, sat in a corner while her family entertained her future husband.

Two days before the wedding, the bride was led to the bathhouse for ritual immersion. On the following day, the groom sent the bride henna which the women rubbed on her hands and feet while chanting and singing. Early on the day of the wedding, the groom was escorted to the bathhouse. When the entourage returned, they — all except the groom, who was fasting — partook of sweets sent by the bride. The bride, in the meantime, donned the wedding dress sent to her that very morning by the groom.

When the wedding ceremony was over, the guests split into two groups — the men and the groom in one chamber, the women and the bride in another. The

wedding feast continued until late into the night, when the entire assemblage escorted the bride to the home of her husband.

When a Persian Jew was dying, all the members of his family were summoned to his bedside to ask his forgiveness. As he breathed his last, they recited the *Shema Yisrael,* and the women wailed and lamented. The body was laid on the floor and covered with a white sheet, and two burning candles were set near the head. The mourners dug into their own flesh and tore their hair.

Forty-one men participated in the purification rites. Each was given a new earthen cup which he filled with water and poured over the body. The cup was then broken above the head of the deceased. The plain wooden coffin (covered with expensive fabric or rough linen, depending on the affluence of the deceased) was carried on poles on the shoulders to the cemetery. Since the spirit of the deceased was thought to hover over his home for a year, study gatherings were held there in his memory on Sabbaths and holidays. At the end of the year, the members of the immediate family were daubed with henna, signifying the end of the mourning period.

Although forced wanderings and hardship in general prevented Persian Jewry from producing scholars of stature, education of the young was highly emphasized. Children studied in cramped school conditions similar to those of their coreligionists in other diasporas, stimulated by the same multi-thonged "prodder" applied to the same parts. The more advanced pupils were able to translate the Bible into Persian and delve into the Mishna and even the Zohar. Only the very advanced studied the Talmud. The younger boys would at first be taught by the teacher, but they would soon be passed on to the older students who would help them practice the lesson by rote. Tuition fees were determined by the parents' ability to pay, in money or in kind. The sons of the very poor were accepted by teachers who were themselves far from affluent. The boys learned to read Hebrew, but very early on went to work, either helping their fathers or serving as apprentices. Even the best pupils had no possibility of furthering their education, since there were no academies of higher learning.

Poor communications between cities, and the often-hazardous distances

A Persian Jew, looking at his new homeland.

separating them, militated against communal contacts between the centers of Jewish habitation in Persia. To compound matters, Jews in far-flung cities spoke different dialects, widening the gap even further. In the individual community, the *mula* was the general functionary — rabbi, legal authority, *shohet, mohel,* and cantor. He performed weddings and conducted divorce proceedings, receiving payment directly from the individuals to whom he rendered service. His position was passed on to his son or son-in-law, if any, otherwise his successor was chosen by the seven heads of the community, whose main tasks were to manage the affairs of the synagogue and represent the community in the royal court (chiefly to avert damaging decrees). They also joined the *mula* in collecting funds for the poor and

A ketuba **from Afghanistan.**

dowries for orphaned girls. Another of their duties was to collect taxes levied on Jews by the Moslem rulers and religious leaders. This collection was often arranged for on the Sabbath, although the actual money was collected at a different time. Other communal needs were also arranged for on the same day and in the same way.

The only Jews who fared well economically were the few in northern Persia who engaged in foreign trade. Elsewhere, Jews lived in abject poverty. The women often wove and knitted in order to help earn a livelihood. Their houses, located in the ghetto, were of mud and clay, set in enclosed, stifling courtyards, clustered about crooked alleys and market places with little to sell. The men did all the buying; women who had to be out of doors hurried on their way, veiled and unobtrusive.

The home of the Persian Jew consisted chiefly of one large room, its floor covered with a mat or rug. Here the family ate (from a large copper tray, each one using his fingers), and slept on mattresses pulled from a corner and spread next to each other on the floor. In the summertime, the mattresses were taken out into the yard.

As did their brethren elsewhere, the impoverished Jews of Persia drew strength from the Sabbath and the holidays. In their difficult circumstances, preparation for these occasions was a challenge in itself, and their ability to meet the challenge and to observe these days properly compensated them greatly for their depressed state. The weekly food budget was always subordinated to the needs of the Sabbath. The menu rarely varied: Sabbath eve brought fried fish, rice pudding, and dumplings made of chopped sour grass and bits of meat. For the Sabbath day there was the omnipresent and eagerly awaited *chamin*, the universal trademark of Jewish gastronomy, kept hot with coals underneath and blankets above. In addition there were hard-boiled eggs, cooked vegetables, and fish.

Sabbath attire was also special. The head of the household wore a multicolored silk undercloak, topped with a woolen *abaya*. Before he and his sons left for Friday evening services in the synagogue, the women lit the wicks in earthen lamps that were either set on a stand or suspended from the ceiling, pronounced the benediction, then kissed the tablecloth and recited the *Shema Yisrael*.

The Sabbath eve began with *Kiddush*. The meal was opened with a fresh citrus fruit and a benediction over a twig of myrtle or some other aromatic plant. They then washed their hands and recited the *Hamotzi* benediction as the father passed pieces of round, flat bread to each member of the family, according to age. He then blessed each one: ''May the Lord bless thee and keep thee.'' Sabbath songs were chanted after the meal. A favorite related to Rabbi Simon Bar-Yohai, father of Jewish mysticism.

Following the Sabbath midday meal, there was an afternoon nap, after which the men went to the synagogue and the women sat together at the doors of their homes, nibbling seeds and chatting to their hearts' content. The *seuda shlishit*, the Sabbath meal eaten towards evening, was light. Later, as the head of the household recited *havdala*, the ceremony separating the Sabbath from the rest of the week, the other members of the family laughed, inducing merriment for the week to come.

Passover was a very busy time of year. Preparations began with boiling the dishes, which was done by an expert in a large communal cauldron. Meals preceding the holiday were mere snacks. On the night prior to Passover eve, the housewife would hide crumbs of bread, wrapped in paper, in all corners, and the head of the family, a lit candle in hand, would look for them in all nooks and crannies. The crumbs were gathered in a special utensil and burned on the following morning.

The *Seder* table was arranged by the women while the men were at prayer. Although Persian Jewry celebrated the same *Seder* ritual as Jews around the world, their ceremony was distinguished by a unique *afikoman* custom. The father would hand the *afikoman matza* to one of his sons: If the son succeeded in keeping the *afikoman* from being stolen, he received a prize; otherwise he had to forfeit something, while the ''thief'' was given the privilege of asking anyone at the table to do a song and dance for him — or else the *afikoman* would not be returned.

In the course of the meal, a few of the participants would slip away and return, carrying bundles over their shoulders. Answering their knock, the head of the household would ask: ''From where are you coming?'' and they would answer: ''From Egypt.'' They would then be brought to the center of the room to recite the story of the Exodus dramatically and with much gesticulating. Often a group would go from house to house and repeat the performance.

Passover actually ended on the day following the festival, when the family would gather up the usually liberal leftovers and go out to the woods or fields for a picnic.

Persian Jewry's esteem for Rabbi Simon Bar-Yohai was given full expression on Lag Ba-Omer, the holiday associated with the great sage. The more affluent prepared festive meals and invited the others to join them; the *mula* went from home to home and recited portions of the Zohar, the mystical tract credited to the great sage, after which the meal was served. Musicians played, accompanying the singing of special ''Bar-Yohai'' songs in Persian. At the synagogue, everyone lit a candle in memory of the sage and his son, Rabbi Elazar, and Rabbi Meir Ba'al Haness, another sage who was also held in great reverence by Persian Jewry.

During the seven weeks between Passover and Shavuot, when the *omer* was counted, Persian Jews kept a piece of *matza* and a bit of salt in their pockets.

Since Shavuot was thought to symbolize the marriage between the Torah and the people to whom it was given, the preparations for the festival were very much akin

32

Right: a cobbler, continuing to work at the craft he practiced in Persia. Below: a synagogue in Esfahan.

to wedding preparations. An elaborate sweet table was the rule in every home. On Shavuot night, people would gather at the homes of families which had suffered a death in the course of the preceding year. There, seated on mats and holding a vase of roses, each person would in turn recite passages from the Bible, ending with the recitation of the Book of Ruth. The women served coffee to the men, to help them stay awake the entire night.

For Persian Jewry, as with other communities around the world, the fast of Tisha B'av (the ninth day of the month of Av) was an outlet for bewailing their own depressed status, as well as for mourning the destruction of the Temple in Jerusalem. On the eve preceding the fast, the family would partake of a simple meal of rice, beans, and hard-boiled eggs dipped in ashes. At the close of the meal, each one would take a pinch of ashes and rub it on his forehead. In the synagogue, the Book of Lamentations was read in the dim light of candles; at the end of the recitation, the candles were extinguished, and the *mula* recounted the story of the destruction of the Temple and other events of Jewish martyrdom.

Before the family retired for the night, the head of the household would give each one a sum of money to put under his pillow for distribution in the morning to the poor. Everyone, rich and poor alike, contributed to the "Atonement Offering" during the recitation of Lamentations the following morning. The services continued with the reading of the Book of Job, in Persian. At *minha* services in the afternoon, everyone gathered in the yard of the synagogue for the slaughter of the sheep purchased with the "Atonement Offering" money; all the males put their hands on the sheep while the *shohet* recited the prayer preceding the act of ritual slaughter.

Among Persian Jews, the spirit of the High Holy Days was intensified by frequent fasting during the *Selihot* period that preceded Rosh Hashanah, and during the Ten Days of Penitence between Rosh Hashanah and Yom Kippur. Rosh Hashanah eve was a time to ask for release from unfulfilled vows and for the distribution of charity. The festive meal on that evening included fruits and vegetables that symbolized a good year: apples cooked in sugar for "a sweet year"; beets, "so that our enemies be beaten"; the seed-packed pomegranate denoting the multiplicity of rights and privileges; fish for fertility; lamb's head "so that we be the head and not the tail."

The two days of Rosh Hashanah were semi-fast days. No food or drink was taken until after prayers, so that the half-days would add up to a complete day of fasting. Individuals who were too weak to fast ate before dawn and went back to sleep. In the synagogue, the cantor recited the prayers in Hebrew and repeated the more important ones in Persian, for the benefit of the untutored, along with explanations of their content. In the afternoon it was customary to recite all the Psalms. The climax of the service was the sounding of the *shofar*. Clear, flowing tones were a promise of a good year, while a quavering rendition moved the congregation to more fervent prayer.

The *kapara* (atonement offering) preceding Yom Kippur was a custom observed most scrupulously. Each member of the family presented his own individual offering: a rooster for a male, a hen for a female, and, for a pregnant woman, a hen for herself and a rooster and a hen for whatever sex the fruit of her womb would be. After the recitation of the *kaparot* prayer, the fowl was slaughtered by the *shohet*.

34 *A carpet repairman.*

The feathers were plucked for bedding, and part of the meat was given to the poor and part was eaten in the pre-fast meal.

The men went to the bathhouse for the seven ritual dips, then proceeded to the synagogue for penitential flaggelations: the *mula* passed a thong over their bare backs as he recited penitential prayers for himself and his flock. After the very moving and impressive *Kol Nidre* service, many men remained in the synagogue all night, reciting Psalms and the "Crown of Sovereignty," composed by the great poet Solomon Ibn-Gabirol, in Persian. On Yom Kippur day everyone, even infants, came to services. At nightfall the congregation went out to the yard for *kiddush levana,* the blessing of the new moon, symbolizing the renewal of Creation, and good wishes for the new year were exchanged.

Construction of the *sukka,* the booth used on the holiday of Sukkot, began after the post-Yom Kippur meal. The *sukka* was a communal affair — one for all the families in the yard compound, with materials stored from year to year. Before entering the *sukka*, everyone took off his shoes, and nothing was eaten outside its confines during the entire festival. The *etrog* and *lulav*, being beyond the means of many families, were also shared. Simhat Torah actually commenced with the festival of Sukkot itself, since dancing in procession with the Torah was held every evening. The ''Torah Bridegroom'' and ''Genesis Bridegroom,'' who read selections from the scrolls, were pelted with nuts and sweets as they recited.

Little notice was taken of Hanukah, other than the lighting of candles and the recitation of prayers relative to the occasion, as well as a recounting of the Hasmoneans' deeds. On the first night, the candle would be lit by the head of the household; on the other nights, the sons would light the candles, so as to become familiar with the ritual. Children of the poor went from door to door for gifts, in each case burning a wisp of grass in order to discourage the ''evil eye'' from visiting the household. On the last of the eight nights, the father brought forth a large tray of nuts and roasted seeds, which the children grabbed by the fistful, to be eaten in school on the following day.

Tu Bishvat was observed by Persian Jews much in the same fashion as it was elsewhere: family gatherings at which fruit of the Land of Israel was eaten.

Purim, the holiday which originated in Persia, was, understandably, *the* festival of the year, and the ritual of its observance dated back, according to Persian Jews, to the days of Mordecai and Esther, around whose reputed tombs in Hamadan they used to gather for the reading of the Book of Esther.

The spirit of the festival moved into high gear on *Shabbat Zachor* — the Sabbath on which Jews remember what Amalek did to their forefathers on their flight from Egypt. The *mula* delivered the gist of the Book of Esther, as the congregation shook its collective fist against the enemies of Israel. The Fast of Esther was observed most scrupulously, and the reading of the *megillah* (Book) of Esther was punctuated with noisemakers and the stamping of feet at each mention of the evil Haman. On the following day the streets of the Jewish Quarter were filled with children in

A coppersmith.

masquerade, *mishloach manot* in hand. The poor were given silver coins. The festivities culminated with the burning in effigy of a towering Haman fashioned by the youngsters.

The high rate of infant mortality in Persia induced many Jews to resort to supernatural means to ward off this evil. The custom also spread to the treatment of illness in general. Quacks and medicine men flourished in all parts of the kingdom, and their practices were many and varied — such as melting lead in a pan above the invalid's head, pouring the molten metal into a basin of water garnished with a pinch of salt, egg, sugar, and cotton, and then having the invalid take a sip, leaving enough to anoint his body and sprinkle the corners of the room.

Anyone suspected of exercising the "evil eye" was subjected to all kinds of harassment. Strips of his clothing were obtained, one way or another, and burned so that the ashes might be used to sprinkle on the feet of the alleged victim. In some instances the patient's body was covered with coins which were then distributed to the poor, since "charity saves from death."

From the turn of the present century, and especially after after World War I, the Jews of Persia obtained some rights, although socially and economically they continued to suffer. The Alliance Israélite Universelle established schools that helped prepare young people to emerge from the ghetto. But any desire on the part of Jews to become part of the Persian cultural fabric was thwarted by the spirit of nationalism which swept the country.

The ties between the Persian community and the Land of Israel had been lax, maintained for the most part by the visits of emissaries who sought funds for the maintenance of scholars. This was enough, however, to induce a few to follow in the footsteps of Ezra and Nehemiah. At the beginning of the twentieth century, families left Shiraz and settled in Safed and Jerusalem, working for the most part as stone masons. The stream continued to grow with the establishment of the State of Israel. With the fall of the Shah and Homeini's rise to power the situation of the Jews deteriorated, and many of them left what is now Iran. The number of Jews still there is estimated at 30,000.

Persian Jews were talented craftsmen, and used their skills to enrich their religious as well as everyday life. Left: 19th century kiddush cup (left) and a twin-mouthed 18th century brass lamp. Opposite, right: two Torah cases. Opposite, left (from top to bottom): excerpt from a ketuba, a silver amulet (with cover), a pair of enamelled earrings.

The Caucasus

Both Caucasian and Georgian Jews trace their history in the area all the way back to the eighth century B.C.E., although archaeological evidence dates back only as far as the first century C.E.

When Christianity was first introduced to this region, the Jews were severely persecuted, and many fled to neighborhing countries. In the eighth century C.E., however, with the spread of the Khazar Empire, the Jews enjoyed a period of prosperity and well-being. Many stories are told of the greatness and influence of the Jews at this time, and of the massive influex of Jews from Mesopotamia and Persia and the countries of the Byzantine Empire.

During the eighth century, the Moslems invaded eastern Caucasia where they enforced Islam on the inhabitants of Daghestan. In Georgia and Armenia, however, the Christians remained entrenched and from that period onward two separate Jewish communities evolved in the Causasus — Georgia in the west and Daghestan in the east. A marked difference that grew with time evolved between the Jews of Georgia and the Jews of Daghestan.

In the thirteenth century Daghestan was conquered by the Mongols and the situation of the Jews deteriorated.

The Jews were driven out of their flourishing towns and into the mountains, and since then have been known as the Mountain Jews. Their precarious position did not improve until the Caucasus came under Ottoman rule. New communities arose, in Kuba, Daraband, and elsewhere, but they were swept up in the revolt against the Ottoman regime by the mountain tribes. In the nineteenth century, at the end of a fifty-year war with Russia, there were 21,000 Jews in the Caucasus; on the eve of World War II, there were 50,000.

The Russian writer Nemirowitz-Danchansky recorded the following description of a Jewish village in the Caucasus a century ago:

> Stone houses cling to the slope, scattered in disorder and separated by narrow lanes. Below, well-cultivated fields and orchards frame the village in green.... The noisy lanes are crowded with people, in colorful attire. The tower of the synagogue resembles a Moslem minaret; it is colorful and is faced with yellow and blue slabs of stone, and it towers above all the houses.... Inside, the houses are unlike any other in the Jewish Diaspora. The oven is built of stone, and the mud chimney goes up to the roof.... The passageway from one room to the next is very low, and one must stoop to get through. The rooms are no larger than niches, but everything is very clean. The walls are apparently whitewashed very often. The earthen floor is packed down and is free from rubbish. Utensils of all kinds glisten from the shelves, and tall, elaborately-engraved pitchers stand in the corners. There is also silverware, displayed on huge copper trays. Here and there are large mirrors, hung about with swords, guns, pistols and daggers; the pistols are holstered in black silver. The guns are decorated with silver mountings.... The roof rests on beams and is stacked with weapons. The mountain Jews are very proud of their arms, and a Jewish youth in tatters which reveal his fine muscular build will readily go about with a pair of silver-handled pistols or a ruby-studded dagger sheath.... The guest rooms are beautifully adorned with colorful silk prints on the walls. Through the windows the bright sunlight comes to rest on Armenian pillowcases, a shiny green bedcover, and the sparkling weapons....

Opposite: the smile of a Jewish mother.

40

The unique life-style of Jews in Caucasian villages molded them into a single family unit. A wedding in the village drew everyone into the celebration and the entertainment of bride and groom. A band of musicians accompanies the groom along the streets of a village near Daraband (top). Women join the wedding festivities (middle), while the men do their bit to heighten the merriment (bottom).

The Jews were always admired by their Caucasian neighbors for their diligence and courage. Unlike their Jewish brethren elsewhere, the Caucasian Jews never wore symbols of degradation. Their attire, for generations, was a long cloak, a tall fur hat, a sword girded at the waist, a rifle at the shoulder, and a cartridge belt across the chest. They had a reputation for bravery that matched their appearance.

The elders of the community glory in describing the daring deeds of the young people, the common theme being: outnumbered, they died while inflicting a similar fate on their ambushers. And yet, they were always known for their kindness, humbleness, and goodness of heart. They always bore a passionate love for the outdoors, and liked nothing better than to canter along the mountain trails,

A Caucasian Jew in traditional garb.

strumming the balalaika.

Hospitality was one of their great joys. Emissaries or travelers from a foreign country would be given warm, cordial welcomes. A visitor from the Holy Land would create a surge of emotion. Long before the arrival of the guest, the table in the main room would be laden with every delicacy available; an empty spot on the table was considered a disgrace.

Upon arrival guests would divest themselves of their weapons. Then, at the table, each person would place a slice of meat on his neighbor's plate. As the preamble to the meal, the rabbi or one of the dignitaries would pronounce the benediction, break the bread, and pass morsels around. The menu invariably included spiced vegetables stuffed with meat. *Shishlik,* skewered bits of broiled lamb, was a favorite, as were *hinkel,* egg noodles boiled in meat stock and spiced with ground garlic, vinegar and sharp wine; *tiara,* a broad-leafed vegetable cooked with meat and raisins in grape juice, and *hashul,* flour and groats thickened with the fat of sheep tail and seasoned with spices, vegetables, and honey.

Only the men sat at the table, and their conversation revolved around folklore, valorous exploits and the like. When the guest was a visitor from the Holy Land, he would fill his fascinated listeners with tales of the ancestral homeland.

Caucasian Jews spoke Tatti, a Persian dialect mixed with Turkish, which led to their being called "the Tatti" by some. Hebrew was known only by the leaders, although boys learned to pray and to read the Bible in the original.

A boy's education began at the age of five, in the *kuns* — a small, low-ceilinged room next to the synagogue. There pupils would sit in a semicircle on a carpet, in front of the teacher who invariably sat with his *keitin,* a long pipe, in one hand, and a prodding lash in the other. Once the child had mastered the Hebrew alphabet, the teacher would get his fee — a bottle of alcohol and a half-ruble. When the child advanced to translating the Bible into the vernacular, the fee was doubled. This second stage generally marked the end of the average child's education, since by this time he was usually ready to help his father earn a living for the family. Gifted students were allowed to go on to study the Rashi commentary, and the best of them, numbering from three to ten boys, went on to Talmud with Rashi, studying with the *dayan*, the community's authority on Jewish law. This course lasted four years. Such boys usually entered the rabbinate, and were obliged to learn the laws of *shehita*, the ritual slaughter of animals.

Final examinations for the rabbinate were a special occasion held in the presence of rabbis and dignitaries, as well as the parents and relatives of the candidates. The *dayan* would sit on a high cushion, long pipe in hand. The relatives held fowls in their hands while the *dayan* and leaders posed questions on the laws of *shehita*.

When the oral examination was over, the entire gathering went out to the yard, where the *dayan* performed the first *shehita* and the candidates followed, each in turn, under the watchful eyes of the rabbis. The slaughtered birds would then be sent to the home of the *dayan* as a sign that the act had been executed properly. If it had not been performed properly, the *dayan* would not partake of the fowl. The successful candidates would then be given the title "rabbi," although they had no authority to ordain others without the consent of the *dayan*. The parents of the new rabbis invited the *dayan* and dignitaries to celebrations at which each newly-ordained rabbi would hold forth in homiletics, mysticism, and legend. Every toast would be followed by the traditional proclamation, "Next year in Jerusalem." The concluding remarks were made by the dignitaries in praise of the father, who had reared his son to study the Torah. In cases where the father was affluent and a property owner, his son would join him in business. Otherwise the young man would receive a rabbinical appointment.

Family life began with the engagement, or *kiddush benzi*, arranged by the two sets of parents. The marriage ceremony itself was held when the boy was thirteen or fourteen, but in some localities it took place when he was ten or eleven. The girl was eight or nine.

Once the parents had their eyes on a girl they would send emissaries to her parents as an opening to the negotiations. The emissaries, usually a man and a woman, would first investigate the nature and character of the potential bride, to see whether she would suit the young man. If their report was favorable, they would be sent back to discuss the price with the parents. Once an agreement was reached, the two fathers would get together to talk terms in the greatest detail. The groom's father would undertake to supply the bridal vestments, five gold pieces, and a silver belt, as well as the silk wedding gown.

The bride's parents, in order to emphasize her worth, would begin by quoting an outrageous price which was eventually pared down to a reasonable figure. Once agreement was reached, the groom's parents would hold a feast for the town's dignitaries, headed by the rabbi and the *dayan*. The formal feast would begin with the groom's father sending the bride's father, through one of the notables at the feast, a "down payment," along with delicacies and slabs of sugar. The bride's parents would welcome them, and the *t'naim* (terms and conditions) would be written, executed, and witnessed right then and there. This done, the emissaries would be fed well and would then return to the home of the groom, singing lustily along the way.

The women would hold a party of their own, and the groom would hold a stag party for his bosom friends, the main feature of which was a troubador who sang popular ballads of heroic deeds. The young people punctuated the merriment with pistol shots fired into the air.

Every evening thereafter and until the wedding itself, the young men would visit their friends, bringing with them a trio of musicians, called *zuranu*, who played drums and pipes. During this period the bride's girlfriends would join in a circle around her and sing love songs. On the second and third days, the girls would accompany the bride to the homes of female relatives for the parting good wishes. The bride would be dressed in rags, and the relatives would give her gifts. If their route took them past the groom's home, his friends would sally forth and "drive off" the party with bits of straw and sand.

A few months after the engagement, the bride's parents would invite the groom to their home. He would come laden with gifts, which he would deposit in a large bowl placed on the table for that purpose. The young lady would be brought in for a formal meeting with her betrothed, at which point the young men who had accompanied the groom would stretch themselves out on the floor and pretend to be asleep.

Wednesday was the accepted day for weddings among Caucasus Jews. On Sunday, ten days before the wedding, friends of the groom would be sent with roast meat and hard-boiled eggs to the bride's home, where they were met by the bridesmaids, who pelted them and made them retreat in "disgrace." This custom, which was very popular with the young people, was repeated through Thursday, at which time the bridesmaids would deck the bride out in her wedding dress and then go out to accept the offering from the young men. That night the bridesmaids slept in the bride's home while the groom's attendants slept in his home. The "best man," usually a boy of about ten, was appointed on the Sabbath preceding the wedding. From then until after the ceremony he remained at the groom's side.

On Sunday, the parents of the groom dispatched two emissaries to invite everyone in the area, Moslems as well as Jews, to the wedding.

On Wednesday, the day of the wedding, the young couple fasted. In the afternoon the rabbi and relatives of the groom would come to the bride's home to appraise the clothes and ornaments she had gathered. Her family would attempt to raise the value of the dowry, and in the ensuing argument the rabbi would act as mediator.

The father of the bride would then add gifts twice the value of the sum he had received for his daughter.

Prior to the wedding ceremony, bride and groom would be taken to the respective bathhouses. The groom's head would then be shaved, and he would be decked out in his wedding finery. His exit would be greeted by his friends with pistol shots. In Kuba and Daraband it was customary for them to come up to the groom, kiss him on the forehead, and slip a few coins into his pocket. On his way home he would be met by girls carrying baskets of red apples on their heads. Tucked among the apples were small tree-like figures with branches made of burning candles. The girls would dance around him to the rhythm of little drums until he reached his home. The same ceremony attended the return of the bride to her home, where older women braided her hair while the bride wept loudly.

Now came the time for the bride to bid farewell to the home of her parents. She would kneel before her mother and ask forgiveness for any pain she might have caused. The mother would lift her from the ground, kiss her on the forehead, and bless her. Then the procession to the canopy would begin.

The groom went through the same procedure at his home, except that his escort to the wedding canopy consisted of a troop of "best men," often mounted on horses and disporting themselves with pistol shots fired into the air.

If the bride and groom came from different villages, a special mission of nine men and nine women would leave the groom's village the day before the wedding to fetch the bride. As they left, the groom's relatives blessed them and poured pitchers of water in the wake of their carriages. When they returned with the bride and her entourage, the groom's friends, arrayed in their full weaponry, would gallop to his home to announce the arrival. The bride would be on horseback, her steed decked out with the finest equine embellishments. As she entered the village, the groom's brother, holding a lighted candle, would catch hold of the horse's bridle and lead it into the village.

At the entrance to the groom's home, the bride would be met with a bowl of

The first immigrants from the Caucasus to Eretz Israel preferred to settle in Jerusalem; no job was too menial. Right: a bootblack.

honey, into which she dipped her fingers and then anointed the *mezuza,* the doorposts and the threshold.

The wedding procession to the synagogue was led by singers and musicians, followed by the bridal party. The palms of the attendants were painted red.

The canopy was set up in the yard of the synagogue. The *dayan* read the *ketuba,* which he translated into the vernacular, then pronounced the traditional Seven Benedictions. The groom betrothed the bride, then flung a glass to the ground, as the audience shouted *Nakke sa'at, mazal tov;* On their way home the newlyweds would be pelted from the rooftops with rice, raisins, nuts, and flour, so that by the time they reached their destination their clothes were white.

The wedding feast would begin with the scattering of dried radishes among the guests, who were seated on mats. The main dish was *waani* — chunks of breast of lamb garnished with raisins, onions, garlic, and milled horseradish, and covered with a thick layer of rice and fat. As the guests ate, each in turn was blessed by the rabbi.

Wedding gifts were showered on the couple at a special *natar,* gift-giving feast. The young husband, flanked by dignitaries of the community, would keep his eyes on the ground. Two of his friends would keep passing glasses of wine to him, and he would hand a glass to each guest who came up to offer a gift. A scribe, sitting at the young man's left, listed the gifts and the names of their donors. This accomplished, the young man and his friends would stroll outside until evening, the time for *sharm wako,* the unveiling of the bride's face.

The husband and his closest friends would enter the bride's room and formally ask the bridesmaids to reveal the young wife's features. The couple was then left alone for a short time, after which the two joined the other guests for merriment until the morning hours.

The seven days of the marriage feast were highlighted with the husband being called to the Torah to read the Scriptural passage, ". . . and Abraham grew old." The bride would bring a box of snuff, which the sexton then proceeded to distribute among the worshippers.

Life would then begin for the new couple as it had for their parents and grandparents. The woman would take over the household duties and live a retiring life. But in the evening, as she joined the other women and girls at the wells and springs to draw water for the next day's activities, she had her moment for chatting and gossip.

The massive iron curtain which clanged shut on the Jews in the Soviet Union did not spare the Jews of the Caucasus. But being far removed from the center of Russia and living as they did in the mountainous regions, they succeeded in retaining their Jewish mode of life, producing their own vitality for future generations, to compensate for their isolation from the rest of world Jewry.

Bukhara

The tall, big-boned and gentle-looking Jews of Bukhara inhabited the plains of central Asia for hundreds of years, isolated from the mainstream of the Diaspora. As a result, they have maintained their uniqueness in the kaleidoscopic mosaic of the Jewish people. It was not until the eighteenth century that they reestablished contact with other Jewries and with the Land of Israel — a contact which caused a spiritual upheaval leading to a mass immigration to the Land of Israel, and to far-reaching changes in their way of life and customs.

The province of Bukhara was once part of the Persian Empire. During the reign of the Samanids in the ninth and tenth centuries, the city of Bukhara (both the province and city have the same name) was already quite important. Later it became the capital of the Bukharan Emirate, which took in parts of Uzbekistan, Kazahstan, and Turkomanistan, and developed into a center of Islamic culture. In the middle of the nineteenth century, the Emirate passed into Czarist hands and was later swallowed up in the upheaval of the Russian Revolution. Today it is a province of the Uzbek Soviet Socialist Republic.

Bukhara's Jews claim descent from the exiles from Judea and Samaria (First Temple period), whose numbers were subsequently augmented by suvivors of the Roman conquest. This claim is quite plausible; many of the exiles chose to live in the Persian Empire, which for the most part allowed Jews to live within its boundaries according to their own traditions, as witness the Book of Esther.

News of the Jews of Bukhara was first brought to world attention by Rabbi Benjamin of Tudela, the noted twelfth-century traveler, who had found them living in large communities in Hurzam and Samarkand. His report told of their great scholars and wealthy merchants (Bukhara, on the main highways connecting East and West, was an important center of Persia's highly-developed commerce). Bukhara's advanced irrigation system, he wrote, provided the land with agricultural abundance and the Jews shared in this prosperity and were quite content with their lot.

Less than a century later, these ideal conditions came to an abrupt end. The Mongolian hordes of Genghis Khan invaded central Asia in a wave of blood and fire. Commerce came to a standstill and the flourishing cultural centers were wiped out. The curtain dropped on Bukhara's Jews for a full three centuries. The circumstances surrounding their return are obscure; the Bukharan Jews themselves claim that the emirs who came into the country, after the Mongolian wave had spent itself, asked the Jews to return in order to reinvigorate Bukhara's trade and commerce, whereupon they came back, but only after the authorities had agreed to guarantee them full protection. Unfortunately, these guarantees proved to be worthless. As in other Moslem countries, the Jews became subject to oppressive and degrading decrees: they were pushed into ghettos, where they were forbidden to build new homes or acquire houses from Moslems to provide quarters for their natural increase.

The decrees took various forms. When venturing forth from the ghetto, a Jew was obliged to tie a rope about his waist (like a lowly porter); later this was replaced by a silk cord. He had to wear a tall hat (the *tilpak*, about twenty inches high) that covered the forehead down to the eyes. Jews were not allowed to ride horses — this was for freemen only — nor to tarry in Moslem neighborhoods after dark. No

Mother and sons, in traditional Bukharan garb, kindle the Hanukah lights (wicks steeped in oil).

Jewish house could be taller than a Moslem house. Jews had to sit on low stools in their shops, so as not to be taller than their Moslem customers. Every adult Jew had to pay a head tax, the *jizziah;* when collecting the tax, the Moslem collector would degrade the Jew further by slapping his face (the Jews evaded this disgrace by having all the money collected first by the head of the community, who turned it over to the Moslem collector and then received a collective slap).

During one period, Jews were required to hang a black rag above the entrance to their homes and were forbidden to open any window facing the street. Transgressors were fined or imprisoned; a third offense could mean the death penalty. Litigation with a Moslem before the *kadi* invariably found the Jew guilty, with no further recourse. If a Moslem felt like beating a Jew, the latter was not allowed to defend himself.

These decrees were so severe that any relaxation was held to be a miracle; the instances were so rare that each such relaxation became a legend. Wise and gifted Mulla She'in, it is said, converted to Islam, rose to a position of eminence in the Emir's court and, mindful of his origins, used his position to mitigate the decrees. After fifty years of apostasy, he repented and returned to the Jewish fold, to which he was welcomed back with gratitude and rejoicing.

Sacred writings, other than the Scrolls of the Law, were very rare in Bukhara; consequently, few sages were to be found in the community. Only the wealthy were in a position to acquire books, and these were used by study groups which the owners of the books organized, but the cultural level was low, even among the spiritual leaders. The mere ability to read Hebrew was considered tantamount to scholarship.

The head of the community, chosen to represent it before the authorities,

48 *Fine fabrics embroidered in all hues were popular among Bukharan Jews.*

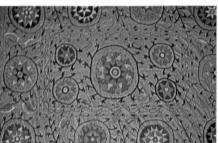

commanded great respect among his fellow Jews. One of the best known among them was Mulla Pinchas Kohen, a man with a keen sense of justice, courage, clarity of reason, truth, and distaste for bribery. One story told about him concerns an order issued by the Emir: The mulla was to deliver to him certain Jewish wine smugglers. When the mulla refused to inform on his brethren, the Emir ordered him taken to the top of a tower and thrown off — unless, so the Emir's men intimated, he would embrace the Islamic faith. The mulla rejected the proposal, climbed up to the tower and was thrown to the ground. To everyone's amazement, he rose to his feet, unhurt. "What saved you?" demanded the emir. "I do not know," replied Pinchas Kohen, "but as I was falling I felt something soft as wool being placed beneath me." The emir understood that this was an act of Divine Providence; he gave the mulla a splendid coat and appointed him and his family to leadership of the community for all generations to come.

The community house of worship was the Great Central Synagogue, which was subdivided into six small sanctuaries. A separate entrance led to the women's gallery. The liturgy followed the Persian rite, and was partially retained even after the Sephardic one was introduced. It was customary for everyone to remain seated at the end of the service and place his palms in front of his chest, as the elder intoned: "The Lord, Builder of Jerusalem, will gather the dispersed of Israel, and may all Israel, from the north and the south, the east and the west, be taken into the bounds of this blessing." At this, the worshippers would raise their palms and pass them over their faces, as a petition for spiritual abundance.

Parts of the readings from the Prophets were translated into the vernacular, much to the delight of the worshippers, particularly the women. The Zohar was especially popular and was recited at most gatherings — each man in turn chanting a chapter. The more intricate his improvised chant, the greater his glory.

49

Left: elderly Jews from Bukhara, in traditional robes and hats, ascend to Mount Zion in Jerusalem. Right: this unique string instrument graced every Bukharan festival. The sound of its strings would set the women dancing, as they drummed their tambours and clashed their cymbals.

According to Benjamin of Tudela, the youngsters received a rather meager education. The school was either close to or in the basement of the synagogue. Learning was auditory and by rote. The lazy pupils were stimulated by a lash — the *falkah* — hanging on the wall. The teacher, none too erudite himself, taught his charges the Five Books of Moses, the Prophets, and *Ein Yaacov*, a book of homiletics which the Bukharan Jews passionately enjoyed.

Boys whose parents could not afford the minimum tuition fees often grew up without any education at all. This situation persisted until relatively recently. About eighty years ago, a spirited dignitary, Rabbi Shlomo Mussah, began paying tuition for these boys himself, and thenceforth all boys had at least some measure of learning. Girls were not taught to read or write or even pray. In the synagogue, the women would stand and listen reverently to the men's prayers. When the Torah was taken from the Ark, the women would blow kisses in its direction and say a prayer in their own words.

Generous and optimistic by nature, Bukharan Jews loved nothing as much as their festive meals, with the tables laden with tasty food and the room resounding with melody and song. Any family event was worth celebrating in the most lavish manner possible. A father blessed with new offspring would invite the entire community for the Sabbath meal. They came in two groups, first the men and then the women. A safe return from a long journey was also an occasion for a festive family gathering at which the traveler would distribute gifts to one and all. When death came, the family would distribute handkerchiefs to everyone attending the funeral — and then invite them to a hearty meal.

All such occasions called for heavy expenditure, and often a host was torn between impoverishment and generosity. The less affluent suffered embarrassment because of another deplorable custom: certain individuals, claiming to be concerned about proper observance of the holidays, insisted on visiting homes and poking their noses into the family pots; if the holiday preparations did not seem grand enough to them, they would treat the owner to a generous portion of pious abuse. These practices were finally nullified by Rabbi Shlomo Mussah, following a stern discourse on the value of modesty and moderation in all festivities associated with the Jewish faith.

From early childhood, the Bukharan Jewess was taught to obey her father and to accept his views on all things. In due course he chose a husband for her, and she usually went along with his choice without protest. Some parents became in-laws while the future mates were still in their respetive cradles. In the infrequent case in which the girl refused the young man chosen for her, every effort was made to have her reconsider, but there was no compulsion.

Girls matured quite early and were considered ripe for marriage at the age of twelve; the more ambitious advanced the event by a year or two. The groom was hardly older than the bride. A woman who visited Bukhara about one hundred years ago went to see a Jewish family and asked for the man of the house. "He's not at home," she was told by two little girls who were playing in the yard. "May I see his wife, then," she asked. "We are his wives," was the reply.

Once the parents agreed on terms and the couple's consent was obtained, an engagement party was held for all the relatives and many guests. Tuesday and Saturday nights were the preferred times. The bride and groom would be placed in

*Bukharan Jewesses
participating in the
recitation of the Passover
Haggadah.*

separate rooms, and all during the meal they would send one another bits of delicacies. One of the chief participants was a "woman of incantations," engaged by the parents to ward off the evil eye from the couple. Carrying burning incense in a brazier, she would swing it among the guests for them to sniff and thus become immune to assault by evil forces.

The bride and groom did not meet each other alone during the engagement period. The agreement between the two sides was oral but binding. The wedding was generally scheduled for a year later, and the entire year passed in an aura of anticipation. Guests were invited for refreshments (fruit and wine) at the home of either in-laws, on festivals and New Moons, or if a very honored relative came to visit. The males sat with the groom, and the women kept the bride company. The men danced and the women kept the beat. At the height of the merriment, a tray of sugar cubes would be pushed along the floor, back and forth, for good luck. The groom, wearing a special hat, would then be placed in the middle of the circle formed by the dancers. His friends, singing as they went, would go around among the guests, collect a silver coin from each, wave the coin above the head of the donor, and toss it into the hat.

On the Sabbath immediately preceding the wedding, a festive meal would be tendered by the parents of the bride. That evening the in-laws would meet for a special ceremony called *Khuda beni*. The guests would stand around a bonfire as the women played and sang. They would then have a modest meal, so as not to attract the Evil Eye to the groom. At the wedding ceremony, the guests were required to raise their hands aloft, to show they had no magic or sorcery up their sleeves, again in an attempt to ward off the evil eye.

Three days prior to the wedding, the groom's kinsmen would repair to the home of the bride to assess the items she would bring to her future husband's home. During this "Assessment Day," the bride's brothers would seat themselves on the parcels to prevent removal until they were paid to release them. A similar custom was observed after the wedding ceremony. When the bride was being led to her husband's home, the brothers would block the doorway until pried away with gifts. All this was intended to add to the merriment.

The wedding feast was an occasion of supreme ostentation. The banquets provided by the affluent on the marriage of their male offspring at times reached legendary proportions.

A Bukharan saying notes that "three times in her lifetime does a woman see the light of day: at birth, on the day of her marriage and on the day of death." Be that as it may, once a woman became a wife and entered her husband's domicile, she would rarely be seen outside the confines of her home. Her duty was to accept her husband's dominion and do his wishes to the best of her ability. He did all the marketing while she did the cooking, spinning, sewing, and everything else that went under the name of housekeeping.

Every man's paramount yearning was for a male heir. If his wife proved barren or a producer of female progeny only, her husband could divorce her and/or marry an additional spouse.

When a son was born, joy reigned supreme. With the family in attendance in the home of the young mother, the midwife would enter with a silver bowl containing a wax candle in the shape of a five-fingered hand set in a circle of plain candles. Each of those present would light a candle and place a silver coin in the bowl. This done, the midwife would light the central candle.

The circumcision rite was performed in the synagogue, in the mother's presence. From the synagogue she went to her father's home until the period of purification was over. Both her arrival at her father's home and her subsequent return to her husband's abode were marked with festive meals.

The Bar Mitzvah was such an elaborate occasion that the father stopped work several days before the event in order to devote his full time and attention to the preparations. At the same time the son would be poring over his speech, to be delivered in the vernacular.

Bar Mitzvah day brought the entire family together from near and far. The principal protagonist of the occasion would officially open the ceremonies by delivering his talk, the father would recite the *kiddush*, and the boy and his teacher would be robed in colorful vestments — the sign that the feast was about to be served.

The wealthy prolonged the celebration for three days. In the case of the less affluent, the boy was already back at work, helping the family earn its livelihood on the very next day. Now, however, he was a man, ready to strike out for himself.

The dual propensity of Bukhara's Jews toward the good life and their faith found its most gratifying expression in the observance of the Sabbath and festivals. Culinary and religious rituals were equally elaborate. The synagogue liturgy was interwoven, as was the liturgy of Persian Jewry, with Babylonian and local melodies sung with special love. They were always in quest of a ''better cantor'' — one who possessed a fine voice and could interpret the chants reliably. Sabbath eve prayers were conducted by any young man capable of reading from the Hebrew prayer book (translating the meaning of the text was beyond the abilities of most of the worshippers).

On Sabbath afternoons, the entire community, old and young, would gather in the synagogue to hear one of the learned men expound on the biblical portion of the week. Homiletical tales about the Garden of Eden or the Messiah would hold them spellbound for hours.

To this day, Bukharan Jews are careful to memorialize the souls of the departed, and they seek every opportunity to be called up to the Torah reading for this purpose. The anniversary of a death is observed punctiliously, with the *kaddish* recited weeks before and after the day itself. At times there are more people in the synagogue reciting the *kaddish* than there are replying ''Amen'' — a phenomenon not uncommon elsewhere.

The spiritual and emotional complexity of the High Holy Days has given rise to many specifically Bukharan symbols that go beyond the spirit of penitence and renewal marked by the season.

On Rosh Hashanah eve the head of every household would light a candle in the synagogue, and on Yom Kippur eve he would hang up and light a lamp filled with enough oil to last throughout the fast day. It was believed that if the lamp burned to the very end, the sins of the owner had been forgiven and he would be inscribed for a good year. If the lamp went out, it was seen as a bad omen. When the community elders concluded that this custom bred depression, they decreed that each man was to give the synagugue trustee, the *gabbai*, the price of lamp and oil, and he would light all the lamps so that no one would know whose lamp went out. At the conclusion of the fast, the elder of the community would wish the congregation a happy year. Later that evening, people would go in groups from house to house to offer their good wishes for the year to come.

The more intricate the commandment, the better Bukharan Jews liked it. And the prescriptions for Sukkot were very much to their liking. They decorated their *sukkot* with gay splendor: the walls were adorned with tapestries and with colorful paper garlands, and the ground was covered with thick carpets. ''Elijah's Chair,'' a symbol of welcome to the Patriarchs, who according to tradition visit the *sukkot* at this time, stood in one corner, decorated with silks and laden with sacred books.

On Hoshana Rabba eve the people were careful not to leave their homes, for they believed — as the Zohar intimates — that anyone venturing abroad on that night who does not see his shadow would meet with tragedy.

Simhat Torah was a day of pure rejoicing. The walls of the synagogue were adorned with tapestry and drapery. Each Torah scroll was wrapped in seven coverlets. The act of removing the coverlets was considered a great honor, and worthy of considerable donations to the synagogue. Removing the last coverlet was the highest honor, and the wealthy worshippers bid for it enthusiastically, much to the merriment of the congregation. The winner would later treat his friends and relatives to a feast.

Immediately after Sukkot, the trustees made rounds of the homes of the wealthy for funds to buy fuel to tide the poor over the long and bitterly cold winter.

Tu Bishvat and Purim were celebrated in Bukhara in the same fashion as in the surrounding countries. On Tu Bishvat, fruits grown in the Land of Israel were served to guests. Purim was an occasion for playing cards and dice games.

Passover preparations were elaborate, bordering on the excessive. Plans for the holiday lasted throughout the year, since orders for next year's wheat, which was to be kept dry after reaping until it could be ground into flour for baking the *matzot,* was ordered by heads of families just after the end of the holiday. The wheat was picked up between Lag B'omer and Shavuot, and each family milled and stored its own flour.

With the advent of the month of Nissan, preparations were stepped up to a feverish pitch. The baking of the *matzot,* the focal point of activity, was done by the women, who were well versed in the laws governing the ritual. While kneading the dough they would keep their mouths covered, and any woman caught talking during this process would have her *matzot* declared unfit for use. As in other Oriental communities, the Bukharan *matza* is thick, round and quite tasty.

After the *matzot* were baked, the woman would prepare a feast for her family, in gratitude for having accomplished the sacred task without a flaw.

On the Great Sabbath, the Saturday immediately preceding Passover, the cantor would address the congregation on the subject of the Passover regulations and admonish his listeners to observe the law meticulously. His warnings of the consequences were so severe that by the time the *hametz* was burned, on the morning before the *Seder,* there was hardly a crumb to be found anywhere.

For the *Seder* each family would slaughter one or more sheep, a portion of which was set aside for the community's spiritual leaders and for the poor. While the men repaired to the public bathhouse, the women would add the final touches to the *Seder* menu. From the bathhouse, the men went to the synagogue for final instructions on conducting the *Seder.* By evening the entire family, scrubbed clean and decked out in colorful clothes, was ready to celebrate the exodus from Egypt. They sat in a circle on the carpeted floor and the *Seder* began. In the center of the circle the *Seder* plate and the *matzot* rested on a white silk cloth, embroidered in dazzling color. Oil lamps set on iron or metal stands provided bright illumination. The head of the family opened the *Seder* by reciting the *kiddush,* and the others joined, each in turn, in reading from the *Haggadah,* ending with the traditional proclamation: "Next year in rebuilt Jerusalem!" The women and children thereupon proceeded to their own quarters, while the men remained behind to chant the Songs of Songs.

During the intermediate days of Passover all work was suspended. At the close of the festival, the oldest man in the family would take a sheaf of green stalks; the other males would then come to him and kiss his hand, upon which he would tap them lightly with the stalk. The oldest woman in the family would do the same for the female members. This done, they would bake bread, and then sit down and eat it in a spirit of joy.

Music was very popular among Bukharan Jews. They played and sang on every festive occasion, and their liturgy was very melodious; the chanting of the cantor was listened to with fervent reverence. They excelled in playing the popular string instruments: the *tamour,* the *cheltar* and the *changui.* The long-necked *tamour,* which closely resembles the mandolin, is made of wood of the mulberry tree and can

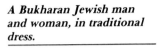

A Bukharan Jewish man and woman, in traditional dress.

be tuned in many ways. The pot-bellied *cheltar* has a sounding board of leather made from the walls of a cow's heart. The zither-like *changui* has 42 strings, is made of oak, and is played with two sticks, like a xylophone.

Bukharan Jews were famous for their musical accomplishment, and were often invited by their Moslem neighbors to play at family festivities.

In literature and poetry, Bukhara's Jews were originally influenced by the traditions of their Persian brethren, but in time the contact was broken and Bukharan Jews developed a literature and poetry of their own. Their poetry flowered in the seventeenth and eighteenth centuries and burst into full bloom in the works of the poet Yossef Yehudi, who composed paeans to the heroes of the Bible and translated poetry of the Middle Ages.

This intellectual endeavor lasted until the end of the eighteenth century, when their entire cultural structure weakened, and did not rise again until Bukhara's Jews came into contact with other world Jewish communities towards the nineteenth century. The strongest stimulus was the reawakening of the yearning for the Land of Israel. Both groups and individuals found their way there and laid the community foundations for the thousands who were to come after the birth of the State of Israel. More than anyone else, Moroccan-born Rabbi Yosef Maarabi brought to Bukhara's Jews the message of the restoration. He settled in Safed about a century ago, and was sent by religious institutions in the city to gather contributions from the Jews of Bukhara. When he saw the cultural backwardness of the Bukharan community, he abandoned his original purpose and set about organizing a network for the study of religion, much to the gratification of the community. He sent emissaries to Constantinople, Vilna, Leghorn and other centers of Jewish learning, who returned laden with sacred writings. Scribes were brought in to prepare Scrolls of the Law. A dramatic note was lent to Maarabi's effort when a group of forced converts from Meshed reached Bukhara, via Persia, shed the Islamic faith which they had been forced to accept, and returned to the faith of their fathers. This act inspired Bukhara's Jews with the feeling of spiritual allegiance, and induced them to seek even stronger contact with their brethren elsewhere.

When Russia annexed Bukhara, the Bukharan community established ties with Russian Jewry. The pioneering Zionist movement there further infected the Bukharan community. More of them went to the Land of Israel, bought land in Jerusalem, and built a neighborhood of fine homes and synagogues which they called Rehovot and which in time became known as the Bukharan Quarter.

Bukharan Jews were well-off, for the most part. They excelled in silk weaving and dyeing, and traded actively with Russia, Persia, and India. They introduced cotton-growing, and manufactured hats and textiles. Some went into agriculture, and pharmacology.

During the first years of Russian rule, the Jews continued to enjoy their established rights. Early in the present century, however, they began to feel the whip of oppression. In 1911, all Bukharan Jews living in Turkestan were ordered back to Bukhara. This dealt their trade and commerce a severe blow.

Following the Soviet revolution, public schools were opened to Jews. The community listed Hebrew as its national tongue and was permitted to teach in that language. In 1921, with the creation of the zealous "Jewish Section" in the Communist Party, Hebrew was displaced by Tajani-Persian, the vernacular. As elsewhere under Soviet rule, Jewish culture was restricted. A seven-man committee, consisting of the rabbi, head of the community, head of the burial society, the sexton, the secretary, the treasurer, and a trustee, was appointed to administer the internal affairs of the community and its institutions, out of the community's own funds and with grants from the government's budget.

In the 1930's administration was placed in the hands of party politicians; the role of the rabbi and the others was limited to the synagogue. Legal jurisdiction was transferred to a People's Court, which took its orders from the Communist regime.

Soviet instructors and the Persian language pervaded the Jewish schools. The Jews resorted to employing private tutors for Hebrew and clandestinely supported Zionism, despite the constant threat of exposure. The successful merchants were stripped of all their holdings. Many Jews left Bukhara and joined their brethren in Jerusalem, where they went into trade, construction, and industry.

North African Jews

In Jewish literature, the countries of North Africa were known as "the lands of the west" — *artzot hama'rav* (in Arabic, the *Magreb*); to residents of the East, these lands were at the end of the world.

The Jews of North Africa were called *ner hama'arav*, "the candle of the west." Despite hardship and oppression, they maintained their Jewish identity and spiritual sovereignty, producing poets and liturgists, sages and scholars, linguists and scientists.

In lands situated along shores easily accessible to conquering powers, North African Jewry survived them all, until contemporary times.

Jewish settlement in North Africa began even before the Jewish people was exiled from its homeland. But the settlements reached extensive proportions when Titus, who received Africa as a gift from his father, the Emperor Vespasian, in recognition of a "job well done" in Judea, proceeded to populate the region with thousands of Jewish exiles — some thirty thousand were taken to Carthage (near modern Tunis) and were welcomed by the Jews already living in the port city.

Egypt had a Jewish community four centuries before the destruction of the Second Temple, when Ptolemy brought down large numbers of Jews from Judea. They proved to be excellent soldiers, and some, sent to defend Egyptian outposts in Libya and Cyrenaica, kept going westward and reached Jewish settlements established by seafaring ancestors who had arrived in the wake of their adventurous neighbors, the Phoenicians, during the reign of Solomon. Unlike the Phoenicians (and the Greeks and Romans after them), the Jews did not assimilate into the Berber tribes of the region. They clung to their faith and its traditions, and kept in touch with other Jewish communities, particularly in the Holy Land. When the exiles arrived and told the story of Roman rule in Judea, describing the destruction of Jerusalem and the Temple, the Jews of Cyrenaica raised the banner of revolt against their own Roman rulers. Emperor Trajan put down the revolt with the usual Roman savagery, but the decimated community went on. Bolstered by refugees from Judea and Egypt, they recovered sufficiently to establish their presence even more firmly. In fact many of the Berber tribes became Jewish in a mass movement of conversion. Jewish habitation spread all along the coast and reached as far as the Atlas Mountains. Jews populated entire villages where they raised cattle, tilled vineyards and produced wine. In the larger cities they were metal workers, weavers, and dyers, while in the port centers they engaged in shipping and trade.

The Romans did not fail to note the influence of the Jews on the native populations, and sought to restrict their activities. This persecution grew after the Roman Empire embraced the Christian faith. When the Byzantine Emperor Justinian noted this influence, which was even more evident in the light of the failure of Christian proselytizing among the natives, he decreed that the Jews cease inflicting their "queer ideas" on the local population. Finally he ordered all synagogues converted into churches.

Faced with extinction, entire Jewish communities withdrew to the south. There they attracted other tribes and went forth to challenge the invading Moslem forces. The Jewish queen of the tribes, Dahiya al Kahina (Dahiya the Prophetess), aroused the hill people to follow her in battling the invaders. She fell in battle in the year 707.

The Moslem wave emanating from the Arabian Peninsula did not find it easy to

North African Jews were distinguishable from their neighbors in features and modes of dress.

conquer North Africa. But when the Moslem rulers finally did become entrenched, the natives accepted both their sovereignty and the faith of Islam. All traces of former civilizations — Greek, Carthaginian, Roman — were obliterated, except for some splendid edifices, fine roads, and theaters. A few among the tribes persisted in

Eighteenth-century North African oil lamp, of bronze.

adhering to Judaism. Along the slopes of the Atlas Mountains and in the oases of the Sahara they still recounted the stories of their origin, claiming descent from the Ten Lost Tribes.

The Moslems, intent on uprooting Christian influence, did not spare the Jews, and they suffered most severely under the rule of Idris, of the Ali dynasty, in the eighth century, after he wrested the western lands of North Africa from the Eabas Caliphate. He established his capital in Fez and shamed and humiliated the Jews even though many of them had supported his rise to power. Every year they had to supply his harem with twenty-four Jewish virgins. Later, however, when Idris' heirs came to power, life became less harsh and soon centers of Torah learning arose in Fez and Kairouan (in Tunisia), replacing the banished yeshivot in Babylon.

Among the pillars of the community in Fez were Isaac Alfasi and Maimonides, the philologists Yehuda ben Kurish and Donash ben Labrat; Kairouan brought forth Rabbenu Nissim and Rabbi Hananel, heads of great academies of learning.

This surge of spirit and scholarship was disrupted and almost overwhelmed by the rise to power of the Muwahaddin, the zealots of Islam. Their scimitars gave the Jews the choice of death or conversion to the faith of Mohammed. Their leader, Abed al Mumin, claimed that the Prophet had granted the Jews five hundred years, during which time they could retain their faith. But their Messiah would either have to come before the termination of that period or they would have to convert. Now the period had come to an end and they had to make their choice. Many chose to perish. Others fled while still others, at least ostensibly, accepted Islam. It was at this time that Maimonides wrote his famous "Epistle on Apostasy," which spoke up for the Marranos — Spain's New Christians.

The Moslems were not convinced of the spiritual fealty of the apostates; they forced them to wear black clothes and a yellow hat, so as to make them conspicuous and easy to trail.

The centers of Jewish scholarship in Fez, Marrakesh, Oran, Sejilmassa, and Tel-Massan disappeared. Even when the scourge of the Almohads dissipated, the lot of the Jews did not improve markedly. The degrading edicts remained in force, and the Moslems constantly sought pretexts to oppress the Jews. Their residence in

Jewish laborer in Marrakesh, Morocco.

Fez was first forbidden and then restricted to the *mellah,* the ghetto. Kairouan was declared sacred to the Moslems, and no unbelievers were permitted to live there. In other cities, too, Jews were crammed into the hovels and alleys of the *mellah.*

Many Spanish Jews escaped the Inquisition by fleeing to North Africa and either settled there or used it as a way station for further wandering. Many of the descendants of Spanish and Portuguese Jews who had settled in Leghorn eventually moved to North African countries, as well.

In the sixteenth century foreign powers began to subdivide the region into a number of political and geographical entities, under the rule of Spain, Portugal, the Ottoman Empire, and other Mediterranean powers. With this disintegration, there also came major changes in the life and structure of the Jewish communities, now separated by boundaries and political loyalties. They developed different Jewish life-styles that reflected both their insistence on maintaining their ancient faith and their integration into the life of the countries in which they lived.

There is a great overlapping of customs and ceremonies among North African Jewry. Algeria's eastern communities shared many customs with neighboring Tunis, whereas in the west the Algerian communities were greatly influenced by their Moroccan neighbors.

Morocco

Morocco, the Maghreb monarchy at the north-western tip of the African continent, has the most colorful history of all the North African states. At the end of the eighth century, Moslems swarmed over the area and held it in the name of the Caliph in Baghdad. Idris, a descendant of Ali, the son-in-law of Mohammed, came to Morocco from Egypt, rallied the Berbers to his side, and set up an independent state. Idris built his capital in Fez, in the foothills of the Atlas Mountains, and proceeded to make it the equal of Baghdad and Cairo. He erected magnificent palaces and surrounded the entire city with a wall that is still a chief tourist attraction.

The Jews fared well under the rule of Idris's heirs, who appreciated their diligence on behalf of the city's growth. In order to protect the Jewish community, Idris II built an inner wall around a section near his palace where Jews could live without fear of being molested. In time, this safety device became a veritable prison camp, choked with a growing population which could not expand beyond its walled-in confines. This was how the first *mellah* — a maze of tortuous alleys hardly fit for human habitation — came into being. The name *mellah* means "salt." Its probable derivation is connected with the degrading task forced upon the Jews by the hostile Moslem populace — that of executioner of state. After a person was decapitated the head was impaled on the city walls. But before it was impaled, the Jewish executioners had to prevent its decomposition, which they did with salt.

Morocco produced many brilliant scholars, among them Rabbi Yitzhak Alfasi, one of the foremost authorities on Jewish jurisprudence, Dunash ben Labrat, one of the great Spanish-Jewish poets, and Yehuda ibn Hiyuj, who set forth the principles of Hebrew grammar and etymology. In the eleventh century, when the Berber tribes rose up against the regime, many of these scholars left Morocco for Spain, taking with them a substantial segment of the Jewish community. The advent of the fanatic Almohads brought to an end a golden age which had lasted two centuries. The Almohads forced many Jews to convert to Islam. Those who converted derived some comfort from Maimonides' "Epistle on Apostasy" which he wrote in order to bolster their hopes for a return to their faith. The converts were also subjected to a variety of indignities and confined to the *mellah*.

The tide turned in the fifteenth century. Many of the refugees from the Spanish Inquisition fled to Morocco and were welcomed with open arms. By now, however, there was a great social and cultural gap between Spanish and Moroccan Jews which resulted in problems of integration. This was accentuated by the success of the Spanish exiles in working for the betterment of the community, which they achieved by their own activities in commerce and trade, by their knowledge of foreign languages, and by their employment as consultants to the more affluent members of Morocco's citizenry. The government quickly grasped the importance of these exiles and granted them special privileges which the other Jews did not enjoy. This preferential treatment caused deep cleavages: the two groups maintained separate synagogues and refrained from intermarrying.

In the sixteenth century, Spain and Portugal attacked Morocco and other parts of North Africa. The Portuguese, who took control of Morocco's port cities, took advantage of the Jewish residents to strengthen their administration. Jewish merchants, who maintained a virtual monopoly on trade in Morocco's port cities,

An elderly Moroccan Jew.

used connections with their brethren in European centers to draw Morocco into the mainstream of foreign trade.

In the beginning of the seventeenth century, as Portuguese rule waned, Dutch mercantile interests came on the scene. Jews played an important role in this new development, too. The Falagi family compiled an amazing record: the brothers Samuel and Joseph were Morocco's permanent ambassadors to The Hague. Of Joseph's five sons, Moshe was secretary and interpreter to the King of Morocco; Isaac was Morocco's ambassador to Istanbul; Joshua was tax and customs director in Safi; Jacob was the representative of the Moroccan *sharif* in Denmark, and David followed his father as ambassador to The Hague. But although many of these Jews held citizenship in a European country, in Morocco itself, despite their overall usefulness, the Jews had fewer basic rights than serfs.

In the first half of the seventeenth century, a Jewish tribe living southeast of Meliliah staged an uprising against the Moslem rulers and under the leadership of Ibn Mishal, a wealthy Jewish merchant, took over control of the region, ruling it from the fortress where Ibn Mishal kept all of his wealth. Ar-Raschid, a Sherifian fleeing for his life, understood the advantages of having a bastion at his command. Knowing that Ibn Mishal was very hospitable, he disguised himself as a wanderer and gained access to the fortress. In the middle of the night he opened the gates and let in five hundred of his followers. Under torture, Ibn Mishal revealed the hiding place of his treasures, after which he was killed and his treasures used to bring Ar-Raschid to power.

For the Jews it made little difference who was, or aspired to be, in power, since all the rulers financed their campaigns by taxing the Jews. News of the death of a ruler was received by the Jews with trepidation. They knew that any change only meant more trouble. They hid their possessions wherever they could, barred their dwellings, and slept with weapons close at hand. A change in rulers that was not followed by anti-Jewish actions was tantamount to a miracle.

These adverse conditions produced a constant stream of Jewish refugees fleeing Morocco. The scholars among them found a ready welcome in the Jewish communities in Turkey, Italy, and Holland. Several of them, on the way to the Land of Israel, remained in Tunisia and Jerba in order to sustain the Jewish communities there.

Far left: a Moroccan Jew blessing a mezuza *prior to entering a building. Below: an elderly woman with colorful wool kerchief (left); an elderly couple (right).*

Left: Jewish woman in typical Moroccan dress, in her drawing room in Fez. Right: Jewish dwellings in a village in the Atlas Mountains.

The passage of time brought no respite to the Jews of Morocco. In the nineteenth century, Mulai Abed ar-Rakhman conspired to deprive Yehuda Abarbanel of his fortune in order to finance his struggle against the French. After Abarbanel was put to death, the ruler's emissaries came to his home to confiscate his wealth. They saw Abarbanel's beautiful daughter and wanted to take her to their master, but her fiance seized the sword of one of the king's men and killed his bride and himself.

In 1831, a remarkably beautiful Jewish girl, Suleika, daughter of Shlomo Hagwil of Tangier, was seized by Moslems and taken to the king's palace. The crown prince saw her and begged her to convert and become his wife. When she refused, the prince called in the elders of the community and threatend to wipe out all the Jews unless Suleika agreed. The girl steadfastly refused and was subsequently executed. The Jews erected a tall monument in memory of her courage.

A spirit of suffering permeated much of Jewish life in the *mellah*. In their ramshackle dwellings (the "wealthy" occupied the more airy second story), the residents maintained tight family relationships based on discipline and respect for elders. The earnings of the father and his sons were pooled for the subsistence of the entire family. When a son married, room was made for the new family member and for future offspring; only in cases where the bride's parents were more affluent did the son change his residence.

Status was determined by material possessions and/or scholarliness, the latter being the weightier factor. The size of the family was also a determinant, and the families that grew into clans often maintained synagogues of their own. Even community matters were of concern to all and holidays were often observed collectively, so as to lend the proper atmosphere to the *mellah* as a whole. On these occasions, the *mellah* underwent a complete transformation, as did its inhabitants.

The Sabbath was a very special day in the life of Moroccan Jews. There was great emphasis on food, primarily the *hamin*, since Sabbath without it, so said the Moroccan Jews, was like a king without a throne. This succulent dish (layer upon layer of potatoes, rice, chickpeas, meat, and eggs) spent Friday night in the oven and emerged in all its browned glory on Sabbath morning. Another favorite was fish cooked with chickpeas, through which, according to popular belief, the souls of the righteous passed prior to their ascent to heaven. When Sabbath was over, worshippers in the synagogues were given fragrant sprigs for the *havdala* ceremony. A fitting conclusion to the day came with another repast, the *melaveh malkah*, escorting the "Sabbath Queen" to her exit. This usually consisted of coffee, pastry, and religious songs sung in Arabic.

Believing as they did in every jot and title of symbolism in tradition, the Jews of Morocco were understandably eager to begin the new year in proper fashion. Rosh Hashanah was ushered in with the eating of many fruits and vegetables, with each benediction pronounced over food adding to the number of pious deeds. The High Holy Day prayers were chanted by three cantors in unison.

Sukkot provided a unique occasion for turning the drab *mellah* into a verdant jewel. Inside the green-covered *sukka* stood "Elijah's Chair," adorned with colorful embroidery and laden with sacred books. Simhat Torah was the most exciting day of the week-long celebration: every family came to the synagogue for *hakafot*, and as the men danced about with the Torah scrolls, the women, much to the delight of the youngsters, threw sweets at them.

Hanukah meant jelly doughnut time. The traditional festival meal was *couscous* and chicken, while games rounded out the celebration.

68

Faces of Moroccan Jews.

On the Fast of Esther, the day before Purim, everyone fasted — men, women and children — in anticipation of the evil days ahead. But Purim itself was a merry affair. The youngsters armed themselves with a variety of implements for the assault on Haman, and their mothers prepared mountains of baked goods for the traditional exchange of gifts. Haman was burned in an assortment of effigies, and the Purim dinner was the climax of the holiday.

Passover also attained several interesting addenda at the hands of Morocco's Jews. The leaven hidden and then searched for on the night before Passover eve also included slices of grilled liver. *Matzot* were not baked until all the leaven had been burned on the morning before Passover. The baking was, of necessity, done in great haste, with a few minutes off for a bite of potatoes and hard-boiled eggs. The work was accompanied by the chanting of Psalms.

Before sitting down to the *Seder*, it was customary to take the *Seder* plate and make the rounds of one's friends, passing the plate above their heads. After the Four Questions were asked, the person conducting the *Seder* picked up a staff and the *afikoman matza,* left the room by one door, and then came back by another. In response to the group's question, ''From where do you come ?'' he would recount the story of the Exodus, embellishing it to the best of his ability. Afterwards everyone commented, ''He that tells of the Exodus from Egypt at greater length is the more praiseworthy.'' The *Haggadah* was then recited, mostly in the vernacular. The traditional stealing of the *afikoman* was not practiced.

Unlike other Eastern communities, Moroccan Jewry prohibited the use of beans and rice on Passover. Fresh green beans, however, were allowed.

Far left: a teacher and his pupils, and a young boy holding his alphabet table. Left: a mother carrying her child on her back.

Since the younger children tended to fall asleep early and miss part of the *Seder*, a special *Seder* was held for them during the intermediate days. Family picnics were also popular on these days. The last day of Passover marked the beginning of the *maimuna*, a festival in memory of Maimonides, which, in color and atmosphere, surpassed even Passover. The women wore velvet dresses embroidered with silver and gold thread. The girls decked themselves out in bridal white or went about disguised as Arab women. The young men masqueraded as Berbers or famous figures and roamed along the alleys of the Jewish Quarter. The young people exchanged *en passant* glances of appraisal and anticipation which, in some instances and in due course, led to the canopy.

Inside their homes, the women set the festive table with a white cloth decorated with green wheat stalks and flowers brought in by Arab villagers. In the center they set a pitcher of milk and a bowl of flour topped with five eggs, five bean stalks, and five dates. Surrounding the bowl were plates laden with honey, fruit, nuts, cookies, *muflita* (a sweet crepe), wines, and lettuce leaves.

En route from the synagogue, the worshippers stopped at the homes of their friends and relatives to chant the *maimuna* benediction, *Alallah maimuna ambarcha massauda* — "best wishes for a blessed *maimuna*." At each stop the visitors partook of refreshments, particularly the lettuce, honey, and *muflita*. They also visited the rabbis and the *kohanim*, to receive their blessing. Bridegrooms sent their fiancées golden ornaments and had dinner at the homes of their future in-laws. The *maimuna* menu consisted of fried pancakes dipped in butter, milk, and honey, and grilled fish (no meat or strong coffee was served). Following the

Artisans in the Jewish mellah in Morocco: a coppersmith (left) and a blacksmith (right).

meal, everyone went out for long strolls, within the limits of the Quarter. The older generation blessed the younger ones by wishing them a "wedding within the year."

In the port cities, Jews went to the sea to dip their feet in water. Elsewhere, rivers, brooks and springs served the same purpose. Maimonides inspired the Jews of Morocco to symbolic manifestations in every phase of life. Even so, some scholars ascribed the name *maimuna* to other sources, pointing to the Hebrew word *emuna*, meaning "faith" (in the coming of the Messiah during the month of Nissan).

The *sefira* days between Passover and Shavuot, when people were supposedly prone to "evil spirits," found the Jews of Morocco carrying as a precaution bits of rock salt, given them by their *shamash*. It was also a time when they paid homage to the sages, Rabbi Meir Baal Haness and Rabbi Shimon Bar Yohai, by lighting candles in their memory.

On Shavuot it was customary to take a few *matzot*, hidden on Passover, and shred them into bowls of milk and honey, since the Torah, given on Shavuot, was likened to milk and honey.

The days between the Seventeenth of Tammuz and the Ninth of Av were keenly felt in the *mellah*. Children began fasting at the age of nine. On Tisha B'Av night the entire family slept on the bare floor. The Book of Lamentations was read as prescribed, with an added passage commemorating the expulsion from Spain; many of the forebears of those reciting it had been among the exiles.

In preparation for *Shabbat Nahamu*, the Sabbath of Comfort following Tisha B'Av, the women whitewashed their homes in the belief that the Messiah might soon come.

Despite their poverty and lack of space, there was no blessing greater than having a large, ever-growing family. Sterility was considered a curse, and barren women tried everything to become pregnant — even turning to miracle-workers and Arab medicine men. In some districts herb experts brewed potions designed to promote fertility. Barren women often sought the intercession of dead holy men whose graves they visited regularly. When such a woman became pregnant, she was inclined to credit the departed *tzaddik* whose grave she had visited, and she often named the new-born child for him. During pregnancy, the expectant mother was careful not to look at deformed people. In the case of a chance meeting, she spat quickly to cast off the "evil eye." Fathers invariably wanted sons, and there were all sorts of formulas for guessing the sex of the foetus.

Two midwives officiated at the delivery, and if the birth was difficult, the rabbi was called in. The women joined in prayer, and the husband stood at the *mezuza* until he was informed that his wife had given birth. A male offspring evoked the cry of *baruch habba,* welcome, and the father was congratulated with exclamations of *siman tov,* a good sign. A female offspring was welcomed with cries of, "May she be blessed and lucky," and the father was congratulated with a simple "good luck."

The infant mortality rate was high, and there was a plethora of methods to prevent it — incantations, amulets, even painting the infant's eyelids blue with a small silver applicator. The teacher and his pupils came to chant prayers and petitions, the text of which was then tacked on to the mother's bed. The most popular method for keeping the child well was assembling in the home of the new-born for night vigils that consisted of Torah study and the recitation of Psalms.

The circumcision ritual was performed at home. Eldest children were named for their grandparents. If the boy was born on a holiday, he was named Nissim ("miracles") for Hanuka, Mordecai for Purim, and Menahem ("comforter") for the month of Av. A new daughter was given a name at the Torah reading in the synagogue, which was followed by a modest *kiddush* at home.

Education was especially emphasized by Moroccan Jews. The foremost ambition of every father was a son gifted in Jewish studies. When a boy was forty days old, he was taken to the school, where the father treated the pupils to refreshments. At the age of three or four, the child was already a student himself. At the age of seven he was proficient in the cantillations. His first "performance" in the synagogue was almost like a Bar Mitzvah celebration.

Membership in the burial society was considered a great honor, and was passed from father to son.

Bar Mitzvah was observed at any time during the thirteenth year. On the chosen Sabbath, the young man delivered an intricate sermon, in verse, plus words of gratitude for his parents, friends, and family. The actual ceremony was held on the preceeding Monday or Thursday, when the Torah was read; the young man and his father had their hair cut the day before, surrounded by friends and musicians. The boy was escorted to the synagogue, his family leading the way with large candles. The boy donned his prayer shawl and phylacteries for the first time. After the ceremony the family went home for a light meal. A big party was held that night. In many districts, this was the teacher's night as well; he passed around glasses of whiskey to all those present, and they in turn placed silver coins in the glass, to

74 *From left to right: weaving on a primitive loom; a blacksmith; a mirror-maker.*

remunerate him for his efforts. If the family could afford it, the boy continued his Jewish education after his Bar Mitzvah. To the Jewish family in Morocco, there could be no greater honor than their son becoming a rabbi.

A wedding turned the *mellah* into a huge catering establishment. For the most part, the bride had not yet reached her twelfth birthday. If she was underweight (not unusual for brides of nine or ten) she was fed fattening food to fill out her figure. There was no official engagement ceremony, merely an understanding between the two sets of parents. The bride and groom exchanged gifts, particularly on Purim and Passover. Two days before the wedding (usually held on a Wednesday), the groom appeared before the rabbinical court to obligate himself to care for his future wife, while the father of the bride did the same with regard to the dowry. Everyone then proceeded to the bride's home to view the clothes and ornaments she would be taking to her husband's home.

A traveler describing a Jewish wedding in Tangier had this to say:

> The steer for the feast was slaughtered in the yard of the bride's home (a ceremony attended by all the invitees) . . . As they left, each placed a coin on the steer's head; this was called *siman tov* (''a good sign'') and given to the ritual slaughterer. As the bride went forth from her father's home, an egg was broken above her head. Preceded by fife and drum, she arrived at her home as though deaf and dumb, as she pretended to be while being decked out, then under the canopy, until she went forth and lay on her bed, a statue of stone . . . .

The bride's attire was prepared with the care worthy of a queen's coronation robes. On her head she wore a maze of colorful kerchiefs, deftly twisted and knotted to form a tall turban. Her bridal gown was ''the great dress,'' worn only for the marriage ceremony, and bequeathed by mother to daughter down the generations.

Fashioned out of brown velvet, embroidered with gold and silver thread and studded with semi-precious stones, it flared out from the waist down. Its long sleeves were puffed, and of light material, as was the fashion of Spanish queens.

Before the ceremony, the women tinted her eyelids, combed her hair in two braids, painted her face, drew odd symbols on her forehead, nose and under her lips to ward off the evil eye, and tinted her palms with henna. Following this, a relative raised the bride aloft on a chair, while the bride made every effort not to bat an eyelid.

The ceremony was held on a raised platform set up in the house rather than in the open air, as was the custom elsewhere. The canopy itself was topped with a large silver crown. Before the rites, a master of ceremonies exhibited the gifts tendered to the couple and called out the names of the donors. The "Seven Days of Feasting" after the ceremony began with a sumptuous meal for everyone, including the poor, while amateur poets vied with one another in singing the praises of the newlyweds. After the wedding the young couple invited all the members of the family to a fish dinner which symbolized the hope for fertility.

Death and grief came often to the *mellah,* and was marked by loud laments by the female relatives, as they wrung their hands, scratched their skin, tore their hair, and beat their breasts. A preacher stationed at the cemetery delivered the eulogy before interment. During the seven days of mourning, prayers were held at the home of the deceased. If the deceased was a man of importance, prayers were held there for an entire year. A somber meal terminated the mourning.

Interestingly enough, Jews and Arabs did not engage in the same occupations, a situation which precluded competition and even resulted in economic cooperation. Some occupations were forbidden to Moslems (manufacturing and selling spirits, money lending), while others were traditionally "Jewish" (working with gold and

silver). Jews also manufactured mattresses, and Jewish merchants dealt in grain and in foreign trade. Since Jews were not allowed to own land, the Moslems supplied them with farm produce, poultry, and beef, in addition to flour and coffee. Where the occupations coincided, the Jews supplied the *mellah* market, while the Arabs took care of the Moslem market. In the rural districts, the Jews were itinerant peddlers.

The rungs of the economic ladder were clearly marked. At the top were the few wealthy bankers and merchants. Then came the goldsmiths and silversmiths, the craftsmen (tailors and carpenters), petty merchants, and storekeepers. The community leaders — rabbis, legal authorities, ritual slaughterers — were paid by the community in the large cities, but in the rural areas they had to engage in other occupations in order to earn a living. These positions were usually passed on from father to son, and long rabbinical lineages were common.

In the communal structure, the *naggid* was the chief leader, selected by the community or appointed by the sultan; when the communal taxes were too heavy, the *naggid* — if he was in a position to do so — contributed a substantial amount.

The rabbis were responsible for all practices and institutions ordained by the Jewish faith. In the rural districts there were circuit rabbis, since not every village had a rabbi.

The rabbis did everything they could to help their poor constituents. They collected loaves of bread and containers of oil drippings for them, and never allowed a festive gathering to conclude without calling for contributions for the less fortunate.

The civilian administration of the *mellah* was in the hands of *Sheikh al Yahudi,* an appointee of the local ruler who acted as the executive branch of the Jewish courts and as police commissioner, assisted by club-wielding deputies. He had the power to punish wrong-doers, disturbers of the peace, drunkards, and violators of the Sabbath. He collected taxes and was paid out of the fines he imposed.

The heaviest punishment that the rabbi could impose on any member of the community was *Herem,* excommunication, in which the culprit was publicly banished from the synagogue and placed outside the community until such time as he repented and paid a heavy fine for reinstatement. This particular punitive measure was credited with the maintenance of law and order in the *mellah.*

In cases where a court could not reach a decision, litigants were made to swear an oath on a Torah scroll. Even litigants who were sure they were right preferred to lose money by way of adjudication rather than swear to a claim over the scroll. Moslems accepted such an oath without question.

Rabbis were aided in their efforts to popularize learning by the emissaries who came from the Land of Israel to gather funds for indigent scholars. The arrival of "an emissary from Jerusalem" was a major event in the *mellah.* To host such a person was an outstanding honor. If the emissary saw the community was in no position to contribute funds, he endeavored to raise its spirits, urging the Jews to devote more time to Torah study.

Time and again, Jews tried to make their way to the Land of Israel, but the tribulations of the long voyage made this very hazardous. One account of such a journey assumed legendary dimensions: Rabbi Hayyim ben Attar, a reknowned scholar, decided to make a pilgrimage to the ancestral homeland. On the way to

Jewish women in North Africa wore a variety of ornaments containing charms and symbols meant to dispel evil, such as these necklaces (left and below) and bride's headdress (far left).

While Jews in the smaller towns maintained more traditional activities, French culture in Morocco's large cities influenced many young Jews to change their life-styles. Right: a young Jew in Casablanca. Opposite: a Moroccan Jew reading from the Book of Psalms.

Italy the ship foundered. Rabbi Hayyim, clinging to a plank, was washed ashore. A lion sought to devour him but was frightened off by the light which glowed in the rabbi's face. The rabbi came to a cave inhabited by forty thieves. As they were about to kill him, one of them held out a restraining hand: he recognized the rabbi as his teacher. Rabbi Hayyim persuaded his former pupil to abandon his evil ways. He then continued on to Leghorn and from there to Jerusalem, where he founded a yeshiva. Worn out from his travels, he died in Jerusalem at an early age.

In the eighteenth and nineteenth centuries, Morocco, eroded by internecine strife, became prey to the European powers in quest of territory in North Africa. Morocco's northern coast was annexed by the Spaniards. After France conquered Algeria on the east and the Sahara tracts on the southeast, its appetite extended to Morocco.

After seizing power in the 1930's, the French set about developing Morocco on a grand scale. They developed railroads, highways, mines and shipping. The Jews hoped for a new era; even prior to the entrenchment of the French, the Alliance Israélite Universelle had set up schools in a number of localities, in which French was the language of instruction, much to the dismay of the rabbis. The latter proceeded to establish modern Jewish schools, which in turn forced the Alliance establishments to include Jewish studies in their curricula.

The French ruled Morocco's Jews far more kindly than they did those of Algeria. They paved many of the streets in the *mellah,*, provided water lines, and allowed the Jews to move out of the *mellah,* into the French sections. Jews streamed from the rural areas into the cities, especially Casablanca, developed by the French from a small town to a city of 700,000.

Assimilation did not fail to make its inroads, much to the concern of the older generation. But as the young Jews — now better-educated and modern in every respect — drew closer to the French, they were unwittingly fanning flames of hatred on the part of Arab nationalists. The Istiklal Party identified the Jews with the French conquerors.

More than 100,000 Moroccan Jews came to Israel in the first few years of its independence. In 1956 Morocco obtained its independence from France, and the status of Jews living there deteriorated. Immigration to Israel was forbidden, and Jewish organizations in existence for generations were closed on suspicion of Zionist activities. Jews were removed from all decent jobs.

During the 1970s, most of Morocco's Jews emigrated to France, Canada, and Israel.

Algeria was still a vassal of Rome known as Numidia when Jews first settled there; Algerian Jews point with pride to the fact that their ancestors, along with the Berbers, were among the earliest inhabitants of North Africa. In the early centuries of the Common Era some of the local Berber tribes converted to Judaism. The descendants of these proselyte Berbers included the *kehina*, the Jewish-Barbary queen who courageously fought off the Moslem invaders.

Like other Jewish communities in North Africa, the Jews of Algeria suffered severe economic and social setbacks in the tenth century when the fanatical sword of Islam put an end to their prosperity. And like the other communities, they, too, experienced a measure of revival in the fifteenth and sixteenth centuries, with the arrival of Jewish scholars from Inquisition-dominated Spain.

Algerian Jews have a legend relating to the arrival of these survivors. The Inquisition was about to put to death the Chief Rabbi of Seville along with sixty community leaders. As the inquisitors were about to lead them to the pyre, the rabbi took out his handkerchief and folded it into the shape of a ship. He then told each of the sixty to touch the handkerchief with his fingertips. At once the handkerchief began to grow until it turned into a sailing craft which the wind took up, along with the rabbi and the sixty men, above the streets of Seville, to the sea and thence to the shores of Algeria. The Moslem rulers of the country — enemies of the Christians — were fascinated by their story and offered them haven.

The Spanish scholars who settled in Algeria were well received and set about improving the educational level of Algerian Jewry. Two of them, Rabbi Yizhak bar Sheshet Barfat and Rabbi Shimon ben Zemach Duran, dedicated their lives to this task. Duran had been a famous physician in Majorca who fled, leaving behind all his possessions. In Algeria his knowledge of medicine was of little value, since people resorted to black magic for healing. He abandoned his profession and devoted himself to healing the spirit of the Jews and to strengthening their communal structure and identity. To this day, Algerian Jews commemorate the two rabbis in the course of the traditional memorial prayers.

Jewish merchants who came to Algeria from Spain were not as favorably received. Their advanced business experience and acumen quickly put them in privileged positions over the rest of the community. Moreover, the Moslem rulers, who quickly saw the economic gains the newcomers could bring them, gave them special privileges. With the passage of time, as the general benefit wrought by the newcomers touched the local residents as well, they were accepted more favorably.

When the Moors withdrew from Algeria, the Christian inhabitants set about instituting their own persecutions of the Jews. In 1563 they fell upon the Jews of Tel-Assan and massacred some 1,500 people. The entire Jewish community of Oran was expelled and its synagogue converted into a church. The Jews fared little better when the Ottoman Empire engulfed Algeria. Like other outpost provinces of the Empire, Algeria was ruled by pashas who were ostensibly appointed by and subordinate to Constantinople, but who in effect did as they pleased. In Algeria, in time, the conquerors selected their own *dai* who was furthermore supported by the *ra'isses,* the captains of the pirate galleons. The plum offered by this lucrative post proved to be poison fruit for many of the *dais,* who were assassinated by ambitious bidders for the post. Under such circumstances, anarchy reigned. Only those Jews

whose commercial ties with Europe made them valuable economic assets could hope for the favor of the rulers. But their very success aroused the envy of the underlings in the *dai* court. The schemes and conspiracies of these underlings invariably ended with an attack on the Jewish *hara,* or ghetto, and its unfortunate inhabitants.

The French occupation of Algeria in 1830 was made possible indirectly by two prominent Jewish families — the Bacris and Busnachs — of Leghorn. Their financial success on behalf of the *dai* made their word at court tantamount to law, and at one time the *dai* supported the Bacris and Busnachs in a dispute between the Jews and the French government.

The Jews of Algeria, especially the young, became infected with French and European culture. Assimilation and mixed marriages were rampant and the leaders of the community felt helpless to bring the situation under control. Among the primary causes was the lack of Jewish schools, either government- or communally sponsored. Only a handful received instruction from Jewish tutors.

A major reason for the eagerness of the young generation to break away was the *hara.* The houses in the ghetto were subhuman: low, crumbling shacks with no air or light, leaning against each other in foul alleys crowded with children in rags and with donkeys. Hordes of poor people in various stages of disarray sallied forth from the *hara* to beg in the more affluent sectors of the city.

The extent of social degradation was dictated by economic circumstance. The *haras* in the relatively wealthier communities, such as Oran and Tel-Massan, were less miserable and the inhabitants more cognizant of Jewish traditions. Oran was also influenced by neighboring Moroccan Jewish communities and their Jewish consciousness. To aid the community in its struggle against assimilation, Oran established a Jewish school and erected a number of fine synagogues. Tel-Massan,

A Jewish grave in Algeria.

on the other hand, had been a center of learning for many centuries, with much of its spiritual stability stemming from Rabbi Ephraim Ancova, a refugee from the massive wave of massacres of Jews in Christian Spain in 1391. After his death he was revered as the "holy man of righteousness," and representatives of the official authorities participated in the Jewish procession held every year to commemorate the date of his death. The Tel-Massan ghetto was surrounded by a wall and presented a much healthier picture than its counterparts in other Algerian cities. Even the wealthier Jews chose to build their homes inside the wall.

In their attempt to neutralize the wave of assimilation engendered by the French presence, the Algerian Jewish communities resorted to the construction of imposing synagogues — visible testimony of Jewish grandeur. By and large, these synagogues reflected French culture: clerical vestments (long black gown and white tie), for the rabbi and cantor, a decorous service overseen by the *shamash* and emphasized by the pounding of his gavel on the lectern. The reading of the Torah was followed by announcements, after which the rabbi proceeded to deliver his sermon, in French. Both the interior of the synagogues and the ritual ornaments were in the French spirit: the Torah crown of the Main Synagogue in Algiers was in the shape of the Eiffel Tower.

Despite these outward embellishments, Jewish tradition as such was taken seriously, particularly where it reflected specific matters of importance to the community itself. On Rosh Hashanah it was customary not to don new clothes, since the occasion was considered not a holiday but a day of judgment. Nor would they buy a new broom, because the term "broom-swept" in the liturgy was used to describe the fall of Zion.

Like other communities, Algerian Jewry had its own holidays that grew out of the past. The fourth of Heshvan was *Purim antzara*. On this day they would read special poems in memory of the miracles performed for their forefathers in the years 1516, 1517, and 1542. "The Lord confounded the plot of the haters of Israel, and some two hundred ships bearing thirty-five thousand foreign soldiers were wrecked." On the eleventh day of Tammuz, 1775, the Spaniards, who had conquered Algeria, were about to annihilate all the Jewish inhabitants. Suddenly they saw flames shooting forth from the tombs of Rabbi Yitzhak bar Sheshet Barfat and Rabbi Shimon ben Zemach Duran. This frightened them and the Jews were saved. Since then, the eleventh of Tammuz has been celebrated as "Red Purim."

The high hopes Algerian Jewry had originally placed in the French did not materialize. They were not given equal rights, freedom of worship, or the personal security France granted to other minority groups. It was only in 1870 that intercession on their behalf by the heads of the Jewish community of France, especially by Adloph Cremieux, then Minister of Justice of the French Republic, finally obtained for them the rights of full citizenship. The law granting them equal rights was called the "Cremieux Decree." In return for their new status, the Jews had to give up all semblance of internal autonomy — their religious courts, educational institutions, communal organizations — and to serve in the French army. But even the complete fulfillment of these terms did not improve the situation. They were caught in a vise betweeen the French administration and Arab nationalism. French anti-Semites exploited the Dreyfus trial to incite Moslems to loot and destroy Jewish property; in this they were aided by the virulent Algerian French press and by so-called "ideological" French writers. In general, it was French administration policy to use the Jews as scapegoats for Arab nationalism. As late as 1934, a Moslem mob attacked the Jews of Constantine, looted and burned their homes and massacred 33 people, while French gendarmes stood by to make sure the Jews offered no resistance. In World War II, Algeria was ruled by Vichy France, and every Jew's life was in the balance.

Still, Algeria's Jews preferred French rule to Moslem domination. When the Moslems began their drive for Algerian independence, the Jews knew the end of their sojourn there was at hand. In 1962, Algeria became a sovereign state, and when Ahmed Ben Bella took control he committed himself and Algeria to aid the Arabs of Palestine in their struggle against Zionism.

The Jews of Algeria had no alternative. They fled the country en masse, going mostly to France, where they settled in communities of their own, chiefly in Paris. Many also made their way to Israel. Of the 130,000 Jews in Algeria at the time of independence, only 15,000 remained — and these bore the brunt of Arab virulence and frustration after the Six Day War.

Such was the ironic fate that marked the story of the Jewish community of Algeria: the community in North Africa that had yielded most wholeheartedly to non-Jewish culture and influence, at the expense of its internal strength, became the worst victim of violent nationalism.

Tunisia and Jerba

When Tunisia became party of the Ottoman Empire in the seventeenth century, its Jews were naturally hopeful that the new regime would not make their lot any worse than it already was. As Moslems, the Turks could invoke the laws of Omar regarding infidels: no walking about erect; no riding on horseback (riding a mule without a saddle was permissible); no wearing of stockings except on extremely cold winter days; no wearing of fine shoes or outer garments other than black linen cloaks.

Since Tunisia, like other Ottoman countries far from Constantinople, was to be governed by a bey susceptible to fat bribes, it was up to the Jewish community to see to it that the wherewithal for the bribes was available. As it turned out, the bey who ruled Tunisia in the early eighteenth century appreciated not only Jewish affluence but also Jewish diligence, and he utilized the Jews' talents to the best advantage of the country.

Tunisian Jews were expert craftsmen, merchants, administrators, customs collectors, and the mint-masters of the realm. They served as the bey's treasurers, secretaries, bookkeepers, and interpreters.

The parents and grandparents of these Tunisian Jews had come from the shores of Italy, especially from Leghorn, to which their ancestors had fled during the Spanish Inquisition. They served the bey in various important capacities related to his European duties and affairs, but even so the Jewish community remained the target of his caprice. When a Jew by the name of Batho Sapoz was brought before Mohammad Bey in the middle of the nineteenth century, on charges of having insulted the Prophet Mohammed, the bey condemned him to death. The Jewish community, after fruitless efforts to mitigate the sentence, enlisted the aid of the Christians, who also had reason to fear the bey's fanaticism. The matter was brought to the attention of Napoleon III of France, and for the next two years the bey's court seethed with negotiations, until France finally sent a warship to persuade the bey to change his mind (and, incidentally, to give France an entry into the area; Tunisia eventually became a protectorate of France). The bey yielded outwardly to the show of force, by rescinding the verdict and promising religious and constitutional freedom to other faiths, but the decrees made by the Ottoman rulers nevertheless remained in force.

The capital city of Tunis was white, with flat-roofed homes neatly arranged along wide streets and tree-lined avenues. Everywhere, proud minarets overlooking the city jealously guarded the demarcation between believer and infidel.

The physical bond that held the Jews of Tunis together was the *hara*, the ghetto, very different from other parts of the city. Horribly congested, and oozing with refuse, the ghetto was a maze of foul alleys cluttered with miserable two-story hovels clinging to one another in clusters around courtyards which served as kitchens, laundry, bathrooms, and playground. At night, the gloom was shrouded in the yellowish light of kerosene lamps which cast grotesque shadows on the straw mattresses that covered every inch of floor.

In the morning, the ghetto awoke to the sound of creaking hinges and wailing infants and steps, heavy with sleep, treading down the rickety wooden stairs from second-story apartments. The women went into the yard to prepare coffee and buy frothy milk from the goatherd who came accompanied by his herd. After breakfast,

the family members went to work and the small children poured out into the alleys, creating their own entertainment until the day waned and the family was reunited at the evening meal. Then, unless the summer heat was too stifling, the father bolted the door, top and bottom, and the family retired.

Abandoned Jewish dwellings in Madnin in southern Tunisia.

Such was the life of the storekeepers, artisans, skilled craftsmen, and unskilled laborers. Only the handful of wealthy merchants and members of the free professions lived in the integrated quarters of the city, among the Moslems, the Italians, and other Europeans.

Jews settled in Tunisia long before it became a Moslem state. Many of their customs were closer to those of the Berbers than the Moslems. Tunisian Jewish

Opposite: a young woman in the traditional dress once popular among Tunisian Jews.

women, for example, went about unveiled. They joined the men in festive gatherings, and were not subjected to polygamy. If they found their husband incompatible, they could sue for and obtain a divorce. Even so, the family structure was patriarchal and the male head was accorded love and respect. His sons came up to kiss his hand after *kiddush* on Friday night and after he had been called up to the Torah reading in the synagogue.

Tunisian Jews had many seemingly odd customs. Any man who became a widower twice, and whose wives had been ten years younger than he, was barred from marrying any woman except a widow; a woman divorced by two husbands was not allowed to remarry; male twins were always named Peretz and Zorach; female twins were called Sarah and Rebecca; twins of different sexes were named Isaac and Rebecca; anyone born on Yom Kippur was honored for the rest of his life.

Male progeny was preferred. As the day of giving birth drew near, the expectant father asked the rabbi for permission to open the Ark prior to the reading of the Torah at which time he would make his request for a son. During labor he stood near a *mezuza* and read from the Book of Jonah. If the baby was a boy, a sheet of paper with a blessing for the mother, the circumcision prayers, a chapter from Psalms and an incantation against the evil eye was tacked on the door of the delivery room.

All through the night before circumcision day, friends and relatives came to the home of the happy parents, offering their good wishes and gifts of money and clothing. The guests were treated to *burekas* — pastry triangles filled with spiced mashed potatoes and cooked beans — *arak* made from dates, and honey cake. Scholars studied the Zohar all night long. Elijah's Chair in the synagogue was covered with a colorful silk cloth. The festivities were repeated on the third day following the circumcision.

The boy's Bar Mitzvah was celebrated during his thirteenth year, often along with some other family occasion, such as the circumcision of a younger brother or the dedication of a new home. The Bar Mitzvah ceremony was held on either Monday or Thursday. On the preceding day, the young man invited his friends to his home to witness a special haircut, following which all the boys went to the public baths at their host's expense. On the morning of the celebration the boy received his small *tzitzit* (ritual fringes, called *talit katan,*) and the standard large *talit,* or prayer shawl. All the relatives took part in helping him dress for the occasion. His friends accompanied him to the synagogue with song. There the young man donned his *tefilin* (phylacteries) the first time. When he went up to read from the Torah he was sprayed with spiced water. A festive meal followed the ceremony.

Courting and marriage rituals among Tunisian Jews were much the same as elsewhere in the Oriental diaspora, with parents negotiating the arrangements, and the exchange of gifts by bride and groom. A week before the wedding the groom sent his bride a basket covered in colorful cloth and containing wedding gifts: shoes, cloths, a variety of perfumes, little bags of nuts, a pouch of henna, and two candles, to be lit under the wedding canopy. On the Sabbath before the wedding, the groom and his friends were invited to the bride's home for a festive lunch. It was customary to hide a stuffed boiled hen in the house, which was served to the guests only after the groom found it.

88

The wedding took place in the synagogue or at either the bride's or groom's home. The *ketuba* was not read beneath the canopy.

When a person died, the body was laid out on the floor and covered with a white sheet upon which was laid a loaf of bread and a nail. All the mirrors in the house were covered and water pitchers were emptied. Candles were burned at the head and the feet of the deceased until the funeral. If the deceased was a woman, the last chapter of Proverbs was chanted to a special tune. A man who died in old age was lauded with hymns of gladness, among them the hymn of Bar Yohai. In the case of a rabbi, the body was carried round the grave. After the recitation of the benediction dried fruit was distributed among those present. Women did not attend funerals and visited graves only on the third day after interment. Mourning went on throughout the first year. Frequent study gatherings were held by friends in memory of the deceased. At the end of the year, a special memorial candle was transferred from the home to the synagogue, to be lit on the anniversary of the death and on Yom Kippur.

Death notices and announcements of study gatherings, printed in both Hebrew and Arabic, were in such profusion that a visitor at any given time might readily imagine the *hara* was suffering from a plague.

When famous rabbis died their graves were revered as shrines, and were visited en

Left: the interior of the El Jerba synagogue on Jerba Island. Opposite: reciting the Psalms, a familiar pastime in the El Jerba synagogue.

masse by pilgrims from all over the country. The most famous shrine was at Al Griba Synagogue, on Jerba Island and the pilgrimage was made on Lag B'omer.

In the gloomy hovels of the ghetto, the traditional sign of the Sabbath and holidays was the light of the *kandil* — a wooden plaque overlaid with silver and decoratively etched containing a glass of oil with a wick. The woman of the house blessed this light on Sabbath and holiday eves. Families endowed the synagogue with *kandils* to memorialize their departed.

Perfumes and fragrant flowers graced the Sabbath table. The entire family pronounced the benediction, *Borei minei besamim,* a benediction in praise of the creation of spices, before reciting the *kiddush.* At the same time fragrant greens such as myrtle twigs were distributed to the members of the family, (as they were at the *havdala* ceremony immediately following the Sabbath). The main Sabbath eve dish was steamed *couscous* with vegetables and meat (fish was looked upon as a cheap dish and was not eaten on the Sabbath); on the following day, *hamin* was the beloved mainstay.

The youngsters, reared in the tradition of their elders, participated in all the ceremonies, including the Friday visits to the public baths. In the month that preceded the High Holy Days, they lit jack-o'-lanterns fashioned from watermelons and accompanied the *shamash* of the synagogue as he made his rounds to awaken the people for the predawn penitential service, *selihot.*

New moons and change of seasons were observed in unique fashion. *Rosh Hodesh,* the first day of the month, was a semiholiday. The advent of solstices and equinoxes were announced in the synagogues; no water was drawn from the wells on those days, and red-hot nails or iron bars were lowered into the wells to drive off demons.

Below: marketplace and main street, Jerba.
Bottom, left: the Tunis synagogue, torn down and set afire by an Arab mob during the Six Days' War.
Bottom, right: traditional symbols on the doorway of a Jewish dwelling on Jerba Island, southern Tunisia.

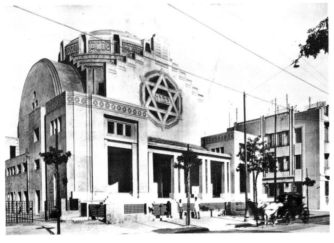

The Ten Days of Penitence between Rosh Hashanah and Yom Kippur were observed in the traditional spirit. On the eve of Yom Kippur, the synagogue was suitably illuminated with handreds of *kandils*. Many worshippers sought to intensify their atonement by standing on hard chickpeas during the Kol Nidre prayer. The fast was broken the following night with *bulu*, a pastry of flour, eggs, and raisins, and by visiting friends (for *jufra*, forgiveness) and the elder of the family, to kiss his hand and receive his blessing.

On Sukkot, booths were constructed of palm leaves, with an arched entrance of myrtle branches built low so that all who entered had to bow slightly. Sacred books covered with a silk kerchief were placed on a low stool facing the entrance. On Hoshana Rabba the men took willow twigs home from the synagogue, tapped the members of the family with them, and wished them "a better and more blessed year."

Simhat Torah was an occasion for joyous outpouring of heart and soul. The Torah scrolls were removed from the Ark, laid down on a nearby table, and were not returned until the new moon of the following month.

On Hanukah, the menorah was placed on the doorpost opposite the *mezuza* and remained there until Purim. A page bearing the festival blessings was hung beneath the menorah. *Rosh Hodesh Tevet*, the new moon of the month of Tevet, which occurs during Hanukah, was known as "the New Moon of the Daughters"; it was a time when girls received gifts from their parents and brides received gifts from their grooms.

The youngsters had a holiday of their own, on the Thursday prior to the reading of the weekly Torah portion of *Yitro*, which is in the Book of Exodus (18:1—20:30). The special feast, eaten out of tiny dishes, included a dove for each child and miniature cookies, all symbolizing the tenderness of childhood. This tradition began when a plague of diphtheria swept the country, taking the lives of most of the children.

Preparations for Purim began on the Sabbath preceding the festival. The youngsters fashioned a large ragamuffin doll, representing Haman, carried it on a wooden bed, and chanted funeral orations. On Purim eve the effigy was burned in a huge bonfire. The girls used to snip off a lock of hair and throw it into a well, with a prayer to Queen Esther that she bless them with her beauty. Triangular *hamantashen* were unknown, but there was a profusion of honey cakes filled with dates and raisins. Tunisian Jews, eager to maintain a "chain" of holidays, saved cookies from Hanukah and ate them on Purim; Purim provided continuity cookies which were eaten on the new moon of the month of Nissan. Likewise, the first *matza* baked for Passover was put aside for an entire year or burned after Sukkot along with the *sukka* foliage.

Passover preparations began on the eve of *Rosh Hodesh Nissan*, when each member of the family dipped a coin or an ornament into the oil of the *kandil*, in the process uttering good wishes for the next year. On the following day, a lamb was purchased, to be slaughtered on the thirteenth day of Nissan. At the time of the slaughter, one of the sons would dip his palm in the blood and transfer it to the outside doorpost of the house, as the Israelites did in ancient Egypt. The lamb was roasted on the eve of the fourteenth and was eaten in haste.

On the morning before Passover, the men, like their brethren elsewhere,

A Jew from southern Tunisia.

completed the study of a tractate of the Talmud, after which they had a festive meal in honor of the occasion. Morsels from this meal were taken home for the eldest daughter and the wife, if she was an eldest daughter.

The main dish on Passover was *masuki* — cooked vegetables, lamb and *matza*. Rice was eaten only after thorough sifting. The children neither recited the Four Questions nor stole the *afikoman*. The housewife retained some of the *harosset* which she affixed to the doorpost to ward off evil spirits. Seafarers took bits of the *afikoman* to guard them against rough waters. On the seventh day of Passover, services were held near a body of water. The men went from there to the synagogue, where they sang biblical songs about the sea and danced around two men dressed up as Moses and Aaron. As the men returned from the water, the women showered them with flowers and perfume.

Left: a Jewish school in Jerba. Below: a group of older Jews engrossed in Talmud study in the El Jerba synagogue.

The end of Passover was marked by the placing of lettuce leaves and other green vegetables in the corners of the house and on its furnishings, to symbolize a fresh and vigorous year.

The period of counting the *omer,* begun on the second night of Passover, marked a time of tribulation. As the worshippers recited the *omer* prayers, they held bits of salt in their palms to ward off demons, which they believed to be prevalent during this season.

Shavuot night was the traditional "night of watching," and it was considered an honor for a man to have scholars come to his home and spend the night in study. The festive meal on the next day consisted of dairy products, seldom eaten at other times. Many ate *matzot* saved from Passover.

Tisha b'Av was the culmination of weeks of mourning, not only for Zion but for the Tunisian community in its days of trial. Lamentations commemorating these days were composed in the vernacular by the Tunisian Jews. On the morning of the fast day, the Torah scroll was placed on a low, black-covered bench, rather than on the reading table. The men came to the synagogue with ashes on their foreheads, while the women went to the cemeteries to pray at the graves of sages. Since tradition had it that the Messiah was born on the day that the Temple fell, the women cleaned and whitewashed their homes, to express their belief in his coming.

The Tunisian Jewish community was cohesive for centuries. But in the course of time, under the impact of immigration, differences arose between the communities in the south and on Jerba Island, and the large centers on the coast, where newcomers from Italy quickly gained positions of economic eminence and instituted Spanish and Portuguese customs and traditions. These new immigrants looked down on the native Tunisian Jews. The result of the subsequent rift was the emergence of two separate communities, with separate rabbis and religious authorities and even separate burial societies. The schism continued until about a century ago, when the liberalization of secular laws towards the Jewish community induced the Jews to abandon their differences and take advantage of the improved climate in the country.

Prior to the period of French influence, the Jewish community was subject to the dictatorial rule of the *ka'id*, who answered directly to the bey. He oversaw the full spectrum of Jewish community life: religious, secular, social, and economic. He collected the taxes, and was known as the bey's treasurer. His signature was required on all documents, public and private. His authority was greater than that of the chief rabbi, and he could call on Tunisian law officers to enforce his dictates. He set the tax rate on the meat sold to Jewish butchers, and determined what sums of charity funds were to be distributed and to whom.

With the advent of the French, community authority passed more and more into the hands of the rabbis, of whom there were many of great renown. Outstanding students were sent to large yeshivot at community expense. Secular education was instituted by the Alliance Israélite Universelle which, responding to the French desire to inculcate French culture and language in the region, set up many Jewish schools throughout the country. Most of the Jews, however, in Jerba and in the south preferred to send their sons to the Jewish school. The Europeans, on the other hand, grasped the opportunity and filled the new schools to capacity. The graduates produced a generation of physicians, teachers, lawyers, pharmacists, engineers, merchants, plantation owners, and senior officials in the French administration. Young women prepared themselves for employment as secretaries, nurses and dressmakers. Many of these young educated Jews sought French citizenship in order to improve their status. Whoever could afford to leave the confines of the *hara* and move to the French-Italian quarter did so as soon as possible.

During World War II, the lot of the Jews worsened somewhat under the Vichy regime, although not terribly, since they were important to the regime. But the situation changed when the Nazis entered Tunisia. They herded the Jews into concentration camps and, before they were defeated by the Allied forces, managed to murder a substantial number of Jews. The native Tunisians regarded the Jews as protégés of the imperialistic French regime, and hence the foes of Tunisian

Squatting at the entrance to their shops, three Jews listen to a friend.

nationalism. This feeling was heightened by the fact that Tunisian Jews were French in every important respect; the younger generation barely knew Arabic, and for that reason many young Jewish lawyers could not appear in Tunisian courts. The establishment of the State of Israel fanned the hatred of the Arab nationalists. Although liberal on the surface, the regime began to restrict the rights of the Jews, taking over community institutions, abolishing religious courts, converting an ancient cemetery into a public park, and demolishing the *hara* and its synagogues. Jews began emigrating, many to France and others elsewhere. All but two thousand of Tunisia's sixty thousand Jews left the country, most of them emigrating to Israel.

The history of the Jewish community on Jerba Island, off the coast of the Tunisian mainland, deserves separate comment.

Thousands of years have passed since Solomon's fleet, seafarers of the tribe of Zevulun, sailed to this area. Tradition states that when the Babylonians destroyed the First Temple, the priests rescued one of its doors and carried it away with them in their quest for a haven, somewhere in the Mediterranean. They found a Zevulunite colony in the southern part of Jerba, *Hara Kabira.* The priests established a settlement, *Hara Zerira,* built a beautiful synagogue, and sequestered in it the door they had brought from Jerusalem.

This synagogue, "the wondrous," still exists. An atmosphere of mystery hovers over *Al-Jeriba.* It has two large chambers, a *sanctum* and a *sanctum sanctorum,* the latter being a gigantic ark which at one time contained sixty ancient Torah scrolls. Two rows of tall, round columns, connected by graceful arches, run the length of the walls, somewhat in the style of a basilica. The columns are adorned with tablets, ornaments and gifts of value; other treasures are kept in the vaults in subterranean chambers.

The liturgy, like the edifice itself, goes back to ancient days, and the service is conducted by the *kohanim*, the priests, who are the only inhabitants of *Hara Zerira*. There are no Levites in the community, despite the fact that they and the *kohanim* have their origin in the same tribe (legend says that Ezra the Scribe had asked the Levites in Jerba to join him in Jerusalem, since none accompanied him from Babylonia. When they refused, he cursed them, and ever since then no Levite survived in the community.)

The fame of the synagogue grew to such proportions that even Moslems began coming there on pilgrimages to seek cures. On Lag B'omer the island is inundated with visitors. At night, a lamp, said to have belonged to Rabbi Simon Bar-Yohai, is carted through the streets by people who, in return for the privilege, contribute liberally to the upkeep of the synagogue. According to one legend, a mob of Arabs, armed with swords and spears, gathered in the yard of the mosque and waited for the cart to go by. But as the cart approached, they were all blinded. Overcome with contrition, they regained their sight, joined the procession, and donated valuable gifts in atonement for their evil intentions.

Throughout centuries of Phoenician, Roman, Arab, and Turkish aggression, the Jews managed to retain their identity and way of life. They produced many rabbis and sages (this occurred after the visit to the island by Maimonides, who found their scholarship standards rather low). Jerba also became the center for the publication of sacred books, supplanting Leghorn.

In the economic sphere, the Jews of Jerba had a large variety of occupations: they spun and dyed wool, were fine metal craftsmen, tended vineyards, and were wine merchants. The wealthy dealt mainly in precious stones and coral, and maintained good relations with their Moslem neighbors. The Jewish women adopted Arab superstitions, rarely venturing forth without a *hamsa* — the likeness of a palm of the hand guaranteed to protect the bearer from demons and spirits — and necklaces of colored stones and fishbones for warding off disease. Likenesses of fish were attached to the entrance of the house in order to induce greater fertility.

The Alliance Israélite Universelle built one of its finest schools in *Hara Kabira*, but the Jews, troubled by rumors that attendance at this school would result in assimilation, preferred to send their children to the old-style school. The rabbis also objected to the Alliance school's presence and declared it out of bounds for the community. The school stood vacant until it was eventually taken over by the Arabs for their children.

The birth of the State of Israel induced many Jerban Jews to immigrate. Others are still there, eager to be in Israel but reluctant to give up their glorious synagogue. They cling to their customs and traditions, in defiance of the disturbing conditions around them. As the Sabbath approaches, the sound of the shofar bids the merchants to shut their stores and the housewives to prepare for candle-lighting.

Wedding festivities in Jerba lasted twelve days, each with its particular ceremonies of gift exchanges between bride and groom, and culminating with the ceremony itself. The groom stood alone under the canopy made of a prayer shawl, and the "Seven Benedictions" were recited before him, after which he and his companions went to the room where the bride was sitting with the women and gave her a sip from the ceremonial wine cup. The bride heard the benedictions at the feast which followed.

There was a time when only bachelors were called to the Torah in *Hara Kabira* and only married men in *Hara Zerira;* in the latter, only the Al-Jeriba Synagogue contains Torah scrolls, so as to compel the entire community to pray there. In all matters of religious observance, the Jews of Jerba were like their brethren on the mainland, only more so. The day after Yom Kippur was celebrated as *Simhat Kohen,* commemorating the safe exit of the High Priest from the *sanctum sanctorum* of the Temple.

Libya

There was a Jewish community in Libya (Tripolitania, Cyrenaica, and Fezzan) as early as the period of the Israelite monarchy. The area was conquered in turn by Carthage, Rome and the Vandals in ancient times, then by the Almohads and the Ottoman Empire. A good deal of the resistance of the native tribes to these invasions was inspired and led by Jews. The Almohads were unable to gain control until Haroun ben-Haroun, the Jewish leader of the tribes, was killed in battle in 1202.

In the fourteenth century, Libya entered into an economic pact with Genoa and Venice. The Italian cities sent metals, glass, silks and wines to Tripoli for distribution in Africa, while in Tripoli ships were laden with dried fruits, fine grains, leather, wool, honey, spices, precious stones, ivory, and peacock feathers for the affluent in Europe. A major portion of this comomerce was carried on by the Jews of Tripoli, and they made this port city a worthy competitor of Tunis.

In 1510, a Spanish armada of fifty ships laid siege to the city. Some of the merchants were able to escape to the hinterlands with their goods. Those who remained were treated cruelly or sold into slavery. According to one account, eight hundred prominent Jews were taken to Naples, where they were eventually ransomed by Italy's Jews.

After ten years of hardship, the inhabitants of Tripoli, unable to dislodge the Spaniards, entreated Sultan Suleiman to rescue them from the *conquistadores*. The sultan sent a fleet of 120 warships, and Tripoli was wrested from the Spaniards. The Spaniards, however, summoned reinforcements from Sicily, then in Spanish hands, and staged a counterattack at Jerba Island, but the Turks won again. Their commander ordered that a triumphal mound be erected, using the skulls of the fallen Spaniards. The gruesome warning to the Spaniards was still in evidence as late as the nineteenth century. It was torn down in 1866 at the demand of the French consul.

The Jews returned to the city, but all were in poor economic circumstances and devoid of Jewish learning. Rabbi Shimon ben Lavi, en route from Morocco to the Land of Israel, was so appalled by what he found in Tripoli that he decided to forgo the privilege of residing in the Holy Land and remained in Tripoli to guide the community. He taught them basic customs and traditions and also drew them to the Kabbala and Jewish mysticism. This undoubtedly revived the spirit of the community, but it also made it prey, in the following century, to the messianic upheaval caused by Shabtai Zvi. The impact of this movement was enhanced by Michael Cardozo, a young physician who came to Tripoli from Italy in 1664 and became the house doctor of the *dai*, the ruler appointed by the sultan.

Cardozo, a descendant of Marranos, was drawn to the Sabbatian movement and in 1674 proclaimed the advent of the Messiah. In time he began to indicate that he himself was the Messiah, pointing to a prominent scar near his ear and the impression of a lion on his forehead as proof. When the leaders of the community realized that Cardozo was gaining followers, they arranged for his deportation. Even so, he returned and continued his preaching. Deported again, he traveled through Tunisia and Morocco, winning over both Jews and Moslems. One of his disciples in Tripoli, Yaacov, rebuffed by the Jews, embraced Islam and was regarded by the Moslems as a holy man, *Sidi Yaacob*. From this period onward, the

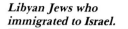

Libyan Jews who immigrated to Israel.

leaders of the community dedicated all their energies to the education of their people, and in time Tripoli brought forth many sages and scholars.

In 1704 Tripoli was invaded by Ibrahim Bey, ruler of Tunis, and violent fighting broke out. This was followed by a plague which decimated the population but which also induced Ibrahim Bey to withdraw. To commemorate the event, Tripoli's Jews introduced *Purim a-Sharif* (on the 23rd day of Tevet) as a regular holiday in their calendar.

The Turkish rulers ruled Libya with extreme harshness and were always engaged in putting down tribal revolts. To finance this warfare they taxed the Jews and framed charges against the wealthy merchants among them in order to justify confiscation of their property. The wickedness of Dai Khalil Pasha finally enraged the Libyans beyond measure. Led by Ahmad Karamenali, a member of an old Turkish family in Libya, whose father-in-law had been put to death by the Dai, the tribes from the hills advanced on Tripoli. The Dai committed suicide and Ahmad became the Dai in 1711.

Aware that the Turkish administrators in Tripoli resented the intrusion of a native, albeit Turkish, upstart, Ahmad invited three hundred of the important officials to his home where he had his servants massacre them. He forestalled the sultan's wrath by sending him shiploads of gifts, consisting for the most part of the possessions of the murdered men. The sultan responded by making him his representative in Libya. The House of Karamenali ruled the country for 120 years, and the Jews experienced generations of tranquility. Ahmad himself enjoyed a long reign — from 1711 to 1745. He turned Tripoli into a beautiful city; among the

Libyan cave-dwelling Jewesses in their original attire and ornaments, including charms against malefactors and the Evil Eye. Their colorful kerchiefs are their own handiwork.

edifices he erected were the Mosque of Ahmad the Magnificent and the Burj al-Mandarin tower.

The Jews continued to prosper. Their trading extended into the heart of Africa. When mobs in Tunis turned on the Jews there, the Jews of Tripoli gave them safe and immediate haven. The only real foe that the Jews of Libya faced in the eighteenth century was plague. The worst, in 1785, was followed by internecine strife between two claimants to the throne, both of whom were determined to control Tripoli. The terrified people of Tripoli petitioned the sultan to reinstitute Turkish rule. Unfortunately, their petition was exploited by an adventurer named Ali Bargal who offered his services to the sultan in restoring law and order. With the sultan's authorization in his possession, he hired a fleet of empty ships and sailed into Tripoli harbor. The populace, believing that an overpowering force was aboard the ships, surrendered. Ali, greedy for gain, instituted a reign of terror which eventually brought the two claimants together. Joining forces, they drove the adventurer out of Tripoli. This event was commemorated by the Jewish community with *Purim Bargal*, a holiday observed in Tripoli and Bengazi with feasting and recounting of the events.

Yussuf Pasha of the Karamenali line, who ruled from 1795–1835, not only restored order but, with the help of the Jews, brought Tripoli to its most prosperous period. Yussuf Pasha was also kindly disposed towards the Jews because of a Jewess named Esther, called "Queen Esther" because of her influence in the court of Ali, Yussuf's father. In the controversy between Yussuf and his brother, she sided with Yussuf and helped him achieve eminence. At the same time, he began the pursuit of pleasure and luxury in a style that quickly depleted the state coffers. He turned to piracy, and this source of income served him well until threats from the governments of his victims forced him to desist.

Yussuf's financial woes played right into the hands of the zealous Moslems. They drew the old pasha's attention to the wealth of the Jews. He allowed himself to be persuaded to levy heavy taxes on the Jewish merchants, until many left the country. Tripoli's prosperity went with them. The Moslems, not content with having the Jews deprived of their possessions, further instigated degrading decrees against them. The Jews were forced to be the executioners of Moslem criminals who were sentenced to death, since the task was deemed dishonorable for Moslems.

With Jewish wealth dissipated, the pasha turned to taxing the entire populace. Here he ran into opposition. His grandson was persuaded by the hill people to lead a revolt against him. Tripoli was besieged; hunger brought on pestilence. Again the sultan was petitioned to send a Turkish ruler and this time the sultan acquiesced. The arrival of Najib Pasha brought the Karamenali rule to an end. The new governor, as well as his successors, sought to enrich themselves at the expense of the Jews, but most of them appreciated the role of the Jews in the economic life of the land and were careful not to give them reason to leave.

Jewish community life in Libya, when not threatened by evil decrees, was exemplary. Spiritual leadership on the one hand, and the response to it by the community on the other, brought about a magnificent growth of Torah scholarship, piety, and mutual aid. The wealthy apportioned a tithe of their income to maintain numerous communal institutions. In all respects, the community reached its zenith in the last quarter of the nineteenth century under the guidance of Rabbi Eliyahu Hazzan. At that point the community numbered 7,500 souls in Tripoli and slightly less that number in the other parts of Libya.

Fine craftsmanship was one of the outstanding trademarks of the Libyan Jew. In the *Suk al atara,* one of the two large market places in Tripoli, the work of Jewish goldsmiths and silversmiths was described by travelers and visitors as breathtaking, featuring ancient styles and designs handed down from father to son. Not far from this section was the former slave market, where captives from Christian lands were brought by pirates of the Barbary coast for sale to the Moslems. Jewish captives were rarely sold into slavery. For the most part, they were ransomed by the Jewish community in Tripoli and became part of it. Many important individuals traced their ancestry from among these captives.

The *hara* of Tripoli was one of the less inviting quarters of the city, but many Jews continued to reside there even after they were able to afford finer homes. Life in the ghetto meant accessibility to vibrant Jewish experience which transcended its surroundings. There were physical distinctions in the ghetto. Most of the houses were low and surrounded with stone enclosures. The homes of the well-to-do had two columns at the entrance, supporting a balcony. The roofs were flat and edged with balustrades — an ideal place for a breath of sea air from the north. In the less pretentious dwellings, the entrance led into a long corridor which ended in a square yard, around which the homes were built. The yard itself was like a miniature market place, and activities ranged from youngsters chasing cats to old men murmuring passages from the Zohar. Food was simple and not too plentiful; the porridge of durra mixed with oil, peppers, and sharp spices was a delicacy.

In their dress, the Jews of Libya resembled their brethren in the other lands of North Africa. The men wore long white cloaks over linen or silk vests, with huge buttons and pantaloons. The women wore their hair in braids tied with colorful

ribbons under a long bright kerchief, but, unlike the Moslem women, they wore no veils.

The Jews of Libya maintained close religious ties with their Tunisian brethren, since many of their spiritual leaders came from Tunisia. This accounts for the similarity in their customs and ceremonies — the exception being the Jews who lived in the hilly regions, where traditions stemmed from ancient times.

The Sabbath began as the *shamash* hastened along the streets with the cry *esh ela shabbat*, "candle-lighting time." After *kiddush*, the members of the family approached the father — *and* the mother — to kiss their hands and receive their blessings. In the synagogue, whenever a man was called to the Torah, his sons and grandsons rose to their feet and remained standing while the portion was being read, then came up to him, kissed his hand, and received his blessing.

Favorite Sabbath dishes were *harimi* (fish cooked with onions, chili peppers, garlic, and tomato sauce, and served as a first course) and *mafrum*, ground meat with onion, parsley, eggs, and various spices, cooked between layers of oranges or eggplant (symbolizing the manna, which lay between two layers of dew). At *havdala* on Saturday evening, it was customary to touch some of the sacramental wine to the eyes and the top of the spine, for good health, and to pour a few drops in the corners of the room for good luck and prosperity.

Rosh Hodesh was a semiholiday when candles were kindled and a festive meal

Jewish women among the cave dwellers in Libya were expert in making colorful rugs. A girl learned the craft of carpet weaving by watching her mother at work. Left to right: a woman prepares the yarn; a young woman carries the wool for weaving the carpet; mother and daughter at the loom; women displaying their hand fashioned carpets.

103

eaten. The first day of Tevet was "Ladies' Day"; the women did not work and spent the day visiting friends and relatives. (This custom was observed in Tunisia as well.) On the eve of *Rosh Hodesh Nissan,* the "night of the *bassisa,*" the entire family came together in the home of its eldest member. Even those who lived great distances away came, since it was believed that whoever did not come would not finish out the year. A special dish of porridge was placed on the table and the eldest, pouring oil into the mixture and stirring it with a key, recited: "Thou, O Lord, Who opens everything without a key and gives to every man bountifully, give us of Your good so that we may give unto others, and send forth Your goodness to all of Israel." He then tasted the porridge, and everyone followed suit. The mistress of the house then dropped an ornament into the porridge, where it would lay all night. The rest of the porridge was eaten the next morning. Other observances of this occasion included the eldest dropping a gold coin into a glass lantern filled with oil (the tabernacle in the wilderness was set up on *Rosh Hodesh* Nissan, and the gold coin symbolized the Israelites' offering).

Rosh Hashanah was a momentous holiday. Before it began women went to the cemetery and lit candles in memory of their departed. In some inland communities, the custom of *kaparot* was observed on Rosh Hashanah eve, with the bones of the fowl later buried in the cemetery. Before the start of Rosh Hashanah and Yom Kippur, it was customary to eat special dumplings, called *spanz,* which were fried in the streets of the ghetto and sold in huge numbers.

For the *kaparot* preceding Yom Kippur, Libyan Jews used only white fowl. On the day before Yom Kippur, morning prayers at the synagogue were followed with a community meal, with rich and poor eating together and wishing one another a good year. This was also the time for the people to pay all the pledges they had made in the synagogue during the preceding year. The trustees of the synagogue sat in the courtyard, at tables covered with flowers and decorative plants, and the members of the community passed by and made their payments. They also made special contributions for the cantor, the *shamash,* and the welfare institutions. Boys from the ages of nine to eleven, dressed in their best, gathered in the yard to sing wedding songs (Yom Kippur, according to the sages, was a "good day").

At *ne'ilah* time, all the children, even the infants, were brought to the synagogue for the priestly blessing. The father lifted his hands, holding his *talit* above the heads of his married sons, who in turn placed their own hands on the heads of their sons, as the blessing was pronounced — a moving sight which the women in the gallery accompanied with whispered prayer. The *kohanim* treated the day after Yom Kippur as a holiday, engaging in no work, in commemoration of the priesthood in the days of the Temple.

Hoshana Rabba eve was "lung and liver night," when the family ate broiled lamb lung and liver. In the synagogue, on the following morning, the men tapped one another with willow twigs; the poor applied the twigs to the rich with complete impunity.

Hanuka and Purim were celebrated in much the same manner as in Tunisia, but Passover had several variations. On the *Seder* plate there was an egg for every member of the family. In addition to the roast shankbone, the Jews of Libya added slices of roast liver and lung, taken from the lamb which every family tried to have for Passover. At the *Seder,* one of the youngsters stole the *afikoman,* wrapped it in a napkin, and walked out of the room, as the others cried, "Thief! Thief!" When the youngster returned and was asked by the father: "Where were you ?" he replied, "In Egypt."

"And where are you going ?" the father continued. "To Jerusalem," the youth said. At this, all those present called out three times "Next year in Jerusalem!" and went on reading the *Haggadah.* Prior to the Four Questions, the mistress of the house picked up the *matzot* and held them above the head of every person in the house, even an infant asleep in a crib.

On the intermediate days of Passover, picnics were held in the orange groves outside the town. The Moslem owners readily admitted the Jews, in the belief that the presence of Jews brought prosperity to the owner of the grove.

Customs varied even within Libya itself. In Malatta some Jews refrained from drinking wine on Passover, using the juice of boiled raisins for the "four cups." In the seaport communities, the men carried with them bits of *afikoman* and a few crystals of salt, provided by the *shamash,* as a means of calming a stormy sea. In some communities, contrary to tradition, the entrance to the home was locked and bolted on Passover; this custom was a reminder of Marrano days. On the last day of Passover, the youngsters roved through the streets, calling: *Ha taruna, ha alhamaman* — "give *natru,* give *kamun*" — ingredients of flour, thereby announcing that this was the last day for eating *matza.* On this day the young men paraded through the quarter, as the young women watched from the windows, balconies, and rooftops. Appropriately enough, the eighth day of Passover was called "have a look day." A young man who had made up his mind about a young lady threw her a flower en route, at which his friends showered him with congratulations. In the evening, all homes were decked out with flowers and lettuce leaves; brides and grooms exchanged baskets of these symbols of fragrance and prosperity.

The *hametz* was brought back on the day following Passover with much pomp and ceremony. Each member of the family received a small loaf of bread with a baked egg inside, the *maimona*, which was eaten with slices of lamb. According to Rabbi Abraham Halfon, one of Libya's great scholars, the custom dated to the year 1204, when Maimonides passed away. The news reached Tripoli during the Passover, and the Jews could not mourn for the great sage in the traditional manner of eating bread and an egg. They therefore postponed the act to the following day and called it *maimona*.

Water, said the sages, is Torah. Shavuot being the festival of the Torah, it was the custom in Libya for youngsters to sprinkle water on passersby. They were also given cookies baked in the shape of the tablets of the Ten Commandments, so that they might digest Torah learning with greater ease and fervor. Cookies were also baked in the form of a ladder, commemorating Moses' ascent to Mount Sinai.

Circumcision rites in Libya were preceded by eight days of rejoicing, marked with daily meals for the poor. On the Sabbath before the *brit*, the father was called to the Torah, and the *shamash* distributed incense to all present. At the entrance to the room where the *brit* was to be performed, the women hung strips of red cloth. So as not to discriminate against daughters, a family gathering was held on the eighth day, at which the rabbi passed the young lady around from hand to hand, three times. Simultaneously a coin was placed in the hand of the midwife.

Young men were ready for marriage at eighteen and girls at thirteen. The match, evidence on "have a look day" notwithstanding, was arranged by matchmakers or the women. Engagements were usually held on *maimona* night. The groom came to visit the bride, preceded by a basketful of delicacies. He was then introduced to her formally, although the two may have met each other previously. The marriage terms were written and the wedding date, on a Wednesday night, was set.

One week before the wedding, friends of the groom came to his home and scattered sweets in the corners for the youngsters to find *(tatzlil)*. A festive meal followed, in the course of which the groom presented his friends with new handkerchiefs, presumably to weep into for the responsibilities he was about to assume. A few days later the groom sent the bride some henna for painting her finger and toenails; whatever she did not use she gave to her girl friends on Friday night, "farewell night," for which she wore her wedding dress, of silk or some other expensive fabric. On Saturday night, the bride's parents gave a dinner for the family, to which the groom was also invited. The bride, hair hanging loose, was led into the room, and all the others rose to greet her. As the music played on, the women applied cosmetics to her face and did her hair. The dinner ended with each of those present giving the father of the bride a gold coin.

Another family repast was held on Sunday. For this occasion the groom sent a basket containing broiled lamb's liver, lungs and heart. The bride ate the heart, first

A newcomer to Israel, in the agricultural settlement of Porat.

dipped in sugar — symbol of a "sweetheart" and a good life to follow. Later in the evening the groom arrived with his musicians, carrying a trayful of spices, a white veil, a bottle of spirits, four eggs, a small mirror, and a pitcher of sweet water. The bride donned the white veil, at which the groom gave her a small basket of white sugar.

The night before the wedding, "rest night," the bride went to bed early in order to be fresh for the next day. At that very moment the groom was entertaining his friends, each of whom was called upon to contribute to the expenses of the wedding, each according to his means. The sums and the names of the donors were noted carefully in a special family journal. As each of the donors had occasion to hold a celebration of his own, the groom was obligated to return to him the sum he had contributed towards the wedding. In case the groom refused, he could be called to a religious tribunal and forced to make the payment.

Shortly before the wedding ceremony, the bride left her parents' home accompanied by her attendants and the musicians, while a master of ceremonies sang and danced before her all the way to the groom's house. The groom went up to the roof of his home with a pitcher filled with water. He poured the water out into the street, then threw down the pitcher, smashing it, in commemoration of the destruction of the Temple. The bride responded by throwing and smashing one egg against the outer wall of the house and another against the inner wall, in the same symbol of remembrance.

Under the canopy, the groom stood during the ceremony, while the bride sat, veiled. The best man read the *ketuba*. Following the benedictions, bride and groom drank from the glass, which was then smashed against the ground, wine and all, as the groom recited: "If I forget thee, O Jerusalem, let my right hand forget its cunning."

In the hill communities, weddings were held en masse on the day preceding Sukkot. On the second day of the festival, all the new husbands and their friends gathered at the town well for the "grooms' race". The newlyweds ran about for an hour after which they were escorted home. The ceremony symbolized, in concrete fashion, the verse, "And He, as a groom energing from under his canopy, would as a man of valor rejoice to run his course."

When a man was nearing death, the *hevra kadisha* remained at his side, to make sure that he recited *Shema Yisrael* before he died. Upon the death of a family member, the wife or daughter hit a table with a stick, and then all the women went outside and symbolically struck a girl across her back, so as to announce the man's demise throughout the Jewish Quarter. All the women undid their hair and began to wail and keen, lauding the memory of the departed.

When the body was ready for interment, a pouch of earth was placed at the head. If death occurred on the Sabbath, a knife and a slice of bread were placed at the heart. If the departed had no sons, the top of his table was fashioned into a cover for his coffin. If he was a man of learning, bits of his shrouds were kept to ward off evil spirits. Two bottles were placed at the head, one of water and the other of oil, with a burning wick. All the neighbors of the deceased poured out all the water in their houses. In a case where two members of one family died in the same year, a rooster was taken to the edge of town and thrown off — a *kapara* for the rest of the family. When the family members returned from the cemetery, they drove a nail into the door of their home, to hold the Angel of Death.

The end of the nineteenth and the beginning of the twentieth centuty brought to power the ostensibly liberal "Young Turks," whose religious zeal nevertheless brought considerable hardship to the Jews in Libya and infringed on their right to study Jewish traditions and the Hebrew language. The Jews were therefore eager to

have a western power gain control of the country, and when Italy took over, the Jews welcomed her arrival.

World War I forced many of the smaller communities to seek escape from impoverishment by migrating to the large cities. This, incidentally, enabled them to give their children a better education.

Zionist sentiment among Libyan Jews began during the days of the Italian regime, when Italy's Jews took the initiative to spread the ideas of the movement. Rabbis and laymen alike joined it enthusiastically. The organization *Hevrat Zion* was formed to propagate the Hebrew language. The blue box of the Jewish National Fund was to be seen in every Jewish home and business enterprise — until the Facist regime in Italy enacted its anti-Semitic policies in 1938, and Fascist influence hit the community. Government schools were closed to the Jews after Jewish children refused to write on the Sabbath. When Marshal Balbo decreed that Jewish businesses had to be open on the Sabbath, many Jews simply gave up their enterprises. Those who remained in business and closed on the Sabbath were flogged in public. The decrees continued in force even when Balbo was killed in an air accident. The rabbis and community leaders were put into concentration camps, and male Jews were taken to work on "civilian projects" in the Sahara; most of them never returned.

When the British captured Libya in 1943, they lifted the decrees. Even so, the Jews were in an extremely insecure situation. On November 2, 1945, an incited Moslem mob broke into the Jewish Quarter and massacred 150 of its inhabitants, looted shops, and burned synagogues. The impotence of the British convinced the Jews that Zion was the only solution.

The establishment of Israel brought the bulk of Libya's Jews to its shores.

The Jewish Cave Dwellers

Beyond Libya's coastal plain along the approach to the Libyan desert, there is a narrow strip of mountains, 500 meters high on the average but at times reaching twice that height, called "Jebel." Its inhabitants live in cave-like dwellings, hidden in the slopes and reached by a gate and tunnel. Built originally as a haven from bloodthirsty desert bands, these homes also shield their inmates from the scorching sun and the biting cold that characterize the climate of the region.

Jewish settlements in Jebel go back to ancient days, as archaeological finds have proven. Despite the differences in their habitations, the Jebel Jews always maintained close contact with their brethern in Tripoli and other communities.

The cave dwellings of this Jewish community are described by Prof. Nahum Slouschtz in his nineteenth-century travel journal: "I saw a series of undulating, man-made hillocks surrounding an aperture in the ground. I looked down as into a bottomless pit, and heard, as from the bowels of the earth, the sounds of lowing cattle, children crying, and the high-pitched voices of women, rising at times to wild laughter.... One of the cave-dwellers led me to a low wooden door half-hidden in the hillside, with a wooden doorknob which he turned until the door swung open. We entered a sloping tunnel with sharp stones underfoot, intended to slow down the descent. Some twenty yards farther the tunnel ended at a huge courtyard, illuminated by an invisible source of light. It was Saturday. Two donkeys stood at a rickety trough. Two or three sheep and a goat jostled one another. In one corner I saw an anvil, hammer, and strips of metal — evidently a workroom.

"Farther on I came to a courtyard illuminated by the aperture I had seen earlier. Along its edges were the dwellings, dug out of the earth and containing primitive utensils, straw mattresses, food stores, all strewn about in disorder. In the courtyard was the common oven, spinning wheel and items which were obviously the children's toys. From this courtyard other tunnels led into similar units of habitation — a maze of dwellings intricate enough to confound any enemy who would seek to break into the community."

The Jewish men and women in these subterranean villages, very much like their

Moslem neighbors, practiced a way of life handed down over many generations. In the entire region, only Jews were iron mongers and silversmiths. But they also engaged in tilling the soil. The women excelled in spinning and weaving carpets and burnooses and enjoyed a reputation for fine workmanship. Their wants were few, and whatever they owned they were ready to share with their neighbors.

Good relations were the rule between Jews and Moslems in the region. Still, in matters of faith, the Jews maintained a strict separation. There is reason to believe that the region was at one time inhabited by Jews only. One legend maintains that Jews were far more numerous in the area, until a quarrel broke out between a Jewish blacksmith and Arab dignitary who wanted his horse shod on the Sabbath. The Jew refused and this led to strife which caused many Jews to move away from the region. But signs of Jewish habitation in ancient days are common — *kassar al Yahud* ("fortress of the Jew") near Tajtat Village; and *hacham al Hajara* ("wise man of Hajara village"), whose ancient grave is a sacred site to both Jews and Moslems.

In time, drought and pestilence reduced the Jewish population, and when the State of Israel came into existence, the entire community left the region which their people had inhabited for centuries and immigrated to Israel.

Opposite: at home and in school. Above: jewelry with a Star of David as its central motif.

Even before Jews had settled in Tripoli, there was a Jewish settlement in an eastern promontory of Libya. In the course of time, five port towns were built along this promontory — a peninsula extending from the Libyan desert and stretching across to the Egyptian border — the most important among them being Bengazi.

A Jewish community existed in Cyrenaica as far back as the third century B.C.E., when the region was known as Berenice, named for the wife of Ptolemy III of Egypt. The community prospered and enjoyed full autonomy, even under Roman rule, until it joined the revolt against the empire and was put down by Trajan. The community was dispered, and no Jewish life existed in Cyrenaica until the arrival of refugees from the Spanish Inquisition. Later, Jews from Tripoli and other parts of Libya also swelled the community.

An English traveler who visited Bengazi some 150 years ago had this to say about its Jews: "They are of a persecuted stock and stubborn in their desire to amass wealth despite everything. They are the leaders of trade and efficiency in the city, and they trade with their handiwork which is done tastefully and in orderly fashion, which enables them to pay the heavy taxes imposed on them and to withstand pillage . . . . Their homes are neat and better furnished than the Moslem homes. It never happened to us that we should enter the home of a Jew and not find him engaged in one beneficial act or another. We have also found that all the Jews are inclined to do good, and they seem satisfied with their way of life . . . . "

By mid-century the Jews of Bengazi numbered a thousand families and there were eight synagogues. In most respects they resembled Tunisian Jews. In Darana, a coastal town so beautiful that the Byzantine Greeks called it the "pearl of the Mediterranean," the Jewish community boasted of a Torah scroll — "the *tzagair* of Darana" — which it claimed had been written by Ezra the Scribe and brought to Alexandria after the destruction of the Temple. In the course of anti-Jewish rioting in that city, one of the looters stole the scroll and made off with it, with the aim of selling it in some distant country. Just as he boarded a vessel he had a stroke, the scroll fell from his hands into the water and was washed up near Darana. Precisely at that moment, the legend goes on, one of the sages of the Jewish community happened to be nearby and picked up the floating object. Seeing that it was a Torah scroll, he hastened with it to the synagogue where, much to everyone's amazement, not a single letter had been erased by the water. The Jews of the town believed it to be a gift from heaven. Since this took place on the first day of the month of Elul, the day was declared to be a holiday for all time, during which pilgrims came to touch the Torah scroll and offer contributions on its behalf.

The Jewish community fared well under Ottoman rule. Its members were entrusted with responsible government positions; many served as judges, city councilmen, consuls, and representatives of foreign powers. As bankers, shippers, and foreign trade entrepreneurs, they added greatly to the city's prosperity. This state of affairs continued under the Italians until 1938, when Mussolini subjected the Jews to the hardships and oppressions of the Fascist regime. In the bombings which Bengazi sustained during World War II, the Italian residents of the city completed the impoverishment of the Jews by looting their shops and homes. In 1942, many Jews were sent to concentration camps in the Jado desert. To the few who returned after the defeat of the Nazis, the sole comfort was the willingness of the British Jewish soldiers to help them rebuild their community.

Libya's independence meant little to the Jews, since it was accompanied by a wave of Arab nationalism which, following the United Nations Palestine partition resolution of 1947, burst into mob violence against them. The British in charge were powerless to handle the situation, which worsened daily until the Jews moved away, first to Tripoli and subsequently to Israel.

Egypt

The Land of the Nile entered the pages of Jewish history in its earliest chapters. Long before the Children of Israel achieved nationhood, Egypt played a decisive role as springboard. Then, many centuries after the Exodus, a new Jewish community arose in Egypt which endured until modern times.

To the world at large, Egypt is the land of the Sphinx and Pyramids, of ancient temples, and ancient treasures. But to Egyptian Jews, the great monuments of the past are the spot on the Nile where the child Moses was placed in days of yore; the places through which the Prophet Jeremiah passed, lamenting for Jerusalem; the sequestered Torah scrolls, said to have been written by none other than Ezra the Scribe; and the synagogues where the immortal Maimonides once prayed.

Because of Egype's centrality in early civilizations, the story of its Jewish community is better known than those of other Jewish communities in the Diaspora. Its proximity to the Land of Israel facilitated a firm association between the two countries. Despite the biblical injunction against going back to Egypt, Jews settled there many years before the destruction of the Temple. Moreover, for decades and even centuries at a time, the two countries found themselves under one rule — often with a foreign power in authority.

The first large contingent of Jews went down from the Land of Israel to Egypt following the destruction of the first Temple in 586 B.C.E., joining earlier refugees from the Assyrian invasion. According to Jeremiah, these were of the lower class, the nobility having been exiled by Nebuchadnezzar to Babylonia. The famous Genizah collection of ancient documents found in Cairo describes a Jewish settlement on the island of Elephantine, in the Nile, consisting primarily of mercenaries who had built a temple and even brought offerings on its altar. Jews continued to serve as soldiers, in garrisons along the southern border, after Egypt was conquered by the Persians. By the end of the sixth century B.C.E., however, internal strife in the Egyptian regime brought about the destruction of the temple, and the Elephantine community never regained its status following the liberation of the country from Persian rule.

The second wave of Jewish immigration to Egypt took place in the days of the Ptolemys. When Jews fled their own country to escape the edicts of Antiochus, the liberal Ptolemys allowed the Jews to follow their own religious precepts and maintain their own institutions. Elders were authorized to oversee the Jewish community, which enjoyed a large degree of autonomy. Onias, son of the High Priest who escaped from Syrian domination, was allowed to build a temple in Leontopolis, in the province of Heliopolis. The temple was modeled after the Holy Temple in Jerusalem and was called the "House of Onias"; Egyptian Jews brought offerings there for two hundred and thirty years.

The largest Jewish community in Egypt was in Alexandria, where Jews engaged in a variety of occupations — artisans, merchants, shipowners — and attained economic and political prominence. The Greeks and the Egyptians of Alexandria, envious of the good fortune that the industrious Jews were enjoying, attempted to bring about their downfall by conspiracy and intrigue, but the Ptolemys continued to protect them. It was only when Egypt came under Roman rule that their situation changed for the worse. Incitement against them grew with the Roman

Haham Eliyahu Hazan of Alexandria, dressed in the traditional robes of Egypt's rabbis.

historian Apion, one of their more vociferous defamers. When the king of Judea, Agrippa, came to Alexandria and was given a royal welcome by the Jewish community, mobs set upon the Jews, burned their synagogues, and despoiled and looted their homes. While all this was taking place, Flaccus, the Roman governor of the city, stood by and even encouraged the terror by declaring that the Jews had no rights whatsoever.

The Jewish community, which numbered one million, did not yield easily. They turned from self-defense to retaliatory action against the attackers. When the citizenry assembled in the amphitheatre to organize a delegation to Rome, a mob tried to set it afire. In the rioting that ensued, and with the aid of the Roman governor, some fifty thousand Jews were killed, according to the historian Josephus. They continued sending emissaries to Rome with protests against the governor's stand. The Romans finally dispatched their legions to put down the uprising; the soldiers stormed the Jewish neighborhoods, killed many thousands, and set fire to the magnificent houses of worship. The turmoil continued until Emperor Hadrian recognized the validity of the claims submitted by the Jews and restored their rights.

Egypt's Jews, with the benevolent aid of Ptolemy II, were instrumental in producing the Septuagint, the Greek translation of the Pentateuch. Jews sent their half-*shekel* contributions for the upkeep of the Temple in Jerusalem, and were always in readiness to aid Judea. Jewish soldiers in the Egyptian army foiled Cleopatra's attempt to annex territory under Hasmonean rule, and in response to the call by King Hyrcanus II of the Hasmonean dynasty, they extricated Julius Caesar when he was besieged in Alexandria. When the revolt against Rome broke out in Judea, many Egyptian Jews took part in the fighting.

After Jerusalem fell, the Jewish community in Egypt tried to strengthen its position by projecting the values held in common by Judaism and Greek philosophy — an approach which attained prominence in the writings of Philo, a noted Jewish philosopher and a member of one of the many delegations sent to Rome to intercede for Jewish rights. Philo's principles turned many traditional Jews against him; as for his influence on others, another factor militated against it — the advent of Christianity.

Byzantine rule in Egypt deprived the Jews of all rights and privileges and caused the Jewish community to be a pariah among the populace. In despair, the Jews helped the Persians in their attempt to conquer Egypt, but the Persians were routed, even though Egypt's strength had been suffiently reduced to enable the Moslems to conquer it in 642 C.E. By the beginning of the ninth century, Moslem rule was firmly established, following a protracted struggle with the inhabitants.

The Moslem Caliphs practiced a policy of indulgence toward the Jews, although they were fanatics in matters pertaining to religion. The Jews were not compelled to adhere to the Laws of Omar, which decreed that they had to wear distinct attire and pay the per capita tax imposed on all non-Moslems. A large Jewish community arose in Fustat, which was then the capital (Cairo, a short distance away, was founded later), and the Jews attained high positions in the economic and political life of the country. They mastered and spoke Arabic with the same ease that their forefathers had spoken Greek. But they sent their finest young men to study in the Babylonian yeshivot. One of these students was to become Rabbi Saadia Gaon, head of the famous yeshiva in Sura.

Under the Fatimid Caliphs, the territories under Egypt's control included the Land of Israel and Syria; this served to strengthen even further the ties between Egypt's Jews and their brethern to the north. The privileged position of the Jews in the Fatimid court was often used to mitigate the lot of the Jews in other areas. The Jewish community in the Land of Israel received a good deal of its sustenance from the Jews of Egypt, who made frequent pilgrimages to the land of their ancestors and, in many cases, arranged for interment in the sacred soil.

The foremost source of information about the old Jewish communities in Egypt is the Genizah — the large collection of documents, compiled over many centuries, discovered at the close of the nineteenth century in the large synagogue in Fustat, the Cairo suburb that was the home of the largest of some thirty Jewish communities in Egypt of those days.

According to Genizah documents, the larger communities were divided into two distinct segments: the arrivals from Judea and the newcomers from Babylonia. Each referred to its own sages whenever juridical Jewish problems arose. In the days of the Fatimid Caliphs, the overall community was headed by a *Nagid*, selected by the community and approved by the Caliph, or appointed by him directly. The second-in-command was the *mukkadam*, charged with supervising the execution of the *Nagid's* policies and regulations.

Egypt became the center of a new Jewish sect — the Karaites — who believed only in the Written Law. Rabbi Saadia Gaon fought strongly against this movement, which had many followers among the Jews of Persia and Babylonia as well, but he was not successful in eradicating it. The Karaites gained a firm foothold in the community and in the royal court. Though they lived in the Jewish Quarter of the capital, they kept apart from "rabbinic" Jews and were organized by the Caliphate as a distinct and separate sect.

According to Rabbi Benjamin of Tudela, eleventh-century Egyptian Jews engaged in trade in oil, spices, wine, and fabrics, utilizing their ties with their coreligionists in Morocco, Tunisia, Algeria and even India. They were also tailors, bakers and dyers.

In 1171 Saladin rose to power. The Fatimid dynasty was replaced by the more fanatic Ayyubids, but the skills of the Jews — particularly in medicine — kept them in favor with the new caliphs. The presence of the great scholar and philosopher, Maimonides (Rabbi Moshe ben Maimon), the great luminary of Jewish erudition, did a great deal for the status of Egyptian Jewry. He wrote a rationalization of the Jewish faith, using Aristotelian concepts, in his *Guide for the Perplexed*. Through responsa with scholars elsewhere in the world, he strenthened the authority of Jewish religious law in the life of the people. His "Epistle to Yemen" made it possible for Yemenite Jewry to weather the catastrophe which came in the wake of the activities of a false messiah.

With Maimonides' death in 1204, responsibility for the community's spiritual future fell upon his son, Rabbi Abraham, a capable scholar and worthy successor. In due course he was appointed by the community to the position of *Nagid*. He was forced, however, to devote much time and efforts to refuting the charges made against his father's writings by extremists in various countries. The disputations died down in time, and the works of Maimonides assumed the important niche in Jewish scholarship that they have since occupied. His descendants continued to serve the community in administrative and scholarly capacities, so long as Egyptian Jewry was permitted to enjoy automony.

In the middle of the thirteenth century the Mamelukes assumed control of Egypt. Disliked by the inhabitants, they attempted to gain their favor by fanaticism for Islam. This expressed itself by decrees against the Jews: Jewish physicians were forbidden to attend Moslem patients; Jews were to wear yellow cloaks and bells or metal coins around their necks whenever they went to the baths; insecurity on the roads ruined trade; the head tax was constantly increased; and mobs were incited against the Jews so as to divert their anger from the regime. Soon, Egypt's Jewish community dwindled to a mere five thousands souls.

Many of the Jews expelled from Spain came to Egypt, where they were welcomed by their brethren with open arms. They settled mainly in Cairo and Alexandria. The scholars among them were accorded great respect; Rabbi David ben-Zemra ("Radbaz") became the Chief Rabbi of the entire community. During his term in office he wrote thousands of responsa, and even when he became wealthy through trade, he devoted most of his time to writing sacred literature, including a commentary to Maimonides' *Mishneh Torah.*

There were, nevertheless, many differences in liturgy and customs between the Egyptian community and the newcomers. As a result, the Spanish Jews formed synagogues of their own, as did the arrivals from North Africa (the Mograbi). At no time, however, did this separation impair the relations between the established community and the newcomers. The Spanish Jews quickly adopted Arabic as their spoken tongue, and the Egyptian Jews accepted the scholarly superiority of the newcomers. Marriages between the two groups was regarded favorably and practiced extensively, and· in due course the two became one.

The Ottoman Turks supplanted the Mamelukes in Egypt in 1517, but the change did not improve the lot of the Jews. They were still subject to the whims of the pasha, the local ruler appointed by the sultan in Constantinople. These rulers, like the Roman procurators of old, sought to attain the good life by squeezing their subjects. Their regimes and private lives were torn with inner strife and intrigue which undermined order and security in the realm. The Jews were the first to suffer, since they were a convenient scapegoat and a ready excuse for whatever disaster overtook Egypt. Only the courageous self-defense action of the Jewish community prevented the complete annihilation of Egyptian Jewry.

The evil decrees seemed as inevitable as they were harsh, and any event which alleviated the situation was regarded by the Jews as nothing short of miraculous and worthy of commemoration. The 28th of Adar marked a deliverance of just this kind. Shortly after the conquest of Egypt by the Turks, one of the pashas plotted to rebel against the sultan and sought the cooperation of the master of the mint, a Jew named Abraham Castro. The master of the mint, aware of the implications of the plot, fled to Constantinople to apprise the sultan. When the pasha heard of this, he decided to vent his anger against the entire Jewish community. But he was slain before he could do so.

At the end of the sixteenth century, Moslem oppressions of the Jews grew in intensity. Long-dormant regulations were revived and enforced. Jews were not permitted to ride horses, only mules. When passing a mosque they had to alight and proceed past it on foot. The same procedure had to be observed when passing a Moslem. The pashas interfered with the internal workings of the community. The position of the *Nagid* was replaced by the *halabi,* Jewish businessmen who served the pasha in economic matters. A *halabi* who failed to please his master was put to death; in the seventeenth century several *halabi* ended their careers in this manner, victims of court intrigue or the jealousy of the pasha himself. Later, the tasks carried out by the *halabi* were performed by the economic advisers of the pasha while the administration of the community's inner affairs was placed in the hands of a Jewish religious court.

The spiritual renewal created by the influx of Spanish Jewry gradually receded. Egyptian Jewry of the period was only slightly better than stagnant. Only a few individuals — engaged in foreign trade or court advisers — were affluent; the bulk of the Jewish population was engaged in inferior occupations, and many depended for their sustenance on public support.

Into this age of spiritual inertia there came, like a bolt of lightning across a gloomy firmament, the "Messiah of Izmir," Shabtai Zvi. Fleeing from the Jewish religious authorities, he descended on Egypt in blazing triumph. Raphael Yoseph, the *halabi,* a dignitary of great wealth but a bedazzled visionary, found in Shabtai Zvi a man after his own heart and gave him full support. He sponsored, in his own home, the marriage of Shabtai Zvi and a strange girl, a refugee from the Cossacks in the Ukraine, who insisted that she was predestined to wed the Messiah. Shabtai Zvi gained a large group of adherents, among them the rabbi of Alexandria. Egypt became the hub of messianic turbulence, which later turned into a rack for the Jewish people.

Shortly after the death of Shabtai Zvi, when the storm he had raised was beginning to subside, Egypt was visited by a series of upheavals and plagues. The rulers again incited the masses against the Jews. Even Napoleon, despite his proclamation about the rights of the Jews, acted against them with a heavy hand, destroying the ancient synagogue in Alexandria and levying a burdensome tax on the Jewish community.

Versed as they were in the meaning of oppression, the Jews of Egypt refrained from ostentation or anything that might arouse the populace against them. They purposely wore shabby clothes and kept the exteriors of their homes in disrepair, in contrast with the neat and well-kept interior. From ancient Fustat the Jews moved to a specifically Jewish quarter — *Kharat al-Yahood* — a maze of narrow alleys unpaved and strewn with rubbish. The wealthy sought dwellings elsewhere, although they were careful to hide opulence from hostile eyes.

The sole glory left to the Jews was the memory of their great sages, and this link was enshrined in the synagogues which these men had frequented. The synagogues, therefore, became the most precious asset of the community and were maintained with scrupulous care, especially since the Moslems forbade any refurbishing. At the close of the fifteenth century, there were in Alexandria (according to Rabbi Obadiah of Bartenura) no more than twenty-five families and two synagogues: the very large ancient one, partly in ruins, and a smaller one where the community prayed and which it prized because the Prophet Elijah was said to have revealed himself there when he came to seek rest from his sojourn in the desert. Much later, as the decree forbidding the renovation or the building of synagogues lifted and the economic status of the Jews had improved, a magnificent structure was built above and around this synagogue, adorned with marble columns and figured marble floors, seats of expensive wood, and stained-glass windows.

The Torah scrolls in these synagogues were no less venerated. In the synagogue of the town of Almahala, according to the seventeenth-century Jewish historian Yossef Sambari, there was a sacred Torah scroll encased in chased brass inscribed with holy names. It was said that anyone swearing to falsehood over this scroll would not live out the year. On the first day of Iyar, the synagogue was visited by many Jews, as well as by Moslems and Copts, for festivities which included dancing around the synagogue and lighting candles; the latter custom was also the source of considerable revenue, which was used for keeping the synagogue in repair. The famous scroll, reputedly capable of inducing many miracles, was brought forth and read only on festivals and on the High Holy Days.

In places where no synagogue existed, the Jews in the locality set aside a wing of one of their homes to serve as a place of worship.

The most famous synagogues were those associated by name with the great figures from the past. The ancient Maimonides synagogue in Cairo, the most

A manuscript from the Cairo Genizah.

hallowed of all, has a cave running beneath it where the body of Maimonides was kept until its transfer to the Land of Israel for burial; the cave became a shrine for myriads of the afflicted, including Moslems, seeking a cure for their ailments. Egyptian Jews claim that King Fuad, stricken with an incurable throat disease, spent a night in the cave and emerged in good health.

Another famous synagogue was named for Ezra the Scribe. In its center stood a small canopied wooden structure, spread with a clean white sheet, like a bed enclosed with slats. It is said to be the spot where the Prophet Jeremiah sat as he pronounced his lament over the destruction of Jerusalem. Just being near it was said to have a positive bearing on childbirth.

The importance which Egyptian Jews attached to their synagogues is reflected in the special customs and traditions which they generated over the centuries. It was customary, for instance, to have non-Jewish musicians provide music in the synagogue on Sabbaths, festivals, weddings, and similar occations. A non-Jew was hired to snuff out the candles after services on Friday night and rekindle them on Sabbath afternoon. In Alexandria, a non-Jew was employed to note the names of the donors as they called out their contributions on Sabbaths and holy days. The post of cantor was held in high esteem; once, an outstanding cantor was allowed to officiate even though he suffered from one of the numerous eye diseases that has always plagued Egypt.

The synagogue was truly the center of the community. In addition to its standard uses as a place of study and worship, it had special facilities for circumcision rites and reserved seats for grooms and mourners.

Egyptian Jews regarded marriage as the cornerstone of life, and their approach to it was more reasonable than in other Eastern diasporas. The daughter was not given in marriage before she reached the age of fifteen, in order that she might have an opinion about the match. They were also careful to ascertain the Jewish status of the other party, particularly when recent immigrants were involved. The ceremony took place in daylight and in the presence of ten official witnesses. The *ketuba* was written with meticulous care, and a copy was deposited with the Jewish court.

On the day of the wedding, all entrances to the Jewish Quarter were decked in red flags dotted with white stars. The canopy consisted of a *talit*, held up by hands at the corners, rather than the standard canopy on poles.

A *brit* ceremony was a community affair. The infant was borne to the synagogue to the strains of fife and strings and the beat of a drum; the music continued during the entire ceremony, while the women in the gallery sang joyfully.

It was customary for Egyptian Jews to prepare wills in order to prevent conflict among heirs; merchants used to include, as protection for their heirs, a list of all their investments. Wills were also made prior to long journeys, such as a pilgrimage to the Land of Israel.

The deceased were buried in their finest attire rather than in shrouds, and interred without a coffin, as was the custom in Jerusalem and Turkey. The family engaged professional mourners, donated to charity, and honored the memory of the deceased in every way possible. Throughout the Jewish Quarter, all stores were closed and all work halted to allow everyone to pay his last respects. On the Saturday after interment, all the Jews in the quarter gathered in the synagogue to extend official condolences to the mourners, and special ceremonies were observed, until the rabbis banned them; the wailing and weeping, they claimed, impinged on the spirit of the Sabbath.

At the foot of Mount Almukattem, southwest of Cairo, is one of the oldest Jewish cemeteries in the world, dating to the period of the Second Temple. Graves were later hewn out of the rock on the northeastern slope, but very little evidence has remained of these early burials; villagers in the area simply stole the headstones and used them to build houses.

One of the tombstones that survived was over the grave of Rabbi Hayyim Hafusi, one of the great scholars of the sixteenth century who was also venerated as a miracle worker. His tomb, as described by a traveler, consisted of a mound of stones dripping with oil libations poured on it by men and women seeking intercession. Visitors removed their shoes at some distance from the grave and crawled to it on their hand and knees. The name of this scholar was so revered that Moslems accepted the oath of a Jew "on the name of Rabbi Hayyim Hafusi" as a binding contract.

A legend concerning Rabbi Hayyim is based on the blindness which overtook him. Since it was said that "bribery blinds the eyes of the wise," some people were led to suspect the rabbi of taking bribes. Whereupon, in the course of prayers at the synagogue, the rabbi said: ". ... If it be true and I am guilty of sin, may my bones wither so that I be not able to descend from this place. But if I am free of sin, may my eyes be opened and my sight be restored, so that the congregation may see that there is a God who judges with goodness and grace." Instantly his eyes were given back their sight; he descended and approached the worshippers, calling each by name. From then on, he signed his name, "The Lord is my miracle, Hayyim Hafusi."

The road to the cemetery led past the Moslem burial grounds. The Jewish mourners were often attacked by Moslems or brigands, until they were forced to bury their dead at night, under escort of armed guards, assigned to them for a fee by the authorities. The Karaites had a special section in the Jewish cemetery.

As life became easier, so did death and burial. The wealthy members of the community preferred elaborate tombstones, monuments, and family mausoleums. The walks and benches added to the comfort of the community when it gathered in the cemetery for vigil and prayer at the graves of saints and scholars on the night prior to Yom Kippur. Tents were put up in the area, and the trustees of the various charitable institutions sat there and gathered contributions for the poor. People brought food with them or bought it at refreshment stands. Members of each family lit candles or oil lamps at the grave of the departed, and everyone left a burning candle on the graves of the sages. Barren women prayed with special fervor at the grave of Rabbi Hayyim Hafusi.

In their observance of the festivals and holidays, Egypt's Jews followed the age-old customs and traditions, with a few innovations of their own. They wore white on all such occasions. On Simhat Torah, as well as on Shavuot, they carpeted the floor of the synagogue with green turf. On Purim they paraded through the streets of their quarter astride horses, mules, and camels — in commemoration of Mordecai's triumphant ride astride King Ahasuerus' horse. Passover was, understandably, the high point on the calendar; the community saw to it that none in need went hungry on the holiday of Exodus.

When Mohammad Ali came to power, early in the nineteenth century, a decided change for the better occurred in Jewish life in Egypt. Mohammad Ali was an energetic administrator who had the interests of the country at heart. He recognized the potential value of the Jews to Egypt's development and removed many heinous obstacles which had been placed in their path. When a blood libel in Damascus threatened the Jewish community there is 1840, Mohammad Ali — Syria was also under his rule — heeded the call of justice and freed the accused. His liberal policy induced the Jews to return from the small villages to the large cities. They settled chiefly in Cairo and Alexandria, as did many thousands of refugees from Eastern Europe and the lands of the Mediterranean basin. In Egypt they resumed their existence, united as a community but separated in custom, habit, and liturgy, according to their lands of origin. They engaged in trade and finance. Many became prosperous, although the number of extremely affluent was never high. They went into the free professions and government work. A few became captains of industry, but even so the number of poor Jews remained constant.

The community structure became more complex and authoritative, and was influential among Jews and Moslems alike. The communal institutions and

Two inscribed amulet rings from Egypt.

agencies — religious courts, schools, hospitals — were administered by a community board of influential individuals charged with obtaining the funds needed to operate the institutions. Education of the young, however, was not on a very high level. Girls remained untutored until about a century ago, when Adolph Cremieux established schools for them, with the generous aid of the Rothschilds of Paris. All schools taught Hebrew and Arabic, French, Italian, and, toward the close of the century, English. Vocational schools were also founded for boys and girls, and these were later amalgamated under the aegis of the Alliance Israélite Universelle.

Jews in the smaller communities, where no Jewish schools existed, sent their children to other schools, including missionary establishments.

The spirit of liberalism in Egypt grew, to the detriment of Jewish life in the country. Professor Nahum Slouschtz, on a visit there late in the nineteenth century, said: "Many among the Sephardim are the wealthiest families in Egypt . . . famous in the realm of trade; some are millionaires ten times over. Most of the gold and precious stones trade in the Khan el Khalili market is in the hands of the Sephardim, as are some railroads and manufacturing plants. Many have high positions in the government." On the other hand, "ethical and spiritual standards of our brethren in Egypt are very low. The Torah has been forgotten for several generations in Egypt. Very few are literate in the sacred writings. The rabbis and sages come from the Land of Israel, and at times from Morocco and Tunisia . . . the vacuous and superficial culture of the French, which bears flowers but no fruit, has infected most of the young people." Slouschtz did find, however, that the alienation of the more recent Ashkenazi arrivals from Jewish customs and traditions was greater than that of the old-time Sephardim. The Ashkenazim were bent on emulating the Italians, and threw off all vestiges of morals and modesty. They spoke several languages but ignored their own, and the only festival they observed was Purim, which they celebrated in the style of an Italian carnival. Nevertheless, these modern Jews did not seek to assimilate — perhaps because they still regarded their own Jewish civilization as more advanced than that of the general community — and they contributed generously to the upkeep of the community structure.

The advent of the British, in 1882, ameliorated the position of the Jews even further. All restrictions were removed. Magnificent new synagogues were built, for which outstanding rabbis and scholars were obtained from all parts of the world. Chief Rabbi Raphael Aaron ben-Shimon, originally from Jerusalem, bore his position like the *Resh Galuta* of Babylonian days. A gifted author and leader, his bearing intimated the pride of the Jewish people in its spiritual legacy. Rabbi ben-Shimon was followed by Torah luminaries, most of them from Italy.

Zionism evoked a warm response among the Jews of Egypt. Zionist organizations were founded in all the larger communities, and Zionist youth clubs sprang up all over the country; even the Karaites were drawn to the movement of national revival. Egyptian Jews were particularly helpful when the Turkish regime in Palestine, aware that Jewish sympathies there lay largely with the Allies in World War I, deported thousands of Jews to Egypt.

By the mid-twentieth century, the Jewish community in Egypt numbered well over 75,000 souls and rivaled many other centers of Jewish life in the world. It took Zionist leaders to its heart, regardless of the particular ideology that each represented.

The formation of the Arab League and the rise of Arab nationalism boded ill for
the Jewish community in Egypt. For some time the Jews clutched the hope that this
was but a passing cloud. But when the State of Israel was proclaimed, that hope was
dashed. Thousands of Jews were arrested for alleged spying on behalf of Israel.
Mobs were incited to plunder and pillage Jewish homes. Immigration to Israel was
forbidden. Young Jews began to leave Egypt in droves for other destinations — and
then proceeded to Israel. Their families followed in due course.

In 1954 Egypt began to hang Jews; two years later, the Egyptians vented their
anger over their defeat in the Sinai campaign upon the entrapped Jews in Egypt.
Some one thousand Jews were all that were left of the once-mighty community. A
few of these were saved when Israeli frogmen spirited them away from Port Said to
Israeli ships in 1956. The peace treaty between Israel and Egypt allowed for renewed
contact with the small aging Jewish population that remained.

Although Syrian Jews dated their "family tree" to Abraham, whose servant Eliezer was a native of Damascus, it was in Aleppo (Halab, the Aram-Tzova of the Bible) that the Syrian Jewish community reached the zenith of its cultural growth. In the eighteenth and nineteenth centuries, this 3,000-year-old community absorbed many exiles from Inquisitorial Spain, Italy, and other countries, who established a textile and clothing industry which became known throughout the region for quality. The Jews from Europe were called Frankos by the local people. They were generally richer and better educated than the old-time residents. The economic decline of Aleppo in the second half of the eighteenth century, however, affected the status of the community. At that time a class of rich bankers arose among the Damascene Jews. They were close to government circles and played an important part in developing the life of the community. They turned Damascus into the center of Jewish life in Syria.

In 1840 a blood-libel charge was leveled against the Jews of Damascus. The threat aroused an international outcry, especially in Jewish communities around the globe. Adolph Cremieux of France and Sir Moses Montefiore of England persuaded the Sultan of Egypt to order the ruler of Damascus to cease and desist from persecuting the Jews.

While there was tension between Jews and Christians, Jewish relations with the Moslem majority were generally correct, and the communities of Aleppo and Damascus enjoyed an active Jewish life.

According to an Ottoman census taken in 1893, there were about 9,500 Jews in the Aleppo region and over 6,000 in Damascus and environs. Most of the Jews were engaged in trade and in various crafts, but the economic decline of Syria at the end of the Ottoman period took its toll on them, too. The Jewish communities in the Ottoman Empire were not directly subordinate to any center, although the "wisest man" — the rabbi — was appointed by the state. The Jews who lived in the small towns and villages would bring their disputes before the rabbinical court in the cities. The factors uniting all the Jews were their common identities and traditions. These factors bonded the Jews living in Syria — whether from Spain, Italy, Eastern Europe or the ancient Jewish communities of Syria — into one society.

Rabbinic authority was very strong in Aleppo until World War I. The rabbi was distinguished from other Jews in his outward appearance by the size and color of his turban and the long wide sleeves of his outer garments. The sage was highly respected in his community and his influence over the people was powerful. The rabbis also had certain powers of enforcement. The rabbinical court could punish by imposing fines, beatings, or excommunication. These punishments, and particularly corporal punishment, were put into practice by the rabbis and by teachers who punished their pupils for desecrating the Sabbath or for disobedience.

The rabbis were believed to have supernatural powers. Many stories were told of the miracles they performed in curing the sick, of bringing rain during droughts, and so on. When a rabbi who was considered holy died, many would go to his grave and beg for his intercession in times of trouble. Veneration of the rabbis strengthened their status and their authority as leaders in all aspects of life.

Rabbis served as members of the rabbinical court, as teachers at various levels, or were simply private scholars. The status of teachers in the elementary schools was

not very high. Scholars who did not serve in the rabbinate were sometimes businessmen or else worked as ritual slaughterers or in similar occupations. Sometimes merchants would hire scholars as private tutors for their children or would support a small yeshiva so that the scholars could gather and study there. The members of the rabbinical court and the heads of the community, including the chief rabbi, were generally appointed by a council which consisted of the dignitaries of the city. In Aleppo the council was a permanent institution. Since there were no elections to the council, it was composed, in effect, of the members of the rich and well-connected families.

The family and the home were the basis of social organization among the Jews of Syria. Until the beginning of the twentieth century, the house generally opened on to a courtyard shared by several families. Customarily, the entrance to the house was through a small gate and a narrow, winding staircase, but it sometimes led to an elegant, luxurious house. It was characteristic of Syrian Jewry, as in other Middle Eastern countries, to jealously guard their privacy and hide their wealth from the eyes of strangers. The women hid their faces with a scarf in the presence of men. In traditional families the children treated their parents with respect and obedience. Older brothers had authority over their younger siblings, who had to obey them. Until the end of the nineteenth century girls, for the most part, did not go to school. Girls from poor families worked as maids in the households of rich families, starting as young as eleven years old. Among the boys there were few who continued their schooling after elementary school. Most of them began to work as apprentices in trade or in the various crafts. Generally, boys continued in their father's occupation, and even public roles in the community passed from father to son.

Marriages were arranged by the parents. People married young, usually before the age of 18, and sometimes even in childhood. But by the twentieth century they tended to put off the time of a boy's wedding until he had established himself in work and could support a family. Marriage of cousins was common in Aleppo.

The marriage terms included special clauses intended to protect the wife. The original *Ketuba* of the Syrian Jews — the *Mustarabim* — granted the man the right to divorce his wife against her will, or to marry a second wife despite her objections, without having to divorce her first; the *Ketuba* of the Sephardim and Frankos, however, did not grant these rights to the husband. There was also a mixed *Ketuba*, which included terms from different types of *Ketubot*. Polygamy was rare and practised only among men who did not have sons by their first wife. Some clauses in the *Ketuba* protected the wife and her heirs. In Damascus and in other places the husband could not force his wife to move from her home town, unless he wished to move to Eretz Israel. In Aleppo an and Damascus the *Ketuba* included terms stating that gifts received by the wife at her wedding would be inherited by her heirs, and not by her husband.

After the wedding the young couple generally lived with the groom's parents. The young couple was given a separate room and the kitchen was shared. There were some couples who lived with the bride's parents or on their own, but in most cases they lived in the town of one of the parents. Mutual visits by the families of the in-laws were common.

Since the women spent a lot of time in the company of male members of their extended families, sharing common living quarters with them, the Jewish women were freer than the Muslims or the Christians about covering their faces. In the eighteenth century the Jewish women in Aleppo, especially those who came from Europe, used to go without a scarf, and this angered the rabbis, who regarded this matter severely and demanded that the women appear with faces covered and in modest dress.

At the end of the Ottoman period the Jews continued in their traditional way of life. The Middle Eastern Jewesses were also influenced to some extent by European culture. The establishment of Alliance schools in the mid-nineteenth century in Aleppo, Damascus, and Beirut also helped to accelerate their integration into a modern way of life. The rabbis did not approve of the opening of these schools, which took the young people away from the traditional lifestyle, but they were unable to stop the process.

Many Syrian Jews developed trade contacts with other countries which led to emigration to Europe and America. After World War I the French protectorates, Syria and Lebanon, contained three large Jewish communities — in Damascus, Aleppo, and Beirut. The first two had almost 6,000 people, and in Beirut there were about 4,000 Jews. The other communities together included approximately 2,000 people. The British conquest of Syria in 1918 did not change the status of the Jews. But the Feisal government (Feisal was crowned in 1920) prohibited the Zionist associations which had arisen in Damascus a short time before. Under French rule there was no discrimination or attacks on Jews, and the authorities even gave them protection from local harassment. With Syria's renewed struggle for independence in the thirties the Jews were the first to suffer. From 1936 on the attacks on, and murder of, Jews increased and reached a peak in the Aleppo riots of December 1947.

The UN resolution of November 29, 1947 sounded the death knell for Syrian Jewry. Stores were looted and burned and synagogues were razed to the ground. The magnificent synagogue in Aleppo, reputedly built in the days of the Second Temple (but more probably in the fifth century C.E.) was among them. Also destroyed was its prize Scroll of the Law, described by the late president of Israel, Yitzhak Ben-Zvi as "the most important and authentic handwritten copy of the Torah in existence." He was able, after many efforts, to salvage part of the Torah.

As soon as Israel was proclaimed, many Syrian Jews illegally left Syria. More than 20,000 filtered through to Israel, but a handful still remains there, basically in a state of siege.

Yemen

egends differ widely as to the origins of Yemenite Jewry. According to one version, a group of Israelites veered off during the forty years of wandering in the desert and headed south to Yemen, before ever having set foot in the Promised Land. A more plausible legend traces the origins of Yemenite Jewry to the days of the Queen of Sheba, who, impressed during a visit to Jerusalem by King Solomon's wisdom, took back with her several of his advisers and their families — who in the course of time grew into a flourishing community. A third legend places the settlement in the period of the Assyrian conquest, and to refugees from the tribes of Judah and Benjamin, after the destruction of the First Temple.

The Yemenites themselves maintain that their community was already in existence during the time of the Babylonian exile and that Ezra the Scribe asked them to join him in the return to Jerusalem. They refused, they say, because, according to their calculations, the time of redemption was not yet at hand. When the Second Temple fell, the community absorbed many Jews who fled to the Arabian peninsula to escape the Romans. This influx resulted in a strongly-knit community, determined to live in the ways of its forebears until the arrival of the Messiah.

They counted the years from the destruction of the Temple. On Tisha b'Av, they would add a special prayer to the regular Lamentations: "Because of our sins and those of our forefathers, we count today, from the destruction of the house of our God and the dispersion of His people from our sacred land, from the fall of the Second Temple, built by our master Ezra . . . . years, and from the fall of the First Temple and the exile to the Diaspora . . . . years."

In the early years after the destruction of the Second Temple, there were large Jewish communities in the northern regions of the Arabian Peninsula. They maintained autonomous rule in several fortified towns, which they defended successfully whenever the need arose. These towns were situated on the main trade routes, and the Jews engaged extensively in the international commerce of the time. Their number was augmented with the voluntary conversion to Judaism of several nomadic Bedouin tribes. The Jews also maintained excellent relations with their Arab neighbors, used their language, read their literature, imparting to them in return their own knowledge of various skills and professions. Their strongest bond was with the centers of Jewry in the Land of Israel and Babylonia.

Yemen was then part of the Hamier Kingdom, which rose to eminence at the beginning of the fifth century C.E. The elevated position of the Jews in that era was underscored by the conversion to Jewry of King Du-Nuas himself. His reign was troubled, however, by the incessant attempts of the Byzantine Empire to acquire this important crossroads of commerce for itself. To achieve this, the Byzantines enlisted the aid of Ethiopia which, having adopted Christianity, was now part of the Empire. The Yemenites successfully warded off these attempts until the defeat of Byzantium by the Persians — which cost the Empire its trade routes to the East. The Ethiopians were exhorted to attack Hamier in full force, and a bitter battle ended in victory. For the next fifty years, until they were driven out by the Persians, the Ethiopians ravaged the land.

The advent of Islam in the seventh century, and the refusal of the Jews to accept the new faith, even under threat of death, brought about total upheaval. The Jews

Opposite: an artisan in his workshop.

*A silversmith fashioning
fine jewelry.*

sought refuge in Yemen, the southern sector of the Arabian peninsula, but the
Moslem conquest caught up with them even in their new refuge. In the course of a
few years, the once proud and prosperous Jewish community was oppressed and
degraded. The Yemenite Jews did the one thing open to them: they disengaged
themselves completely from the other inhabitants and surrounded themselves with
the impenetrable wall of their faith. They also maintained their communal vitality
through a voluminous exchange of responsa with the centers of Jewish learning in
other parts of the world. Their writings drew heavily on Gaonic sources, both in the
Land of Israel and Babylonia. When these centers dwindled in importance, the Jews
of Yemen turned to North Africa, where Jewish scholarship had begun to flourish
in the eleventh century, and accepted the authority of its sages.

Conditions deteriorated with the conquest of Yemen by the Ayoub dynasty at the close of the twelfth century. Its eighty-year rule oppressed Yemenite Jews as never before; the sword of conversion to Islam hung over their heads constantly, and the community seemed doomed to extinction. But then, Maimonides sent his now famous "Epistle on Apostasy" to the dwindling community. This bolstered their spirits immeasurably and the Jews of Yemen managed to bear up under their burden. To this day, Maimonides is regarded as the great leader who saved the Yemenite Jewish community and enabled it — seven centuries later — to return on the "wings of eagles" to its ancestral home.

Little is known about the Jewish community in Yemen during the thirteenth, fourteenth, and fifteenth centuries. The sixteenth-century conquest of the country by the Ottoman Turks brought the Jews to the brink of total disaster. The Ottoman authorities in Sana, the capital, and the princelings and chieftains elsewhere, engaged in endless skirmishes which invariably claimed Jews as victims. Their lot was so bad, it was no wonder that Yemen's Jews received news of Shabtai Zvi, the false Messiah, with almost hysterical fervor. This fervor was taken by the authorities as a sign of revolt, and the Jews were suppressed even further and finally deported to a desert area. One of the exiles was the renowned poet and religious lyricist, Rabbi Shalom Shabazi, who commemorated the deportation in his writings.

It did not take long for the Arabs to feel the absence of the Jews. Commerce languished and the quality of merchandise declined. The Jews were brought back and settled in separate neighborhoods, since they were considered "unclean" to live in Moslem neighborhoods. Their diligence, however, was dissipated in the course of the following centuries by the incessant internecine struggle going on in the

Yemenite Jews were known for their diligence and craftsmanship. From left to right: a woman weaving straw baskets and mats in vivid colors; a smith fashioning exquisite silver jewelry; a mother weaving baskets, with her daughter embroidering with gold and silver threads; The nargileh (in their foreground) was smoked by both men and women.

134

*Below: weaving cloth.
Right: a scribe writing a
Torah scroll.*

country between the authorities and local brigands, or the Ottoman rulers and the Yemenite chieftains. Drought and hunger followed in the wake of fields left untilled.

The sole pleasure left for the Moslems, it seems, was the intensification of misery for the Jews. It was decreed that the Jews clean the public latrines and gather the dung for heating water in the Turkish baths. Special taxes were levied on Jews, and those who could not pay were arrested and tortured. A few Jews succumbed to the relief offered them by conversion to Islam, but the great majority bore the evil decrees with great fortitude. Throughout these trying times the community was bolstered by an amazing number of sages and scholars who rose above the misery to shed light and warmth.

Ottoman rule ended and it was only then, with the installation of the Yemenite Imamate, that Jews could draw a free breath. Rabbi Yihye ben Moshe Yitzhak was appointed Chief Rabbi *(Hacham Bashi)* of Yemenite Jewry. He worked a miraculous cure on his people and restored them to a measure of vitality which kept them going until the entire community was flown to Israel.

Yemenite Jewry was far from homogeneous. The Jews of Aden in the south, for instance, were sedate, even-tempered, and spoke with a languid drawl while the residents of Bitza, three days' journey on foot away, were sharp in everything — speech, temper, even food — and industrious in the extreme. So great was the difference in temperament that these "sons of Zechariah," as the Bitza Jews were called, refrained from intermarrying with the Jews of southern Yemen. The farther north the community, the more marked the differences. In hilly Dialso, a town of tradespeople, the Jews tended toward mental and manual agility and were notorious for their impatience. The Jews of Shar'ab were excessively quarrelsome, especially when it came to disputation over the Bible and commentaries. At times issues were decided by fistfights. In Ta'is, the southwestern capital, the temperament was entirely different: the Jews there, mostly merchants, divided their time equally between business and leisure. The residents of Sana, the capital, were — if the reports of travelers are to be taken at face value — snobs.

Throughout the entire community, however, there ran an unmistakable thread of solidarity. Yemenite Jews preferred to dwell apart, even when they were under no obligation to do so. Living in their own neighborhoods made it easier for them to enjoy the practical manifestations of their faith, as well as to provide more efficient protection against potential Moslem attackers. Their homes, rarely higher than two stories, were unpretentious, in accordance with the law. Mud and lime were in most cases the main building materials, since only the wealthy could afford kiln-baked brick. On the inside, houses were adorned with brass shelves for flower boxes and decorative utensils. The lower story generally served as a workshop and storeroom, while the upstairs was used for living quarters. To safeguard against robbers, walls facing the street were windowless, and doors were made of strong timber. The small courtyards invariably contained a few trees (dates and pomegranates were the most popular), a chicken coop, and a goat shed.

The second story was built around a large guest room. At one end, two or three steps higher, was the entrance to a small chamber, the "intimacy room" used by newly-wed couples. The kitchen had several wood-fueled ovens built along one wall, separated by fireproof partitions of earth. Small windows on the opposite wall served as exhaust outlets. Next to the kitchen was a niche built around the mouth of a well (each house dug its own), and quantities of water were kept in large earthenware crocks near at hand. Baths, sanitary needs and laundry were provided for in a shed outdoors.

Floors of guest rooms were covered with goatskin rags; on entering guests and family members alike took off their footwear in order to preserve the rug. Cushions and pillows of wool or cotton lined the base of the walls for comfortable reclining. Shelves overhead contained sacred writings; a man's material possessions were often appraised by the number and the scholarly level of books which lined his walls.

Yemenite Jews were always blessed with extraordinary diligence, a love for cleanliness, and a strong feeling of familial cohesiveness.

Their day began at dawn, when father and sons went to the synagogue, while the mother, dressed for housework, recited a brief prayer for the welfare of the family and plunged into her chores — milling flour for the day's needs, lighting the oven, and preparing breakfast. Food for the day was bought by the man in the market place on his way back from the synagogue and carried in the fold of his cloak. According to an old Yemenite adage, a bachelor is like a candle — unfettered — while a husband is like a basket — laden with commodities.

After breakfast the father went down to his workshop, the boys went off to study, and the daughters helped their mother draw water, bake, sew, and embroider. The very young girls were allowed to play in the yard, but never in the street. After lunch, women would gather at each other's homes and spend a few hours embroidering and chatting.

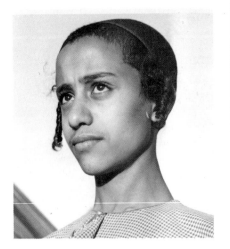

Young Yemenite Jews.

Bread could be, and was, baked in fifteen different ways. It had to be eaten while still fresh, almost warm, and was therefore baked separately for each meal. The flour — of both grains and legumes — was sifted several times, the more the better, and the costlier, which linked the quality of the flour to the occasion. When bread was baked in preparation for a long journey, it was given the texture of crumbly toast, which lasted for days on end. Bread for the Sabbath was made of high-grade flour, and the sesame "rings" were soft and chewy.

The Yemenite menu consisted of cereals, porridge and the like, and were distinguished by their painstaking preparation and delicateness. Certain foods such as *harish,* a wheat meal, boiled to a thick consistency and flavored with spiced butter, honey, and sugar, were prepared especially for convalescents. The Yemenite version of oven-baked *hamin* contained wheat meal, rice, lentils, and other beans built around chunks of fatty meat. Soup of meat and vegetable stock, fragrantly

spiced, was the standby of every meat meal. *Hashwaya* — strips of meat broiled on a spit — was a delicacy that deserved to be eaten with wine or *arak*. Wherever feasible, condiments were applied vigorously: *zakhouk,* a sharp allspice, ground fine and mixed with finely-chopped leaf vegetables; *hilbeh,* a fluff made of clover soaked in water, finely-ground, then mixed with the *zakhouk.* Roasted seeds of all kinds, as well as all varieties of nuts, graced the table on the Sabbath and at special occasions.

One of the most popular delicacies was locust (the *kosher* species). Swarms would come sweeping in towards evening. Special scouts would locate their landing area and light bonfires around it to let others know. Before dawn young people armed with stick and bags, would come into the snake- and scorpion-infested areas to gather the locusts. The locusts were dried, cleaned, and cooked, and served together with other delicacies.

Wood for the stoves was purchased in the market place from woodcutters who

Above, left: a Jewish family in Sana — great-grandfather, grandfather, father, and sons. Above, right: the shofar (ram's horn) used by Yemenite Jewry.

used camels for transport. There was no fixed price for the commodity, and the wood market was invariably the noisiest bargaining place in the vicinity.

Trade and commerce, other highly-charged occupations, were relatively rare among the Yemenite Jews. Most were craftsmen and artisans, and by virtue of their industriousness they were able to elevate their occupations into true artistic expression. Forbidden to own land, they were neither farmers nor farmhands, although they provided local farmers with tools and various services. Gold and silver smithing was highly regarded, and the Jews passed their skills from one generation to the next. They preferred this type of work because it suited their temperaments and also enabled them to work at home and thus keep an eye on the children and their education. Earnings were also quite substantial, since clients included district governors, whose orders included not only jewelry for their wives but the minting of coins for their realm. Many of the smiths trained other apprentices, in addition to their own sons. Yemenite Jews also worked in brass and iron, fashioning hand tools and weapons of all kinds.

The ingenuity and industry of the Yemenite Jews led them into many productive occupations: weaving, engraving, calligraphy, bookbinding, blanket sewing, milling, carpentry, tailoring, pottery, and painting, plus a host of lower occupations; no manual labor was below the dignity of the Yemenite Jew, so long as it was honest and provided a livelihood. Income was in certain instances precarious: Moslem farmers paid their Jewish creditors when and if crops were good; otherwise, the debt was automatically written off, since the Jews had no recourse to law.

The Jews of Yemen depended on only one compensation for their toil and distress — the inner contentment they derived from their faith and traditions. The education of their sons was their highest priority, and they knew that the success of this education depended on the example they themselves set for their progeny.

Yemenite boys were formally introduced to the commuinity during the first

The wedding ceremony topped all other happy events in Jewish life in Yemen. Left: a Yemenite bride and groom in traditional attire before their wedding in Sana.

Simhat Torah of their lives, when fathers took them to the synagogue, and asked for worshippers' blessings. The ceremony was a joyful one and culminated with a festive *kiddush*. At the age of three, their hair was shorn — except for earlocks. During the next two years, they learned biblical and prayer book passages from their fathers. Then came the *khanis* (the schoolroom) and the *mori* (teacher). Since books were scarce, several children would sit around a single volume and they learned to read from different angles. Sessions were opened with "O Lord, open my heart and make me wise in Your Torah .... Blessed be the Lord, giver of the Torah." High priorities were placed on learning the prayers, reading the Torah in accordance with the traditional cantillations (faulty reading heaped disgrace on both parent and teacher), and understanding the commentaries and homiletics. The boys were taught Hebrew script as well as Rashi, although from a practical standpoint it served only the would-be scholars, scribes, and community officials.

There was no fixed time limit for study, but by the time boys reached Bar Mitzvah, they generally became only part-time students, and started learning their father's occupation. But after they became proficient in their vocation, the young men would still devote some time to study. If he was fortunate enough to have a learned father, the two would "talk Torah" while working side by side. More than any other community in the Eastern diaspora, the Yemenite was distinguished for the large number of scholars and well-informed laymen which it produced.

In regard to religious observance, the Yemenite boys became Bar Mitzvah long before they reached the age of thirteen. They were given a pair of *tefillin* (phylacteries) as soon as they could recite the prayers; they would also be called to the Torah as soon as they could read.

Girls received no formal education but their mothers saw to it that they became familiar with the laws necessary for running a Jewish home. Instead of a women's gallery in the synagogue, the women listened to the prayers while seated in an adjacent house. On the other hand, girls were exposed to table talk on religious

Right: young Jews from Yemen on their arrival in Israel. Opposite: Torah study was the main preoccupation of Yemenite Jewry. A shortage of textbooks forced four and more boys to share one book, learning to read upside-down as well as right side up.

subjects, and quite often they were able to listen in on Torah talk between their fathers and brothers, with the result that many Yemenite Jewesses were remarkably well-informed.

Since government decree ordered all Jewish orphans to be converted to the Islamic faith, the death of a father with small children was a great calamity. The community sought to avert the decree by spiriting the children away to other towns, where their identity could be kept secret. When there was no alternative, however, orphans ten years of age and under were given in marriage in order to escape the decree.

The extent to which the synagogue played the role of a community center is another aspect of the uniqueness of the Yemenite diaspora. Aside from traditional prayer and study, the synagogue also served as a community forum. Announcements of public interest, ranging from government edicts to personal announcements, were made here. Anyone guilty of improper behavior, socially or in business dealings, was told, immediately after the reading of the *Haftara:* "Arise and be respectful towards this place." The culprit than had to leave the synagogue and was not allowed to return until he was ready to repent. He would then return to

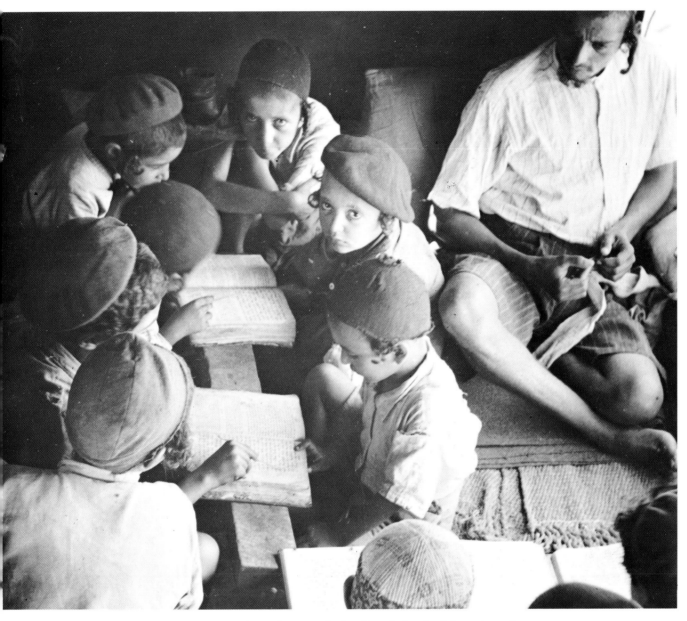

the synagogue and confess: "I have sinned toward the Lord God of Israel and toward this Torah and toward you," to which the congregation would respond: "You are forgiven, you are allowed [to return], now that you have accepted the judgment."

In its appointments, the synagogue reflected the simple and unpretentious life of the congregants. Torah scrolls were housed in plain, unadorned arks. Pulpits were small, mobile boxes. Worshippers sat on mats and cushions.

Synagogues were seldom empty. Morning services were followed by study of the Torah and commentaries. After work the men and boys went to the synagogue for afternoon and evening prayers, and lecture by the *mori* on the rudiments of Jewish law. On Sabbath and holidays, the regimen was augmented by study of the Zohar and the works of Maimonides.

Yemenite Jews found it inconceivable that anyone should make his living from the Torah or be subsidized while studying. There were, therefore, no professional scholars or yeshiva students among them. Rabbis and other religious functionaries earned their livelihood from other callings. The learned amonog them were considered the aristocracy of the community, far more than the wealthy. Yemenite mothers considered it a privilege to deny themselves bread so that their sons might become learned men.

Proficient in Arabic though they were, the Yemenite Jews, unlike their brethren in Moorish Spain, kept their distance from Arabic culture. Yemenite Jewish poets and lyricists dedicated their works to purely religious themes: longing for the redemption of Zion and supplication for the grace of God. Secular subjects were given no expression whatever. For this reason, many of Jewry's hymns and prayers today come from this source.

For the numerous ills and hardships that beset them, the Jews of Yemen had one overriding cure — the Sabbath day. Actually, the Sabbath provided a preoccupation that consumed most of the week. Preparations began on Wednesday (for the housewives) and ended on Friday, when the males went to the public baths and the head of the household readied the wicks and oil for the Sabbath lamps. The males donned special *talitot* over their clothes. The mother put on her wedding dress *(lulu)*, skillfully embroidered with silver thread, donned her bonnet *(matzuan)*, put on a silver necklace, slipped bracelets on her arms and rings on her fingers, applied eye shadow — and then kindled the Sabbath lights.

When the men returned from the synagogue, they were met by the women and girls holding fragrant boughs in their hand.

Kiddush was followed with *geala* — a trayful of fruits and roasted beans, the standard appetizer preceding every festive meal — and washed down with wine or *arak* and accompanied with *zemirot* (special mealtime chants) and Torah talk. Next, a tray laden with *shoiya*, roast meat, was placed in front of the head of the household, and he would proceed to serve it to the others, each in turn according to his age. All but the young quaffed wine in varying amounts. On the Sabbath everyone joined in singing; on weekdays, one person would lead while the others responded. And only at this point did the formal meal commence, with the males washing their hands in the *majassal*, a water basin used only for this purpose. Each had his pair of *hallot* (Sabbath loaves), which he dipped in the bowls of *hilbeh* and soup. In conclusion, following the grace, the assemblage partook of sweets, coffee, and dates.

Bedtime came early on Sabbath eve, since the men and boys would arise the next morning while it was still dark and go to the synagogue, carrying with them the *jamma*, a silver urn containing thick, aromatic coffee. The worshippers treated one another to the sweet drink, vying for the honor of serving the rabbi. After the prayers, the men would go home to wake the small children and take them back to the synagogue.

The Sabbath day meal was very much like the one the evening before except that it was interrupted to allow the father to test his children's progress in their studies and in the week's Bible reading. A nap was then enjoyed for an hour or two, after which the men and boys went to the synagogue for further study, while the women, boughs in their hands, went visiting their relatives, a new bride, or the ill. They walked in groups, keeping within the confines of the Jewish quarter, and were careful to return before dusk. Evening prayers on Saturdays were always said at home. Before the *Havdala* service, everyone would recite a unique prayer: ''Our God and God of our fathers, begin for us the coming six days of work in peace, and whoever advises ill against us and against Your people, the House of Israel, whether

Left: two elderly women, with typical hairdos and jewelry. Below: an elderly man smoking a nargileh at his doorstep.

he be one of ours or not, for the sake of Your name may You do away with him, confuse him, cut him down, demolish him, shun him, destroy him, annul his advice, and spoil his thought."

Preparations for the High Holy Days began a month before Rosh Hashana with the pre-dawn recitation of the *selihot* (penitential prayers). The *almada'i* trudged from street to street, calling each inhabitant by name to arise and come to the synagogue, while groups of youngsters ran ahead and blew the *shofar*, making sure no one remained asleep.

Rosh Hashanah differed very little in content from the ritual followed in other Jewish communities. At one time the *shofar* was fashioned from the horn of a mountain goat, until the rabbis of Sana ordained that only a ram's horn be used.

The *tashlich* ceremony was not practiced in Yemen in public; individuals who wished to "cast away their sins" did so at their own well.

Preparations for the Yom Kippur fast were a serious matter. A large meal was eaten at noon, followed by the pre-fast meal following the afternoon prayers. This meal usually consisted of buttered bread, honey and much fruit, particularly grapes and pomegranates.

Yom Kippur vestments were predominantly of white silk; on their feet, they either wore rope sandals or else went barefoot. Many spent the entire night in the synagogue. At *minha* services everyone went home to exchange the wite silk vestment for the regular Sabbath attire, and to bring a quince with which to break the fast after the *shofar* blast had announced the end of the Day of Atonement.

Back in their homes, the women set about kneading dough for the night's repast, while the men went out to the yard to drive in the first pegs for the *sukka*. Sukkot was so popular that many houses included a room without a ceiling so as to provide a permanent *sukka;* the room was covered the rest of the year with mats, to keep the rain out. *Sukka* roofs were made from durra or corn stalks or green cactus leaves. Inside, the floor was covered with mats and carpets, and bowls of myrtle leaves hung in the corners.

Possession of a *lulav* and *etrog* was imperative. Some fathers used to acquire a set for each of their sons who were capable of holding them.

It was customary, in some areas of Yemen, for several families to jointly buy an ox or a sheep, so as to have an abundance of meat for the holiday. On Sukkot nights, the entire family slept in the *sukka*.

Hoshana Rabba differed from its observance elsewhere in the Diaspora in one major item: the *shofar* was sounded between each *hakafa* (circling of the pulpit).

Hanukah was distinguishable from ordinary days only because of the candles, which were set in alabaster bases. Purim, on the other hand, received elaborate attention. Children began studying the Book of Esther two months before the festival. An effigy of Haman was fashioned in the form of a scarecrow in Arab dress, mounted on wheels, and paraded throughout the Jewish Quarter. The youngsters gathered with their creations and formed a caravan which wound its way to the "gallows." In contrast with custom elsewhere, the effigies were not burned but hidden until the following year.

Purim dress, worn to the synagogue for the reading of the *megillah*, consisted of a blue shirt striped with white, and a black hat. Draped in their prayer shawls, the men and boys read the Book of Esther. At the end, the reader cried out: "Cursed be

Many Yemenite Jews became skilled farmers in Israel, establishing scores of agricultural settlements. Right: a farmer in a workers' settlement. Opposite: a Hadramaut Jew on a combine.

Haman!" to which the congregation replied: "Blessed be Mordecai!" This was repeated three times and then three times again with the phrases reversed. All the characters of the Book of Esther, plus any oppressors of Jews that particular year, were mentioned by name, one way or another. There was no noisemaking or stamping of feet at the mention of Haman's name, out of respect for the synagogue. At home, the males would read the *megillah* to the women, at the conclusion of which all would say: "Thus shall all Your enemies perish, O Lord, and those that love You be as the sun, setting out in its might."

The Purim feast was the chief gastronomic event of the year. Between courses, the housewife would set aside a portion for the poor. Couples married that year received special gifts from their parents and, at the home of the young husband's parents, they received a copper tray laden with sweets and a bag of silver coins. The sweets were distributed on the following day among neighbors and relatives.

Preparations for Passover began while the echoes of Purim were still in the air. First emerged the earthen crocks with the preserved wheat. The women cleaned the kernels and milled them on stone, then sifted the flour until it was as white as snow. This was done by an ancient process which softened the outer layer of the kernel: the wheat was placed on a wild plant called *harmel*, covered with another layer of the plant, which was in turn covered with a mat and placed in the sun. The vapor given off by the *harmel* loosened the outer layer and made the milling easier.

Fresh *matzot* were baked daily throughout Passover by the women. The dough was salted slightly in order to make them more enjoyable. The women also prepared as many as thirteen varieties of *harosset*, which was served throughout the holiday.

The main arrangement of the *Seder* table was a multiple layer of large-leafed lettuce, radishes, parsley, and horseradish. This bed of vegetables was piled high and covered the entire table. In the center, several kinds of *harosset* were set out and sprinkled with grains, to effect the appearance of "straw" on top of the clay-like *harosset*. The other ingredients of the *Seder* plate were placed alongside and the entire table was covered with a white cloth. This done, the members of the family put on their holiday clothes, which had previously been sprinkled with incense to lend aroma to the atmosphere.

The *Seder* began as soon as the males returned from the synagogue. The white cloth came off the table and everyone partook of the vegetables before him. The youngest asked the *makvar*, the Four Questions, in the vernacular. The *Haggadah* was read in Hebrew and then translated. No special cup was set aside for Elijah nor were songs such as *Had Gadya* sung. The ebullience of the *Seder* was in accordance with the total enjoyment which the Jews of Yemen derived from their faith.

On Shavuot eve, mindful of the tradition that the gates of heaven open at some time between nightfall and dawn, it was customary to stay up all night studying. A shooting star was held to be a key to the gates, and many a tall tale was spun concerning luckless individuals who made the wrong wish at the right time.

On Shavuot it was customary to read the *ketuba,* the marriage contract, between God and the Community of Israel, in the cantillations of the Book of Esther. The Book of Ruth was read in the original and in the vernacular, each man reading in turn. As was the custom of the Ashkenazi diaspora, dairy delicacies, including *blintzes,* were served.

The "three weeks" between the Seventeenth of Tammuz and the Ninth of Av were observed as a mourning period. No business ventures were initiated during this period, which was regarded as persecution-prone. Meat was permissible until the last meal before the Tisha B'Av fast. Everyone — the weak, the ill, the pregnant — fasted punctiliously. The Book of Lamentations was read in the dim light of small candles, and the wailing in the synagogue was like the mourning for the dead. The scrolls of the Torah were decked in black. As the fast drew to a close, spirits were uplifted. The final parting words were: "May the mourners for Zion be given splendor in the place of ashes," and each worshipper went home with hope and faith in his heart.

The Ninth of Av fast day gave full expression to the yearnings of the Yemenite community for the return to its ancestral home, and it also voiced the pent-up pain of life in the Diaspora. Yemenite Jews maintained an unbroken affinity to the land of their ancestors: their most fervent aspiration was to be able to make a pilgrimage to the sacred sites and pray for the restoration of Israel.

In 1882 a messianic impulse seized the community. Disposing of their meagre possessions, many banded together in groups and set out, on foot or astride donkeys, for distant Alexandria in Egypt, where they boarded small steamers to Jaffa. Exhausted but not dispirited, they undertook to do whatever was at hand. Others came after them, in a ceaseless trickle, settling in Rehovot, Rishon Lezion, Nes Ziona, Petach Tikvah, and Zichron Yaacov.

Yemen was deep in the throes of civil turmoil when Israel was born. When news came that Israel had smitten its neighboring enemies, the Jews of Yemen abandoned everything and streamed to Aden, joining the Jews of that community in the British detention (which they renamed "Redemption") camp. From there they were airlifted to Israel "on the wings of eagles" in what has come to be known as "Operation Magic Carpet." In just over one year, 50,000 members of the community were transferred to the land of its dream.

Hadramaut

Living in the midst of a tough, sun-baked people who had never allowed the yoke of Yemen's Imam to be placed around their neck, the Jews of Hadramaut — a region along the southern coast of the Arabian peninsula — enjoyed a degree of respect among their neighbors unparalleled in other Arab lands. In appearance, too — long hair and daggers at their side — the Hadramaut Jews were indistinguishable from their Moslem compatriots.

Little is known about the early history of this exotic Jewish community. What is known is that the region was subject to plagues and famine, and that large numbers of townspeople took up a nomadic existence, and this led to turbulence, brigandage, and highway robbery, which kept all but the most dauntless visitors at a safe distance.

One such traveler was the Zionist emissary, Shmuel Yavnieli. He was determined to penetrate into this remote province and make contact with its Jews, even though others had not penetrated past the first brigands. On the road between Hadne and Hebaan, in 1912, he and his caravan were attacked by robbers; he was stripped of his money and bedding and taken to the thieves' village, where he was held until ransomed by the Jews of Hebaan. Yanvieli had this to say about his redeemers (in *Journey to Yemen*):

"The Jews in these parts are held in high esteem by everyone in Yemen and Aden. They are said to be courageous, always with their weapons and wild long hair, and the names of their towns are mentioned by the Jews of Yemen with great admiration."

Hadramaut is sparsely populated. In all of Hebaan, Yavnieli found eleven houses (called "towers" because of their structure of three or four stories) and a community of thirty Jewish families. Most of the heads of the families were engaged in silversmithing; a few were herdsmen, and they moved from one village to another in quest of work.

Bidda's larger community of several hundred souls was relatively new — only seven generations had been reared there at the time of Yavnieli's visit. "The first ones are the heads of the Zechariah clan, who come from Hebaan . . . they sell wares in the neighboring villages, work in silver, leather pelts, cobbling, and say they are poor . . . . Here, meat is eaten only on the Sabbath, and even coffee is a luxury . . . . Some have small fields which they plant with durra, which does not require water . . . . The impression is that everywhere here the Jews dwell in security and are content and healthy."

Legend has it that the fair treatment accorded to the Jews of Hadramaut began fifteen centuries ago, when the King of Hadramaut was engaged in a war with the King of Hameer. Saliman Alhakeem ("Solomon the Wise"), a Jew, advised the Hadramaut ruler how he should carry on the campaign, and was credited with helping to win the war. In gratitude, the king accorded the Jews the status of honored citizens (not merely "protected people") and allowed them to carry daggers in their sashes, a sign of high standing.

"Young and old," says Yavnieli, "go around bareheaded, like the others, with but an oiled thong around their very long hair. They have nothing of the earlocks which the Yemenite Jews foster so diligently. The Arabs here are totally unfamiliar with the Yemenite Jew and his long earlocks. Mustache hair is plucked most

154 *Three Hadramaut Jews upon their arrival in Israel.*

merilessly, by both Jews and Arabs. The young people braid their hair and oil it and take care of it with infinite reverence."

The upheavals caused by man and nature prevented the Jews from developing stable spiritual formats, as did the week-long absences of the men from their homes. "In all of these places," writes Yavnieli, "most of the Jews have only one wife. Girls are married off at the age of twelve . . . The bride is conducted to the groom's village by married people, but not her parents; it is considered a disgrace if they follow her any earlier than seven days thence. She is placed on a donkey, her hair covered and dressed in white. Her arrival is announced with shots in the air, and the general populace greets her in the same manner. For the wedding the women wear long red dresses. The groom arrives with his entourage, linked arm in arm, singing and dancing."

When a woman gave birth, a ewe would be slaughtered in her honor and then passed over her head three times.

The manner in which the Hadramaut Jews greeted one another is worthy of note. Yavnieli writes: "When they greet one another, after a journey, they clasp each other's hands and raise them to face level. One kisses the hand of his friend and inquires about his health, whereupon the other does the same and replies. The procedure is repeated several times."

Despite the precarious travel conditions, the Jews of Hadramaut managed to keep close contact with their brethren in Yemen and to draw from them the spiritual sustenance denied them by circumstances in their own country. In the possession of Hadramaut's Jews were sacred writings of noted commentators and the *tachlaal,* the Yemenite prayer book, and the poems of Shalom Shabazi.

B'nei Dan, "the Sons of Dan," constituted a tribe of mysterious, unseen Jews, said to be direct descendants of the Ten Lost Tribes, whose whereabouts have intrigued travelers and explorers for many centuries. *B'nei Dan*, according to Moslem travelers, were to be found along the road to Mecca; they were called the "Haramin" and used to travel about wearing phylacteries and thongs on their arms. The Moslems claimed that the prayers of these Jews caused them to be petrified by a strong wind, at which the Jews would rob them of their possessions. Yavnieli attempted to get some reliable information about the mysterious tribe, but the answers were evasive and entirely unsatisfactory.

Yavnieli succeeded in persuading the Hadramaut Jews to settle in the Land of Israel. They made their way to Aden and there were put aboard ship for the journey. The first families to arrive caused quite a stir by their strange appearance. At the end of World War II, Palestinian Jews were thrilled whenever any group came from anywhere. But the amazing sight of the Hebaanese Jews excited them beyond description. They could not believe their eyes. It was as though they had come straight out of the Arabian Nights.

The vanguard of the Hadramaut Jews was led by Zechariah Hebaani. He kept after the officials in charge of immigration to Israel to accelerate the transfer of his brethren to the Land of Israel. They were in dire distress, he reported, suffering from hunger and from the edicts of Hussein Abdallah of Hebaan and his sons. They were also in debt to the Moslems, who charged them exorbitant interest.

Although a few families left Hadramaut, most of the Jews remained until they were gathered up in "Operation Magic Carpet" and, together with their Yemenite brethren, were flown to Israel.

Aden

There is an understandable tendency to lump the Jews of Aden with their Yemenite brethren, but they are two distinct groups, just as the two countries are distinct.

Aden, situated on the Arabian coast at the southern end of the Red Sea, is the main commercial distribution center for the entire Arabian peninsula, on the sea lanes that cross to Europe, Africa, Asia, and Australia.

The Romans sought to conquer Aden for passage to Arabia Felix, land of gold and incense; then, in turn, came the Portuguese, the French, and the Dutch. In the middle of the eighteenth century, as the Ottoman Empire weakened, other countries became interested, until Britain finally conquered Aden in 1839 and settled the issue of control over the area.

The state of Aden became a Crown Colony and Protectorate. The city, also named Aden, was declared a free port and attracted many merchants, among them Jews from surrounding territories. Most of the Jews came from Mukka, a port city on the western coast of the Arabian peninsula and an important way station for commerce from India to Egypt and to the Mediterranean, as well as the exit port for the fine Yemenite coffees.

The Jews played an important role in this commercial activity, even though they were oppressed by the Imam of Yemen and forbidden to dwell within the walls of the city. When the British took over Aden, the Jews of Mukka moved to the Crown Colony — taking along Mukka's commerce. Under British rule, the number of Aden's Jews rose in 100 years from 250 to 8,000.

Aden's Jews lived in the crater of an extinct volacno that overlooked the Bay of Aden. The British dug a tunnel connecting this section to the commercial section of the city centered about Steamer's Point.

Prior to the advent of the British, Aden's Jews worked as bookbinders, porters, silversmiths, money-changers, and shipping agents. They also had a monopoly on the ostrich feather market. With the change in regime, they became liquor distillers.

Close contact was established with Jewish merchants elsewhere, particularly in India and Iraq, and many of Aden's Jews attained considerable affluence. In time, Jews from India and Iraq, as well as Jews from Yemen on their way to more favorable climes, settled in Aden. The customs that became prevalent in the Aden community therefore reflected the modes of these other far-flung Jewish communities.

Among the customs peculiar to Aden's Jews which remained intact were some prayers (attributed to Rabbi Saadiya Gaon) and a unique text of the marriage contract. The reading of the Book of Esther on Purim was reserved for bridegrooms. When a woman gave birth to a boy, a goat would be slaughtered and placed under her bed. For the wedding feast, the main dish was the meat of a female calf.

The British presence brought law and order to the region, and the Jewish community responded by organizing itself along efficient lines of discipline and cooperation. Zionist emissaries were given unlimited aid. When Yavnieli, prior to World War I, went to Arabia to implement his vision of the ingathering, he established his headquarters in Aden.

This migration continued into the 1940s, despite British attempts to prevent the Jews from leaving for Palestine. The British tried to force the Yemenite Jews to return to Yemen — where they would have been put to death by the Imam — but

Aden's influential Jews interceded with the British authorities and instead, the Yemenite Jews were placed in a detention camp near Aden.

The birth of Israel aroused Arab nationalism in Aden. An Arab strike against the United Nations resolution of November 1947 grew into a wave of violence against the Jews. Schools were set afire, homes and stores were looted, and scores of Jews were murdered. The rioting spread to other towns in the region.

The Jews of Aden began to leave for England and India, where they had business connections, and for Israel. When the British evacuated Aden in 1968 there were only 150 Jewish families in Aden, and they left with the British, knowing full well the fate that would have overtaken them otherwise.

Thus, in 1968, the history of a once-proud Jewish community came to an end.

The Balkan Jews: Turkey

Turkey, the vital and strategic bridge between Europe and Asia, has been the crossroads of intercontinental culture for centuries. Jews have lived there since the period of the Second Temple, when the region was ruled by Greeks and Romans. They continued to settle throughout the Roman Empire's Eastern area and in time developed divergent customs and traditions. Under Ottoman rule, they again became a homogeneous community, extending from one end of the Balkans to the other and sharing common reservoirs of Jewish scholarship and practice.

The communal structure of the Jews in the Balkans was strong enough to absorb streams of Jews from France, Italy, Hungary, and Poland, as each of these countries, in turn or simultaneously, during the thirteenth and fourteenth centuries, issued anti-Jewish decrees that led to the departure of the Jews.

The Ottoman regime recognized the newcomers' value to Turkey's economic development. According to one account, when Sultan Urham captured Brussa in 1326 and made it the capital of the Ottoman empire, he deported its residents — and imported Jews from Damascus and the lands of the Byzantine Empire to populate it. Jews were allowed to live anywhere in the sultanate and could own land and houses. In return they paid the *haraj*, the tax levied on all non-Moslems. Jews living in countries conquered by the Turks were generally happy to welcome the new rulers. When Murad I captured Thrace and Thessalia, the local Jews asked their brethern in Brussa to teach them the Turkish language and thus hasten their integration.

The center of Jewish life in Turkey, from the second half of the fourteenth century on, was Adrianople, whose *yeshiva* drew thousands of students from neighboring countries. For two centuries, the Jews enjoyed a freedom and prosperity unmatched by any other diaspora. They held posts of prominence and responsibility. Isaac Pasha was the Sultan's private physician, the first of a long line of medical men who held this position. Jewish soldiers served in the Turkish forces. When Mohammad the Conqueror (1451—81) took Constantinople (which the Ottomans renamed Istanbul), Jews were invited to settle in the city, build a synagogue, and establish schools. They in turn urged their brethern in the lands of distress to come to Turkey, where "each man dwelt under his vine and under his fig tree." The call received a swift and extensive response; thousands of Jews came to Turkey and augmented the flourishing Jewish community.

The high status of Turkish Jewry was reflected in the authority and influence of its chief rabbi, the *Hacham Bashi*. The first to bear this title, Rabbi Moshe Cashsaali, was a member of the National Council. This put him on equal footing with the Moslem *kadi* and higher than the Greek Patriarch. His authority extended to all facets of Jewish community life. His successors were chosen by the community and merely approved by the sultan.

A significant step was taken by the Jews of Constantinople to bring the Karaites back in to the Jewish fold. Once a powerful sect, the Karaites had sunk into ignorance and spiritual inertia. They admitted to this, and now sought to come closer to the "rabbanites," the adherents of Jewish oral as well as written law. The rabbis were divided on the possibilities of reintegrating the Karaites. Finally, these efforts came to naught, and the Karaites split away. Many settled in the Crimea and others lived apart in the Turkish capital.

The greatest impact on the Jewish community in the Ottoman Empire resulted from the expulsion of the Jews from Spain, after several centuries of a golden era on the Iberian peninsula. It should be noted that while the Sephardic communities that arose in England, Holland, and other European countries stemmed from Marrano families who eventually returned to their original Jewish faith, the refugees who came to the Balkans were those who preferred to retain their faith and suffer flight to ostensible conversion to Christianity. Among them were men of great scholarship, and their arrival in Constantinople, Izmir, Adrianople, and Salonika ushered in a new era for those centers of Balkan Jewry. The prosperity which their sagacity and diligence brought to the Empire caused Sultan Byazid II (1481—1512) to exclaim: "I am amazed with those who say that Ferdinand of Spain is clever, since he is impoverishing his country and enriching my lands." And the sultan was correct: in every phase of human endeavor — the arts and sciences, trade and industry, diplomacy and administration — the Jews at the heart of the Ottoman Empire gave it the finest hours in its history. The sultan had another reason for favoring the Jews, namely, their role as a check and balance vis-a-vis the Christians in the Empire, whom the sultan suspected of secret loyalty to his foes, the European powers.

The benign attitude of the sultans toward their Jewish subjects was reflected outside Turkey, particularly in Jerusalem, whose Jewish community had been uprooted by the Crusaders. Two centuries after this disaster there were still only seventy Jewish families in the city of David, but a few decades later the Jewish population rose to 1,500, while Safed grew to a community of 2,000 Jews and even superseded Jerusalem in importance. Jewish communities sprouted in the Middle East; Damascus had 500 Jewish families, and a large community arose in Egypt. Constantinople's kaleidoscopic Jewish community of 30,000 boasted no less than forty-four synagogues. It also took pride in its printing establishments. The Nehemias family, which had been printers in Spain, set up the first print shop in Constantinople in 1503. Soon hundreds of books — sacred, semi-sacred, and general literature of Jewish content — came off the hand presses in Constantinople. As the arts and sciences developed in the Turkish metropolis, so did books on philosophy, philology, music, and mathematics (Rabbi Eliyahu Mizrachi, the *Hacham Bashi* who succeeded Rabbi Caphsaali, wrote a commentary on Euclid's

Above: the new synagogue in Izmir (left); the Portuguese synagogue in Izmir (right).

162

*Right: a Jewish couple in
19th-century Turkey. Far
right: a Jewish police officer
in 1890.*

basic treatise on geometry). In the academies of learning, Torah and general knowledge were taught side by side.

Many outstanding Jewish personalities came to the fore in this golden age, and the brightest among them were Dona Gracia Mendes and her son-in-law, Don Yossef Nassi. Their influence in the courts of Suleiman the Magnificent and Salim II was boundless, and they used all of it on behalf of their brethren. Don Yossef even obtained the sultan's permission to rebuild the ruins of Tiberias, which he saw as a nucleus of a free Jewish state, under Turkish patronage. It may rightly be said that in no other country did Jewish genius have so free a rein, and no other country benefited so much from it.

Many significant chapters of Jewish history were written in other Turkish centers.

Izmir, for example, was settled by Jews in the days of the Second Temple (as evinced by Jewish tombstones and inscriptions dating back to the first centuries of the Common Era). Izmir became famous in Jewish history because of Shabtai Zvi, the false messiah of the seventeenth century.

Shabtai Zvi was born in Izmir in 1626, on Tisha b'Av — the date, according to tradition, on which the Messiah will be born — at a time when Jewish suffering in many countries set the stage for messianic yearnings. Zvi, steeped in Kabbalistic mysticism from his early youth, calculated that 1648 would be the year of redemption. The combination of the two dates led Shabtai Zvi to regard himself as the Messiah, and his personal charm influenced others to accept him. In order to gain the favor of the community, he annulled many commandments that were particularly bothersome. The leading rabbis of the time condemned him and banned him from Izmir.

Shabtai Zvi went to Constantinople and then to Salonika, where he symbolically married the Torah, Daughter of Heaven. Forced to wander still further, he made his way to the Holy Land and prayed in Hebron, where, he subsequently told his adherents, many wonderful things happened to him. The next stop was Egypt, where he married an eccentric girl — a survivor of the Cossack massacre in Poland who insisted that she was destined to marry the Messiah. He also met Natan Ashkenazi of Gaza, who spread the name and fame of Shabtai Zvi across the Diaspora so convincingly that many Jews liquidated their possessions in anticipation of accompanying the Messiah to the Promised Land. The enthusiasm of the Jewish populace reached such heights that the Turkish authorities, worried lest the movement turn into a problem for their Empire, threw him into a cell in the Avidos fortress, on the shore of the Dardanelles. When the movement did not abate, the sultan ordered him put to death, unless he agreed to convert to Islam. The "Messiah" chose to remain alive, much to the disillusionment of his followers — except for those who regarded the conversion as a step toward the ultimate goal; they, too, took to wearing the turban and were known as *dunama,* the apostates. The movement continued to seethe for generations and plunged the Jewish community into turmoil and controversy. For some time the *dunama* played an important role in Turkey, with Salonika as their central point of strength; with the annexation of Salonika by Greece, they returned to Constantinople and gradually disappeared.

As for Izmir itself, the energence of Shabtai Zvi did not bring it either peace or good fortune. Aside from the issue of the false messiah himself, which divided the Jewish community, the city fell victim to earthquake and fire, and many of its inhabitants removed their families to Constantinople. Taking a page out of Constantinople's experience, the elders of the Izmir community sought to restore its former standing by means of the printing press. A publishing house that was founded when the messianic movement was in ascendancy, in 1658, now became one of the community's foremost institutions. The greatest Jewish luminaries of the times, including Rabbi Hayyim Falagi, the *Hacham Bashi* of Izmir, who wrote more than one hundred books on various topics relating to Judaism, had their books printed in Izmir.

Salonika

Greece was one of the first countries of the Diaspora, but for generations no special Jewish tradition evolved there. The Jewish community of Salonika, however, stood out not only in Greece but throughout the Balkan countries, and became famous throughout the Jewish world. This ancient community developed an active life, and imparted a distinctly Jewish stamp on the entire city. This influence also carried over to communities in the neighboring countries of Turkey and Bulgaria.

Generally speaking, the size and importance of Jewish communities in the Diaspora has been in direct proportion to the same criteria of the non-Jewish community. But there have been exceptions, and Salonika is one of them.

Salonika was founded and built by Cassandros, eldest son of Antipatros, Governor of Macedonia after its conquest by Alexander the Great. The city changed rulers several times before it was captured by the Turks in 1430. The Turks then held it for almost five hundred years before Salonika reverted to Greece in 1912, following the war between Turkey and the Balkan States.

A Jewish community existed in Salonika for over two thousand years. Paul came there to seek believers for the new faith, but, according to his own account, was hampered by the community. The Jewish population grew to impressive size and influence in the eighth and ninth centuries. When the Bulgarian kingdom was first established, the Jews of Salonika almost succeeded in having it adopt the Mosaic faith.

Suceeding centuries found the community somewhat stagnant; Rabbi Benjamin of Tudela visited Salonika in 1173 and found there only 500 Jews, but in the course of the next two centuries, as a result of expulsion decrees in France, Poland and Italy, many Jews moved to Salonika. When the Ottoman Empire came into power it granted the Jews full rights. The Jews responded by contributing greatly to the development of the area's economy. Word of the liberal Ottoman policy soon spread throughout Europe, and Salonika's Jewish community grew by leaps and bounds. By the beginning of the sixteenth century, the community was sufficiently important to attract to its leadership Rabbi Shimon Ashkenazi of Frankfurt, one of the greatest preachers of his day. Rabbi Yossef Karo, author of the *Shulhan Aruch*, lived in Salonika. The flourishing libraries of the community were further enriched by the arrivals from Spain and Portugal. These libraries, containing rare manuscripts and editions, were lost in the fires which attacked Turkish cities in the sixteenth and seventeenth centuries.

The number of exiles from Spain who settled in Salonika was so large that they were divided into groupings, according to their home towns on the Iberian peninsula. Certain joint projects were undertaken, however, such as the founding and maintenance of central institutes for Torah scholarship.

Towards the end of the sixteenth century, the Ottoman Empire began to show signs of deterioration. The Jews of Salonika held firm until the middle of the nineteenth century, when natural disasters shook the entire city and forced the closing of many schools. The community maintained strict adherence to its faith, and only the very wealthy started to stray away, particularly when the advent of the railroad in the region brought the rest of Europe closer.

Salonika had no ghetto and Jews accordingly mixed freely with the non-Jewish

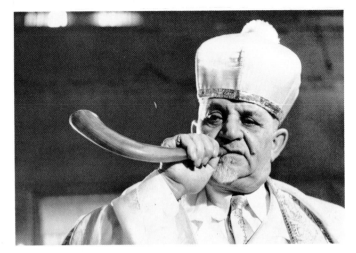

A cantor and shofar *blower from Greece officiating in a synagogue of Greek Jews in Tel Aviv.*

community. Jewish commercial involvement in foreign trade and port work was so extensive that the port of Salonika was practically immobilized on the Sabbath. The Jewish day of rest could be noted in residential quarters as well as in business centers. The Jews (reported Norwegian author Alexander Kyrland, who visited Salonika early in the twentieth century) could be seen strolling along the seafront promenade, dressed in their Sabbath best, in Oriental or Western style. Non-Jews — the employees of Jewish merchants — could also be seen enjoying the extra day of rest. "I have never seen more beatiful people," summarized the Norwegian author, "than the Jews of Salonika, as they go forth on a Sabbath promenade."

In many respects, the reflection of economic status was the same as everywhere else — the poor lived in rundown neighborhoods, while the wealthy had their homes and gardens in the Campanas Quarter. The middle class, however, adopted a unique mode of existence which contributed to the fine spirit that characterized the community. Middle-class families lived in large two- or three-story buildings, in quarters that opened on a central square which served as a "community room": each housewife had her own section for cooking while they all shared a common oven for baking. A well which extended from the ground up through a shaft to the upper floors provided water for washing and laundry; drinking water was purchased from water carriers, while spring water was stored in a *tanaja.* a huge earthen crock. The well also served as a refrigerator, where baskets of fruit and wine were kept in the summer for cooling.

This semi-communal style of living experienced its finest moments on the Sabbath and holidays, when all the rooms, their table decked with white, resounded to the singing of *zemirot,* the festive mealtime chants.

In the early years of Ottoman rule, the Jews had to wear distinctive clothing, yellow turbans and long cloaks, as did other non-Moslems. Jewish women were under orders from the rabbinate to wear nonostentatious clothes so as not to arouse the envy of their Moslem neighbors. This ruling applied even to wedding dresses.

In Salonika brides were selected by the father of the groom, after due consultation with friends and an examination of the bride's family tree. The groom was permitted to have a say in the choice — he could say that he considered his father's choice impeccable! The traditional formula was for the father to say, "Come near, my son, and kiss my hand, for you are about to wed." During the past half-century, young Salonikans have achieved much greater freedom in their choice of marital partners.

The formalities began with a meeting arranged by the parents of the bride. As the groom and his parents were seated, the troubador hired for the occasion sang,

"How radiant is the face of the gracious bride," at which the bride came in, kissed the hand of her future mother-in-law, and proceeded to receive the gifts which the groom's contingent had brought. The young couple exchanged sweets at the start of each new month until the wedding.

The bride began to prepare her trousseau months before the wedding. Somewhat later, her relatives and neighbors would gather at her home for "wool washing day." The wool that she had prepared for making blankets was then washed and dried with much pomp and ceremony, after which it was converted into blankets by a craftsman.

On the Saturday night before the wedding, the bride's friends gathered at her home to cheer her up, now that her period of maidenhood was at an end. The next morning, her relatives gathered for the *ashugach*, the appraisal of the trousseau. Once this was done, the trousseau was packed and sent to the home of the groom.

For the wedding the bride was decked out by her friends in a long, trailing white gown embroidered with gold thread, a white scarf which covered her figure and a veil in the form of a coronet of artificial flowers. The mother of the groom then arrived to present a precious ornament, the gift of the groom. The bride's father and brothers, holding her arms, led her behind the groom's mother, as relatives and neighbors showered the entourage with sweets. As the group came to the home of the groom, the young man himself met his bride at the entrance, holding in his hand a plate laden with sweets, rice, and gold coins, which he poured at her feet — a sign of good fortune.

Now the bride was led to her seat under the canopy. For the ceremony, a prayer shawl was held above the heads of the couple. The marriage contract was read out, the customary bendictions were pronounced, and the groom then broke the traditional glass. The gathering then sat down to a festive wedding meal, which was highlighted by the "Flower Dance," executed by two women to the hand-clapping accompaniment of the guests.

The next day, the young wife appeared wearing a *Kuffaya*, which distinguished the married from the unmarried women. Appropriately, this was called "*kuffaya* day." On the last of the "seven days of festivity" following the wedding, called "fish day," the young husband brought large fish which he placed in a copper basin on the floor in the middle of the room. His young wife jumped across the basin three times — symbolizing their hope for many sons — to the applause of the gathering. The fish was cooked and eaten and washed down with suitable beverages.

If the fish ceremony was successful, the future mother was subjected to all sorts of superstitious precautions, along with serious care for her well-being.

During pregnancy, closet doors and shutters were left open for good luck. The custom was abandoned when it was discovered that this was a help to local thieves. Toward the end of pregnancy, the family — and the expectant mother, if she was able to — went to the cemetery to pray at the tomb of a saintly man, and to hold a picnic on the burial grounds,

At the moment of birth, the family gathered near the *mezuza* on the doorpost of the mother's room for prayers and incantations. If the newborn babe was a boy, everybody present would shout *ninyo*. The crib was fortified immediately with a fragrant branch and pieces of garlic, while a blue bead and a piece of ivory were placed around the baby's neck to ward off the "evil eye."

The night before the circumcision was known as *biola*, and a watch was maintained in the infant's chamber until morning. Songs befitting the occasion were sung by a children's choir, accompanied by the guests. At the ceremony, there were musicians as well as singers, so that the infant received a taste of music as well as of wine. A first-born son was often named *Behor*, "first-born." A daughter was given her name at a festive gathering, in the presence of the rabbi. She was usually passed from hand to hand, with a pause for good wishes, during the name-giving party.

The *pidyon ha-ben* — redemption of the first-born — ceremony was marked by the dramatic. Mother and son were covered with a long white scarf. As the baby lay on a white pillow, the *kohen* (member of the priestly class) approached, picked up the boy, and pretended to make off with him. The parents barred his way, gave him the redemption money, and the boy was returned to his mother.

The Bar Mitzvah ceremony was introduced in the Salonika community only after the arrival of the Ashkenazic Jews from central and eastern Europe.

In the well-organized, tightly-knit communities of Balkan Jewry, each family had its own status, but they were all welded together by close adherence to the practices of Judaism, although these were expressed in different ways. For instance, during the month of Elul, itinerant booksellers passed through the Jewish neighborhoods with wagons of High Holy Day prayer books, for the thirty-three groupings in Salonika's Jewish community.

The economic differences between rich and poor did not impair relations between them. The daughters of the wealthy did a great deal of welfare work, and the community arranged many events to bring the sons of the rich and the poor together. It was common for the wealthy Jews to send baskets of food to the poor by messenger, without the recipient family knowing the identity of the benefactor. One legend states that the Prophet Elijah often disguised himself as a porter in order to participate in this activity. Another story concerned Carlo Altini, a very wealthy man, who gave up riding in a fast carriage and went around on foot so as to be able to distribute alms to the poor in the streets.

The rabbi was the undisputed head of the community. He set an example in piety, learning and integrity. Children were taught from infancy to accord him the utmost respect. He also carried much weight with the authorities. One legend tells of one of the early rabbis of Salonika, who went for a walk along the beach one warm day. The rabbi spread his cloak on the water, sat down on it, and was carried by the wind to Constantinople, where he saw that people were upset by the escape of a lion that belonged to the sultan. The rabbi approached the beast, took it by the ear, and led it back to its cage. The sultan, understandably impressed, ordered the royal treasurer to give the rabbi the funds needed to construct a synagogue in Salonika. The rabbi himself was appointed *Hacham Bashi*.

One of Salonika's outstanding rabbis, Rabbi Yaacov Meir, was appointed Chief Rabbi of the Sephardic community on his arrival in the land of Israel. His twelve years in Salonika came during a period of upheaval and strife, but his personality and influence shielded the community from these vicissitudes. Once, when he was invited by George I, King of the Hellenes, to attend a function at the palace, he informed the king that he could not accept the invitation because the date coincided with Yom Kippur. The king postponed the function until after sunset, enabling Rabbi Yaacov Meir to come to the palace directly from the synagogue, still dressed in his *kittel*.

The Salonikan Jewish community was among the first to have a communal center. In 1520, a Talmud Torah school was founded, which also served as a meeting hall and a place for public functions.

The Community Council, as in all Jewish population centers in the Balkans, consisted of the rabbis, legal authorities, and prominent public figures. One of its chief responsibilities was to collect taxes on behalf of the Turkish authorities. The taxes imposed by the Turks were many and varied, ranging from a head tax to real estate taxes. There was also a sizable list of fines: a town in which a corpse was found had to pay a fine to compensate the relatives of the deceased. In the Jewish community, additional levies were made by the Council, for such purposes as the ransom of captives. Members of the community were taxed in accordance with their means. Scholars, and their widows, were exempt.

The Council was strict in matters of litigation. Any member of the community who sought adjudication in commercial matters through the civil courts rather than the Jewish court was subject to punishment. The area of *hazaka*, a "staked claim." brooked no infringement. A Jew who leased any property or assets from a non-Jew was protected by the Council from infringement by any other Jew who would come along with a higher offer for the leased item.

A unique service rendered by the Council was the publication of *halila*, a special calendar which set forth all the important events to take place during the year, the fairs to be held, holidays and festivals, weather forecasts, financial information, as well as a listing of the services rendered by the Council. The calendar first appeared in 1848 and was published for many years.

Ladino, a dialect of Castilian Spanish, to which the Spanish Jews gave their social imprint, was the language most in use among Jews in the Balkans. In Turkey, Ladino became the official language of the entire Jewish community. Its importance lessened, however, when Ladino, originally written in Hebrew characters, began to be written in Latin characters. As in other countries where Ladino was spoken, Salonika's Jews had their own version of Ladino, which included their own words and idioms. Ladino was not only the major spoken tongue of Salonika's Jews: it was widely used by the city's non-Jews as well.

The arrival of the High Holy Days brought an atmosphere of sober repentance to the community. Even the most hardened souls took part in the *kaparot* ritual and the Yom Kippur services. A famous Jewish brigand, Rabino, the scourge of the countryside, was reportedly ready to seek atonement before the rabbi, on Yom Kippur eve.

The most impresssive Jewish holiday in Salonika was Sukkot, when the holiday booths, festooned with colorful fabrics and decorated with fruits and flowers, were to be seen in yards, on roofs, and on balconies. The *lulav* and *etrog* were to be seen everywhere. It was customary to carry them through the streets even when visiting friends. The festivities reached their climax on Simhat Torah, when the beadle moved among the celebrants, spraying them with scented water from a silver flagon.

The various synagogues in Salonika all had their own ways of adding to the Simhat Torah merriment. Curiously enough, each synagogue had a nickname, often derisive, which the members accepted good-naturedly on Simhat Torah. In the Mograbi Synagogue, nicknamed "the chair," it was customary to seat the guest of honor on a special chair and bind him to it, as he held the Torah scroll. He was then lifted by a quartet of brawny men and carried around the synagogue. At each of the synagogue's four corners he was tossed high and caught on the way down.

The Hanukah *menorah* was in the form of a triangle, with the eight oil-and-wick holes along the base and the *shamash* at the apex. The theme song of the festival was the thirtieth Psalm; the traditional "Rock of Ages" *(Ma'oz Tzur)* song was unknown.

Tu Bishvat was the "Festival of Fruits." Fresh and dried fruits were in abundance in the market places, and many families kept fresh fruit in storage in their cellars for the occasion. The fruit, however, was only the trimming for the main dish — a delicious *hamin* of wheat grits in fat and large chestnuts, served on a huge copper tray. The standard benedictions were complemented with Spanish songs that extolled the qualities of the fruits.

On Purim the market stalls and bakeries were laden with colorful sweets in the form of the main components of the Book of Esther: Haman and his ten sons, the gallows, the royal palace. Youngsters in masquerade carried gifts from house to house. In the afternoon, neighbors held a joint dinner, graced with an abundance of food and wine and marked by singing and dancing.

Passover was ushered in with cleaning, scouring, burnishing, polishing, and buying of new pots and dishes. On the Sabbath before Passover, all schoolchildren were given new clothes for the holiday. The distribution took place in the largest synagogue in the city, in the presence of rabbis and dignitaries. The children responded with songs and dramatic skits about the generosity of the community.

The *Seder* was conducted by the eldest in the family. Explanations of the ritual were in Spanish, so that all present could understand. The *Haggadah* was read in Hebrew and Ladino; the hymns at the close were sung in Turkish, Greek, and Spanish. Elijah's Cup and the stealing of the *afikoman* were unknown in Salonika.

At the close of the holiday, when the men returned from synagogue, the children brought home clumps of grass which their mothers sprinkled with sugar, saying, "a green year, a good summer."

As elsewhere in the Jewish diaspora, Salonikan Jews spent Shavuot night studying Torah until dawn. The women brought coffee to help the men stay awake. In the morning they were sprinkled with rose water during services. Families later went out for a stroll in the fields, carrying picnic baskets filled with cheese pastries, hard-boiled eggs dipped in oil, rice, milk, sugar, and fruits of the season.

On Tisha b'Av there was a pall on the entire city. In the synagogues, all candles were extinguished except one, and the rabbi called out the number of years since the destruction of the Temple: "Brethren, O House of Israel, give heed: Today marks . . . years since our Temple and glory was destroyed. The crown of our heads fell. Woe unto us, that we have sinned." The reading of Lamentations was followed

Opposite: the entrance to the courtyard of Shabtai Zvi's home in Izmir (Turkish Asia Minor).

ספר סדר זמנים

by readings from Jeremiah and Job. Some communities held a simulated funeral, walking in procession with lighted candles in hand. The women gathered in their homes and chanted old melodies about the fall of the Temple, and about Hannah and her seven sons.

Balkan Jews loved to sing, especially melodies based on the Spanish ballads that refugees from the Spanish Inquisition brought with them. Many melodies were also composed in the Balkans, some dealing with family and community life and other devoted to the festivals. Composers offered their ballads for sale as they stood on the street corners and sang their compositions. Also popular, and numerous, were the musical trios made up of a fiddler, a drummer, and a mandolin player. The *tayanedra,* a female drummer, entertained the women with rhythmic songs and stories at women's gatherings. Rabbi Israel Najara, the noted poet, founded in Adrianople an association of lyricists and composers who met in the Portuguese Synagogue before morning services and sang their compositions, which then spread throughout the Ottoman Empire. A similar group was later established in Istanbul.

To offset apprehensions about ill winds which might blow over the Jewish communities in the Balkans, all sorts of "cures" and "devices" came into existence. The ailing were given the milk of a nursing woman. Marjoram dipped in sugared water was placed on the windowsill and given to the ill. Sometimes a sick person's undershirt was soaked overnight in salt water. Those who scorned superstition recited from the Psalms.

Evil spirits were thought to be driven off by horseshoes or the shape of a hand nailed to the front of the house. Amulets made of paper, parchment, or engraved metal were hung around a child's neck for safeguarding.

In 1912, Salonika was annexed by Greece and the Greeks regarded the Jews as competitors, rooted as they were in commerce, shipping, and finance. The Jews helped to bring King Constantine back from exile, but the economic situation was so poor that many of Salonika's leading Jews moved to Athens and other centers.

In 1923 a law was passed forcing Jews to keep their business establishments open on Saturdays and closed on Sundays. This measure undermined the community. Combined with heavy taxes, the new development produced a constant population drain. Many immigrated to the Land of Israel. The young Salonikans bought land in Tel Aviv and built their homes in the Florentin Quarter.

On June 30, 1930, a suggestion by a Bulgarian Jewish politician that Macedonia be annexed by Bulgaria brought violent reactions against Salonikan Jewry. As a result the flow of Jews to Israel grew substantially.

In April, 1941, the Nazis invaded Greece. Thousands of Jews were sent to the death camps; of Salonika's 50,000 Jews, nearly 46,000 perished at the hands of the Nazis. When World War II came to an end, 70 people were all that remained of the Jewish community in Salonika.

Bulgaria

Archaeological records indicate that Jews first came to this central region of the Balkan Peninsula before the destruction of the Second Temple, accompanying the intrepid Phoenician seamen into the Aegean. Their lot was unenviable: a letter sent by Emperor Theodosius I in the fourth century to the governors of the province mentions persecution of Jews there, and requests that order be restored.

The barbarian invasion of Bulgaria in the fifth and sixth centuries evidently wiped out the extant Jewish community. Records do not show a Jewish presence there until the ninth century when refugees from Byzantium and Salonika were brought there as captives by Czar Krum. The Jews proselytized among the idolatrous Bulgarians, but the Christian missionaries were more successful; the Bulgarians accepted a combination of heathen customs and Jewish traditions. In applying to Pope Nicholas I for information on 106 points of religious import, they asked, for example, which was the true day of rest, Saturday or Sunday; which fowl and animals were allowed as food and whether women were to keep their heads covered at prayer. Many Bulgarian noblemen bore Jewish names such as David, Moshe, Aharon, Shmuel.

When the Crusaders left a trail of Jewish dead in Europe, many Jews sought refuge in Bulgaria. Even as late as the twelfth century, Bulgarians still bore Jewish names; they greeted the new Jewish arrivals seeking refuge as brothers. When the Bulgarians became independent of Byzantine rule, they invited settlers from other countries to help develop the country's economy. Many Jews accepted the invitation: their influence and importance grew to such proportions that in the fourteenth century the Christian clergy sought to impose restrictions on the Jews. The clergy was further incensed when Czar Ivan Alexander, having divorced his first wife, married a converted Jewess, Theodora, who used her influence on behalf of her former coreligionists. She saved the rabbi of Tarnovo and other influential Jews from execution.

When Bulgaria became part of the Ottoman Empire, the Jews could breathe freely again, which they did for nearly five centuries. In Bulgaria, too, the Jewish refugees who came from various European countries, Hungary and Germany among them, set up sub-communities of their own. In Sofia there was a synagogue named *Kahal de los Ashkenazim*. There were also synagogues for the Jews from Moldavia, Italy, from southern France, and from Dubrovnik.

The Jewish refugees who came to Bulgaria brought with them, aside from their diligence and resources, excellent business contact with the countries of their origin. Jewish scholarship was not particularly widespread, and even primary schools existed only in the larger towns.

Community life suffered when the Ottoman Empire began to disintegrate in the nineteenth century. Brigandage disrupted trade and communications, and Jewish communities were the first to feel the breakdown. Later, the Bulgarians stepped up their struggle against the Turks and sought the aid of the Russians. The Jews, aware of Russian hatred for their people, reluctantly joined in the attempt. Following the defeat of the Turks by the Russians in 1878, the Jews were promised equal rights and Chief Rabbi Gabriel Almoselino participated in the founding assembly of the new state.

In 1883, the duchy of northern Bulgaria was merged with eastern Rumelia, a step which caused Serbia to declare war upon it. The Jews fought bravely in Bulgaria's ranks, and were lauded by Prince Alexander Batemberg as "true and valiant descendants of the ancient Maccabees."

There followed a period of autonomy for the Jewish community, but authorization to that effect brought about internal controversy, chiefly between the "liberals" and the "conservatives" and, later, between the Zionists and the opponents of the movement. The Zionists gained the upper hand and prevented the assimilation of the community, proposed by the non-Zionists, especially the Communists. As a consequence, the Jews of Bulgaria were among the first to immigrate en masse to Israel — in 1948, 40,000 of Bulgaria's 45,000 Jews arrived in the new Jewish state.

All through the ages, travellers to India have advanced theories and conjectures about the origins of the Indian Jewish community known as the Bene Israel. One favored theory was that these Jews were descended from the Ten Tribes exiled by the Assyrians. This theory based itself on the fact that they have been calling themselves *Bene Israel* (related to the Kingdom of Israel) rather than *Yehudim* ("Jews," related to the Kingdom of Judah). Other theories contend that they did not arrive in India until the seventh century, driven there from the Arabian peninsula by Moslem fanaticism.

India is mentioned many times in the Bible as the land "of incense, fabrics, and precious stones," but there is no mention of any Jewish settlement there.

The oldest written records of a Jewish presence are bronze tablets inscribed in the Tamil tongue and found in Malabar, on the west coast, which refer to special privileges accorded to Yossef Raban, a Jewish dignitary and his family, by the ruler of Malabar. They were allowed to hold a splendid wedding for which they could make clothes from five different hues, sound musical instruments while riding astride horses or elephants, and illuminate the procession along white linen runners and under canopies inscribed with verses in honor of the bride and groom, who were to be carried, bedecked with flowers, beneath the wedding canopy.

Yossef Raban was also given an estate, named Anjobanam, large enough to build seventy-two houses, and was exempted for life from paying taxes. The date of these tablets is between the first and eleventh centuries of the Common Era. By the twelfth century Rabbi Benjamin of Tudela as well as a variety of Christian and Moslem travelers, noted several Jewish points of habitation along the west coast.

Information about Jewish life in India became readily available in the sixteenth century, with the advent of the Portuguese, followed by the Dutch and the English. From the standpoint of community organization, vernacular, customs and traditions, the Jews of India were divided into three groups: Bene Israel, centered in Bombay, which claims seniority of settlement; the Jews of Cochin, concentrated in the city and its environs; and the late arrivals, Jews from Portugal, Holland, Iraq, and Syria, who came after the penetration of the European powers.

The Bene Israel resemble the native Indians to such a degree that many historians insist that they are the descendants of Jews who intermarried with the natives, centuries ago — a contention which the Bene Israel reject outright. They claim that their ancestors reached India, by way of Egypt and the Red Sea, before the fall of the Second Temple and even before the Maccabee uprising, which accounts for the fact that neither Hanukah nor the fasts marking the destruction of the Temple are observed by them.

According to their own account, their ancestors, seven men and seven women, were shipwrecked near the village of Naugaoon, where they settled. The bodies of other on the hapless ship were washed ashore and buried in a cave now marked with mounds of soil.

The Torah scrolls and other religious articles, they say, went down with the vessel and they therefore had no Torah scrolls or sacred books. Nothing remained with them other than the passage *Shema Yisrael*, Sabbath observance, and circumcision: their neighbors called them *shanabar talis*, namely, pressers of oil (this was their chief occupation) who rest on the Sabbath. The Kunkan province, in

which Naugaoon was located, was relatively isolated and not conducive, geographically, to foreign trade or even extensive agriculture.

A single individual reinvigorated the Bene Israel to an extent that his name became legend in the annals. David Rahabi was a merchant in the port of Chaoul. He learned about the existence of a strange tribe called *shanabar talis* which observed what were obviously Jewish customs and traditions. His curiosity took him to Kunkan. From what he gathered as he talked with them, he realized that he had come upon an ancient Jewish tribe. The paucity of its Jewish content was a challenge; he undertook to teach them the Torah and its commandments, as observed in the Jewish world.

Rahabi evidently came from Egypt (*Rahab* is a name given to Egypt in Jewish liturgical poetry). Some scholars identify him with Rabbi David, brother of Maimonides, a merchant who met his death in shipwreck. Rabbi David, they contend, traveled as far as India and was the source of Maimonides' knowledge about the life of the Jews there, which he described in his letter to the sages of Luneil. At any rate, the visit of David Rahabi taught the Bene Israel community a great deal about Judaism.

The use in India of the lunar calendar made it simpler for the Jews to observe the few festivals and holidays with which they were familiar. The first day of Tishri was *Nabiasha-san*, Rosh Hashanah, observed for one day only. The Fast of Gedaliah, evidently introduced by Rahabi, was observed on the day following Rosh Hashanah and was accordingly called *Nabiasha-ruzha*. Three days later came *Kirusha-san:* the family gathered around a large bowl of porridge *(kir)*, fresh cereal mixed with coconut milk and served with sweets, sat next to an incense-burning brazier, recited the *Shema,* and ate the porridge; *Shema* was recited before every meal. Incense was frequently used for similar ceremonies until about a century ago, when the Cochin Jews persuaded them to discontinue the custom. The *Kirusha-san,* the Bene Israel equivalent of Sukkot, was celebrated two weeks earlier than the prescribed date and before Yom Kippur, which they called *Darfalnisha-san,* "the festival of closed doors.'' On Yom Kippur the Bene Israel sat in their homes with doors closed and fasted, having prepared for it on the previous day *(malma)* by ritual immersion and by a pre-fast meal. They wore white and spoke to no one who was not of their faith until nightfall. The following day was *Shilah-san*, ''rejoicing of the priest,'' commemorating the feast of thanksgiving held by the High Priest in the days of the Second Temple when his celebration of Yom Kippur passed without mishap. *Shilah-san* was marked with home-to-home visits and the distribution of alms to the poor.

During the second half of the month of Heshvan, both men and women fasted on Mondays and Thursdays. The Fast of the Tenth of Tevet, *Sebavi-ruzh*, commemorating the encirclement of Jerusalem by Nebuchadnezzar's forces, was adopted by them in comparatively recent times. Tu Bishvat had an entirely different basis; called *Eliya hanaviasha oros* (Miracle Day of Prophet Elijah), it commemorated the alleged revelation of Elijah to their ancestors in Kandala, a village in Kunkan, and thence his ascent to heaven. The event was celebrated with a tray full of fresh fruits and *malida*, bread made of a mixture of rice flour and sweets, which was placed on a white cloth next to the brazier of incense. The fruit was eaten after the recitation of the prayer of bounty *(vayiten lecha)*.

The Fast of Esther and Purim *(Hulisha-san)* were observed as special days, although the Bene Israel did not remember the reason for the holiday. Nor did they remember the background of the Passover, although they observed it, at the proper time, by abstaining from bread and *anas*, a sour syrup used all year long. The festival of Shavuot was reinstituted only about two centuries ago, when the Bombay synagogue was built. The fast of Tisha b'Av was introduced by David Rahabi and called *Birdiasha ruzha* — *birda* being a species of beans which the women wrapped in fabric and soaked for several hours, then cooked with mixed spices. This was served before and after the fast on banana leaves, to symbolize the loss of utensils in the fall of Jerusalem.

Sacrificial offering was common among the Bene Israel. The Thanksgiving Offering *(kundasha nawa tabak*, a ''gift given in the name of God'') was made on recovery from a serious illness or return from a dangerous journey, occasions marked by other Jews with the *hagomel* blessing. The elaborate ceremony attending such an offering involved certain ingredients prescribed in the Bible: loaves of bread and *matzot* mixed with oil and slices of ram's or calf's meat, liberally salted, and a measure of wine or liqueur, all placed on a tray resting on a white cloth next to the brazier with white incense. After reciting the *Shema* twelve times and *vayiten lecha*, those present recited the *kiddush* over the wine, some of which was poured on the ground and the rest drunk by the individual making the offering and by the one conducting the ceremony. The latter tasted each of the ingredients and distributed the remains among all who had fasted together with the donor.

Litigants who had come to terms, as well as purchasers of a new home, field, or garden, presented a ''peace offering'' which was eaten over a period of two days. A ''gift offering'' marked the dedication of a home or a change of quarters. The ''vowed offering'' was made by those who had taken on a vow. Other offerings prescribed by the Bible were not made, because of the absence of both Temple and High Priest, but the ''Nazarite offering'' was made by a woman who, after having

Left: two young Jewesses from India in colorful saris. Below: an older woman, dressed in white.

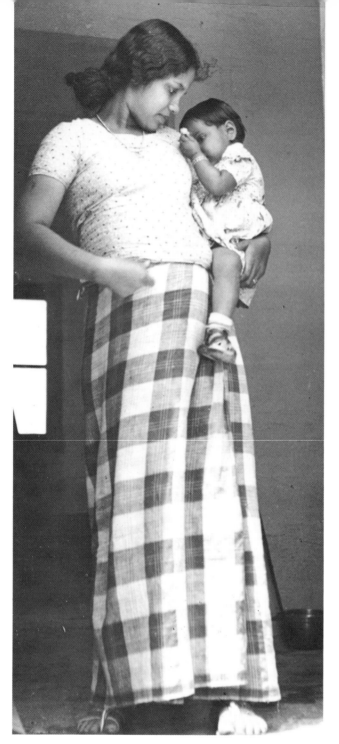

A mother and daughter from India, now living in Dimona, in the Negev.

failed to give birth to male progeny for ten or twelve years after her marriage, vowed that if she were given a son, she would raise him as a Nazarite up to the age of seven. On the morning of his seventh birthday, the boy was led to the synagogue, where his hair was cut. The hair was weighed and the equivalent in gold or silver, as pledged by the mother, was distributed among the poor or given to the synagogue. The hair was not burned (there being no altar) but cast into the sea. The assemblage then went to the home of the parents for the offering. The person conducting the ceremony placed before the mother a bit of each item on the tray, and asked her for the details of her vow. He then proceeded to declare her free of her vow and asked her to eat. He, too, ate, and the remainder was apportioned among the guests. In time, the custom of letting the boy's hair grow for several years became generally widespread, and the day it was cut was celebrated with no less pomp than the time of his circumcision. The youngster was decked out in his finest clothes and driven to the synagogue in style, accompanied by fife and drum. At the synagogue, each of the guests was given the honor of snipping off a few strands. Once the initial haircut was administered, only the earlocks were allowed to grow; the rest of the head was shaven.

When the mother became "purified" (forty days after the birth of a son and eighty days after a daughter), she made a "purification offering."

Many biblical tenets were observed by the Bene Israel in the course of their daily life. Women set aside a bit of dough whenever they baked for the Sabbath and the holidays, and burned it with great reverence and piety. On Yom Kippur Eve, each contributed one rupee (the half-shekel), no more and no less, as was set forth in the Book of Exodus.

In addition to the "sacrifice offering," the Bene Israel also made gift offerings of oven-baked, pan-baked, and pan-fried bread and cakes. This was done by the women, whose familiarity with every jot and tittle of the procedure has been used to refute the allegation that the Bene Israel tended to intermarry with the native populace: such meticulous knowledge of the minutiae, they claimed, would not be available to any woman who was not born a Jewess. Also, Jewish women did not go about with a red dot on their forehead, the popular symbol of good fortune in India. Those who did marry outside their faith (or even proselytes) were called *kaala Yisrael*, "the black Jews" as opposed to the *gurrah Yisrael*, the white Jews. The latter did not intermarry with the *kaala* and did not allow their men to don a *talit*. When wine was drunk in the synagogue, the *kaala* drank only after the other had finished, and no effort to erase this discrimination ever succeeded. When the head of the Bombay community, who had married outside his faith, insisted on having his son participate in a public banquet, all the others arose and left the hall.

The Bene Yisrael were particularly careful not to engage nurses for their children before making sure that they ate kosher food only. *Kashrut* was observed in almost Karaite fashion. Although they did not "boil a kid in its mother's milk" or any other milk, they ate fowl with butter. Beef was not eaten because the cow was held to be sacred in India. As for smaller animals, the thigh muscle was removed, but other laws of *shehita* were unknown, except for the act of ritual slaughter itself. They did not eat the meat of an animal that had been slaughtered by non-Jews, and their meat was soaked and salted before eating. Fish were restricted to the traditional fin-and-scales variety. Swine flesh was considered abhorrent. In time, as contact with the outside Jewish world was established, all the ancillary dietary laws were also adopted.

Rice was a staple at the diet, and chicken or fish soup was a perennial favorite, especially when spiced with red pepper, which was said to contain medicinal powers of considerable potency. Meals were eaten while the diners squatted on the ground; the furniture, made of black wood called *sisam*, was used only on Sabbaths and holidays, and then only by the men, since women were busy serving them. At meals associated with a *mitzvah*, the head of the community sat at the place of honor (he also received a double portion of everything), flanked by the *gabbai* and the cantor. Soldiers serving in the Indian forces were always invited to such dinners; at times their numbers were such that the party had to take place in the street.

According to travelers, the Bene Israel dressed in good taste and fashion. They dressed " . . . more beautifully than any in East India: white trousers fully half a

meter wide at the bottom, a white shirt covering down to the middle, and a white jacket to below the waist, made of cotton or linen, imported from Europe, or, on the holidays, silk brought from China. Their headgear is a red or white hat emboidered with silver along the edge, and they carry a red kerchief in their hands or over their shoulder. They wear leather shoes, as do all Indians, and their hair grows as in Poland — shaven heads and ringlets at the temples . . . . The women wear a laced bodice of silk or cotton, covered with a long cloak to the knees. The young women wear gold nose rings and gold combs in their braids, even though they walk barefoot in the rain." As modern dress came to India (tall white caps, white jacket and tight white trousers), the Jews adopted this attire.

Opposite: dignitaries of the Kadagan (Lake Cochin) community in their synagogue, on the eve of their immigration to Israel. Above: celebrating the installation of a Torah scroll in an agricultural settlement of immigrants from Cochin.

"In general, they were considered honest and straightforward in their speech and dealings, and are therefore respected by all the inhabitants. They are also gracious and charitable, and are kind and hospitable to strangers. Any other Jew who comes to them is called *Hacham babai;* being untutored in the Torah, they assume that any other Jew is a sage."

When it came to marriage, the parents of the groom were the initiators. Each family made sure that the other was of unquestionably Jewish origin and that the other young person was in good health. This done, the two parties sat down to a discussion of finances and preparations for the wedding.

During the engagement period, which usually lasted several months, the bride went about with her long hair let down. On the day of the wedding, the groom was crowned with a garland of flowers and taken on horseback to the home of the bride, where the wedding took place. As soon as he placed the wedding band on the bride's finger, the guests exchanged greetings of *Shema Yisrael.*

When the bride was about to leave for her husband's home, her mother turned to the guests and mournfully told them that her daughter was being taken from her, at which the guests consoled her, in similar style. The mother then turned to her daughter and entreated her, again poetically, not to forget the home in which she had been raised.

A woman suspected of infidelity was divorced. This bill of divorce, signed by the husband in front of witnesses, was unlike the standard one used anywhere else

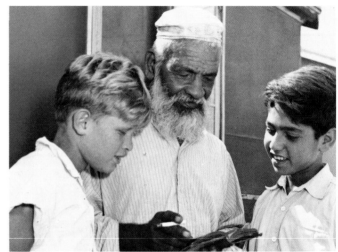

among Jews. It was also written in Hindi and later in English. The dissimilarity accounts for objections to intermarriage with the Bene Israel, since, according to Jewish law, a divorce is not valid unless the document conforms to the prescribed text and format. The Bene Israel for their part contended that there were very few divorces among them and that furthermore, in accordance with Hindu custom, a woman married only once in her lifetime, and a divorcee who remarried was banished from the community and regarded as a *kaala Yisrael,* with whom the Bene Israel did not intermarry.

There was no divorce on grounds other than infidelity. The husband simply took another wife, but he was obliged to provide for the first as well.

When a member of the family passed away, all the water in the house was poured on the ground. The deceased was buried in the kind of raiment believed to have been worn by the first arrivals in India: ankle-length trousers, knee-length cloaks girdled at the waist, blue ritual fringes around the head for men, and a kerchief for women. The body was laid to rest in a whitewashed grave, with the head turned toward the east. After the funeral the mourners bathed themselves and laundered their clothes, and on the third day they cleaned the entire house *(titzoba,* "cleaning of the third day"). The first three days were "weeping" and the following four (of the traditional *Shiva* period) were "mourning." On the seventh day, the family observed a special mourning ritual *(aharut):* a large plate filled with slices of liver and a cup of wine was placed on a white cloth, and the assembled, after reciting *Shema Yisrael* a few times, partook of the wine in honor of the deceased and then ate the refreshments. This done, they placed new turbans on the heads of the mourners — a ritual repeated at the end of the first, sixth and twelfth months.

With the advent of the British, there came a migration of Jews from the rural areas of the Kunkan province to Bombay, Karachi, and other urban centers. There they engaged in construction (several became important contractors) and became known for their diligence and honesty. Others went into the army and achieved high-ranking posts. In the 1857 uprising, the Bene Israel soldiers stationed in Bombay prevented disorder in the city. Despite their loyalty, the Bene Israel were

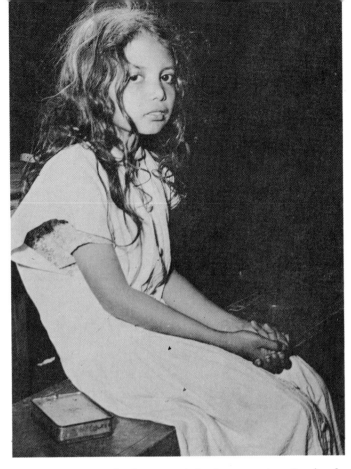

Opposite: Two young Bene Israel men in Israel (far left); an elderly Jew from Cochin with his grandson and a young friend in the agricultural settlement of Nevatim, in the Arava (left). Left: A Bene Israel girl.

later forced out of the military ranks by the rule that a unit had to consist of a single ethnic group; the size of the designated unit was too large for the number of Bene Israel soldiers in service.

Shmuel Ezekiel Dibakar, a senior Bene Israel officer in the India forces under the British, took part in the fighting against Sultan Haidar Ali and his son Tipo at the end of the eighteenth century, and was taken captive. The mother of the sultan, curious to know more about the Bene Israel, asked that Dibakar be spared (he refused to convert to Islam), and several years later he was freed when the influential Rahabi family of the Jewish community in Cochin interceded in his behalf.

He came to Cochin and was very impressed by the fine synagogues and Jewish life there. He vowed to institute the same in Bombay. He kept his vow. Above the entrance to the "Magen David" Synagogue (also known as "Gate of Mercy"), a marble tablet bears the following inscription in Hebrew: "The Gate of Mercy is the Lord's Gate through which the righteous enter. This house shall be called a house of prayer for all people. And this stone set in commemoration shall be a sign to Bene Israel for generations that it was built by Commandant Shmuel Ezekiel in the year 5556 [1796], and being a small structure it was rebuilt and enlarged by the Bene Israel in the year 5608 [1848]. " The street was named "Shmuel Street."

When the synagogue was completed, Dibakar went to Cochin to purchase Torah scrolls, but he died en route. The Jews of Cochin, however, saw to it that scholars and spiritual leaders went to all Bene Israel centers and familiaraized them with the tenets of the Jewish faith. This activity took place precisely at the time that the British missionaries set out to convert the Bene Israel to Christianity. The missionaries translated the Bible into Marathi, the spoken tongue, and established a school for teaching Hebrew. The Bene Israel rejected the missionary effort, but learned a great deal about the Bible from the translation.

The laxity of the Bene Israel in regard to Jewish law and ritual, prior to the fruitful efforts of the Cochin Jews, is illustrated in Shlomo Risman's account of his visit to India in 1840: The *shohet*, called *kaazi*, was generally selected at a gathering at which the foremost notable handed a brand-new knife to someone deemed proper

and qualified, saying, "This knife is given to you that you may perform *shehita* therewith and no other of the fowl and the flock, and be a *kaazi* to us, and circumcise our sons and conduct weddings in accordance with our customs, the customs of the Children of Israel that are scattered among the nations." The *kaazi* accepted the knife, kissed it, and said: "In the name of the God of Israel, I am prepared to do your bidding," and then proceeded to perform *shehita*. Later, when Shlomo Sharabi came from Yemen and informed the Bene Israel that there was more to *shehita* than a brand-new knife, they obtained qualified and learned *shohatim* and generally followed the instructions of the Cochin Jews in all matters pertaining to ritual observance. They also established two aid societies, one to take care of the aged and the handicapped and the other to have copies made of the Bible, prayerbooks, and other sacred writings which were then distributed at cost.

In 1875, thanks to the generosity of Sir Elias Kadouri, a Jewish school was founded in Bombay for teaching Jewish law, literature, and history; the subjects were taught first in Harathi, then in English, with Hebrew as the second language. Many of the school's graduates attained high positions in the free professions, army, and government; one became Mayor of Bombay, and another represented India in the International Labor Organization.

The Jews of Cochin began their history under favorable circumstances. They enjoyed autonomy in the Karanganoor region as far back as the early centuries of the Common Era and were called *Shingali*, the name given to all the Jews along the Malabar Coast. The elite among them were the Yossef Ravvan, Ezer, and Zakkai families, who claimed descent from the House of David. They held sway over the lower class — which consisted, in the main, of descendants of slaves — until 1471, when the lower class families spread out and formed communities of their own. At that time they outnumbered the privileged class by some nine to one, but the Portuguese and other Jews who came to India early in the sixth century gradually gravitated (once they had achieved affluence) toward the elite, claiming, incidentally, that the "black Jews" were of questionable Jewish status because of their slave origin and intermarriage. Relations between the two groups became very strained, and the Jews of Cochin decided to turn the problem over to the Torah authorities in other countries, among them Rabbi David ben-Zimra of Egypt. The Rabbi's response was brief and to the point: "This large congregation is to be allowed to join the household of Israel, and the hatred and quarreling is to be dissipated, and since they live in accordance with the commandments of Israel they are not to be called slaves." Similar responses came from most of the other authorities.

The Jews of Cochin received a helping hand from the Jews of Holland, who first came to India in the middle of the seventeenth century. Later — relations with the Jews of Cochin had improved considerably by this time — more families came to Cochin from Amsterdam and brought with them many religious articles and books.

The head of the community, the *modiliar,* was appointed by the maharaja and empowered to be the community's judge and tax collector. The first *modiliar,* Shemtov Castial, assumed office in 1683, and the position remained in his family, with Dutch approval, then passed on to the Haliguwa family, until it was canceled by the British regime.

The gap between the "white" and "black" Jews considerably narrowed by the nineteenth century, but then widened with the presence of the British. The "white" Jews grew wealthy and powerful, outdistancing their less privileged brethren. This influence grew even stronger when they were joined by the affluent merchants who had come from Iraq. Soon the higher caste numbered only fifty families, and nothing took place in the Jewish community without their approval. On the other hand, these families spared no effort or means to add beauty and meaning to the life of the community, both in the splendor of the synagogue and the vibrancy of communal life. Emissaries from abroad, however, found the schism most disturbing from the standpoint of Jewish unity.

A totally new element came into Jewish life in India after World War I and again when Jews from Europe came to India to escape the wave of Nazism. What could have become a major center of the Jewish Diaspora was dissipated when the Moslems and Hindus became involved in bloody riots and the British announced their intention to withdraw from the sub-continent. The more recent Jewish arrivals decided to seek refuge elsewhere.

When the State of Israel was proclaimed, the Jewish population in India numbered some 24,000 souls — 15,000 Bene Israel, 3,000 Cochin Jews, and 6,000 Iraqi Jews. Many of the latter subsequently moved to England. Most of those who immigrated to Israel were Bene Israel.

Georgia

According to Georgian-Jewish tradition, the first Jews to reach this region came following the exile of the Ten Tribes from the Kingdom of Israel. But most of their memories date from the Kuzari dynasty, apparently a time of well-being for Georgian Jews, which lasted from the eighth through the eleventh and twelfth centuries, when the fate of the Jews changed as a result of the spread of Christianity in Georgia. With this new era came a period of persecution, and many Jews were forced to flee, while others converted to Christianity. Nevertheless, a fairly large community remained true to Judaism.

After the Mongolian invasion (1234) the situation of the Jews deteriorated even further. Many were forced into the service of Christian feudal lords, and their status was that of slaves. This state of affairs continued until the Russian conquest at the beginning of the nineteenth century. The suffering of the Jews under feudalism was great; many feudal lords treated their serfs like animals. Those who were vassals on the estates of churches and monasteries suffered most. They were under constant pressure to convert to Christianity. A Jewish serf who converted would be liberated, be given a plot of land, and turn from a slave into a master. But despite their great suffering and their poverty most of the Jews remained true to their faith. And despite their bitter fate the Georgian Jews were not a sad people; they were well-known for their merriment and love of life.

In the year 1804 Caucasia was conquered by the Russians. Jews were forbidden to live anywhere in the empire save for the Pale of Settlement — primarily in Poland. Caucasia was also recognized as an area of Jewish settlement, because of the many thousands of Jews there. In the middle of the nineteenth century the Czarist regime tried to expel the Jews from Georgia, but the Georgian administration refused, claiming that the Jews were essential to the economy of the State. The Jews suffered greatly under the Czarist regime. Nevertheless, their numbers grew. At the end of the nineteenth century some 30,000 Jews lived in Georgia. In 1921 the Soviets took control of Georgia and put an end to its autonomy. Many Jews moved from the villages to the larger communities and some left for Istanbul and Palestine. At the same time, several thousand Jews came to Georgia from Poland, Lithuania, and Russia. The Georgian Jews welcomed them. Russian rabbis and ritual slaughterers worked hard to improve Jewish education in Georgia, and to raise the religious and spiritual level of the Georgian community.

Georgian Jews lived in extended families which included grandfathers and married sons with their families. It was a patriarchal framework in which the head of the family had unquestioned authority. This structure kept them within the bounds of Judaism and prevented assimilation. The community lived apart in its own neighborhoods, in very crowded conditions. As many as 16 people often shared one room. The Soviet authorities tried to ease their crowded conditions by moving them to other neighborhoods but the Jews resisted, preferring to live among Jews.

The Georgian Jews' financial situation at the end of the nineteenth and the beginning of the twentieth centuries was very poor. A few were farmers, but most were peddlers or small-time traders. The peddlers wandered from village to village selling their wares, careful not to eat the gentiles' food, and sleeping under the stars rather than in non-Jewish homes. The establishment of the Soviet regime abolished private trade, which threatened the livelihood of most of the Jews of Georgia. In the

Painting of a Georgian Jewish woman in typical dress.

1920s and '30's their financial situation was grave. The Soviets set up communal government workshops, but despite pressure from the authorities the Jews refused to work in them on the Sabbath and festivals.

The Georgian Jews faithfully preserved the Hebrew language. They spoke Georgian in dealing with non-Jews and in everyday speech at home and in the street, but the Hebrew language maintained a special status. Every Jew used it three times a day in his prayers, and heard Hebrew verses from the Bible spoken in the synagogue. There were always families in each community who spoke Hebrew as well as Georgian.

Learning Hebrew was an important part of Georgian Jewish education. The holy language was generally taught in a *heder* in the synagogue. The students were divided into three groups according to their levels. The first group, after learning the Hebrew alphabet, moved on to read the prayerbook. Gradually, they joined in the life of the synagogue and on Saturdays would be allowed to read passages of the prayers in place of the cantor. This was their reward for diligence in learning. The second group studied the translation of the Bible, beginning with the Book of Genesis and ending with the last book of the Bible. They also learned to chant the biblical verses and the more advanced pupils studied the Rashi commentaries on the Bible. This group included boys who were about to have their Bar Mitzvah and they took part in reading the Bible in the synagogue on the Sabbath. The third group studied the Oral Law and the Commentaries, and the Legal Commentaries (Mishnah, Gemara, and Halacha). The graduates of this group, usually few in number, became the rabbis and ritual slaughterers in the community.

Georgian Jewry was very rich in rituals and ceremonies in which the entire community took part. As with other Jewish communities, the ceremonies were primarily connected with synagogue, festivals, and family events such as birth, marriage, and mourning. Of all these, the wedding celebrations were the most elaborate.

Marriages were arranged by the parents. Georgian Jewish women, particularly the young girls, rarely left their homes, and there was hardly any opportunity for a young boy and girl to meet by chance or in mixed company. It was the custom for the parents or relatives to arrange the match, and the young couple did not meet until the wedding ceremony. The families agreed to make an alliance between themselves and the date of the engagement was set. The bridegroom's father then invited friends and relatives to his home, which would be lit with candles and many lights. The bridegroom's father gave the rabbi two gold coins and some precious stones, with which the rabbi, as the father's representative, would sanctify the bride. Then the father and all his guests walked to the bride's house in procession carrying lighted candles. One of them carried a large tray holding candies and special pastries, nuts, and fruit. The tray was covered with a silk kerchief, and it was given as a gift to the bride.

The bride's family and guests waited at her house. The rabbi gave the bride's father one of the gold coins and the precious stones he had received from the bridegroom's father. These served to bind the agreement between the families. The rabbi then entered the women's room where the bride sat with members of her family. He gave her the second gold coin he had received from the bridegroom's father. When the rabbi came into the room the bride removed the scarf from her face

Pupils in traditional Caucasian dress on a school celebration, Sackhere, Georgia.

so the rabbi could see her. Then a feast was held. Later the master of the house distributed lumps of sugar and candles, which guests lit as the procession returned to the bridegroom's home.

Sometimes several months elapsed between the engagement and the wedding ceremony, and during that time the two families continued sending each other gifts, especially on festivals, when special delicacies would be exchanged. During this time the articles required for the wedding were prepared — clothes, dishes, furniture, and so on.

Marriage celebrations went on for two weeks. The wedding was generally conducted on a Thursday night. The celebrations began on the previous Sabbath, with feasts held at the homes of the bride and bridegroom and attended by the members of both families. During the week preceding the wedding the bride's relatives held feasts and she was guest of honor in one home after the next. Other relatives were also invited to these feasts, and there was dancing to the accompaniment of drums. On the third evening, the families of the bride and groom held feasts at which they ate and drank and exchanged gifts. A procession set out from the bridegroom's house, carrying lighted candles, a tray holding round loaves of bread with candles stuck in them, and a bowl full of henna to paint the hands of the bride and the fingers of her relatives. The henna ceremony went on until the morning, when the bride was led in procession with singing and dancing to the ritual bath house.

On the day of the wedding ceremony the celebration reached its height. The guests gathered in the bride's house and gave her gifts. The dowry the family had prepared for the bride was put on display — clothes, household articles, bedlinen. The monetary value of the items and gifts the bride had received from her relatives was assessed and written on the reverse side of the *Ketuba* in witness of the dowry brought by the bride to her husband's household.

Later the bride and her relatives, carrying lighted candles, set out for the bridegroom's house, accompanied by Armenian musicians playing tunes on violins and balalaikas. The bride wore a long silk dress with a white veil that reached down to her ankles. The wedding ceremony was conducted in the center of the synagogue, on a platform. The canopy consisted of a prayer shawl spread over the heads of the bride and groom. The rabbi conducted the ceremony. It was the custom for the groom to hold an earthenware jug of wine in his hand, and after betrothing the bride with the ring to dip the ring in the wine. Then the bride drank wine from the jug, after which the bridegroom smashed it. The wedding feast was held in the bridegroom's house. The celebrations continued during the Sabbath following the wedding, and for the entire week ensuing feasts were held in the houses of the couple and their relatives.

After the days of feasting were over, any of the bride's possessions that still remained in her parents' home were taken to the bridegroom's house. The bride kept away from her parents' home for a specified length of time, as a sign that the marriage was successful. If a quarrel arose between the couple the groom sent his wife to her parents' house or she ran away to them. If their married life was smooth the bride's parents invited the young couple to visit them after a number of weeks or months, and held a feast in their honor. This visit lasted several days and sometimes even weeks.

For generations Jerusalem occupied a central place in the consciousness of the Georgian Jews. In many homes there were Stars of David and paintings of scenes from the Land of Israel. The first of the modern immigrants from Georgia to Israel came in the mid-nineteenth century. They established a new neighborhood outside the walls of the Old City of Jerusalem and called it ''Faithful City.''

After the establishment of the State of Israel many Georgian Jews attempted to immigrate to Israel, but the USSR prevented this. After the Six Day War, Georgian Jewry embarked on a bitter struggle to be allowed to leave Georgia, and during the 1970's approximately 30,000 immigrants — about half of the Jewish population of Georgia — were allowed to leave.

The members of the dark-skinned tribe who live in northwest Ethiopia, around Lake Tanna, call themselves "the House of Israel." The local people call them *Falashas* — a derogatory name which means foreigners, invaders. The members of this tribe are indeed different from the other tribes they live among, but they are certainly not recently arrived foreigners. The house of Israel is one of the oldest tribes in Ethiopia. Anthropologists associate them with the Agau tribal group, namely, the original Hamite population of Ethiopia which preceded the Semite conquerors from southern Arabia and founded the Aksum dynasty, giving the country its name and language.

In religion, too, Judaism preceded Christianity in Ethiopia by hundreds of years.

In the fourth century, when the royal household at Aksum became Christian and decided to make Christianity the state religion, some of the population refused to adopt the new faith. These were the forefathers of the Ethiopian Jews.

When did Jews come to Ethiopia? They maintain that they are the descendants of King Solomon. According to their tradition, when the Queen of Sheba (whom they claim was the queen of Ethiopia, and whose name was Makeda) came to King Solomon in Jerusalem, a romance developed between the two, and she bore a child whom she called Manilk. She returned home with the child, and when he grew up she sent him to Jerusalem to his father, King Solomon, who tutored him in the Jewish religion. When Manilk reached manhood his father appointed him king of Ethiopia. Manilk, accompanied by a group of his father's best advisers, went off to this new kingdom — and the House of Israel are the descendants of those young men.

The first historical evidence of the existence of a Jewish settlement on the west coast of the Red Sea is found in Greek books that date from the second century B.C.E. It is assumed that the settlement was founded by Jewish traders who came there on business prior to the destruction of the Temple. On the trade routes they crossed both sea and land along the length of the Nile. There was an ancient Jewish settlement on the island of Elephantine in Upper Egypt as far back as the sixth century B.C.E. It is assumed that the settlement in Ethiopia was one of the trade satellites of this community. Another hypothesis is that Jewish traders in the Second Temple period engaged in missionary activities, and apparently had considerable success in Ethiopia among the Agau tribes. Many converts joined the Jewish settlers. It is commonly accepted that Judaism was prevalent in Ethiopia before Christianity reached there.

Persecution of the Jews commenced after the royal household at Aksum adopted Christianity. The Jews were banished from the coastal area and cut off from international travel routes. A long period of isolation from Jewish communities throughout the Diaspora set in. Nothing whatsoever of the development that took place in Judaism during the period of the Mishna and the Talmud reached the ears of the Ethiopian Jews. Because of their severe persecution by the Christians, there was no immigration of Jews from other countries to Ethiopia, and the Jews there remained an isolated tribe unknown to other Jewish communities. It was not until the ninth century that world Jewry became aware of the Ethiopian Jews. Eldad Hadani appeared before Jewish communities in North Africa, Spain, and Babylon, and spoke of Jewish tribes living in Havilah. He was most probably referring to the tribes of Ethiopian Jews, and there are some who believe that Hadani himself was an Ethiopian Jew.

According to Ethiopian sources, the Jews established an independent kingdom which existed in the ninth century, ruled by a king named Gideon and his wife Judith. According to the tradition of the House of Israel this kingdom grew strong in the tenth century and rebelled against the Christians, burning churches and monasteries. This period apparently lasted for several generations, until the Christians reconquered the area and the Ethiopian Jews were again banished to the mountainous area inland. The Christians continued the persecution for centuries to come. In the seventeenth century, the king of Ethiopia — the Negus Sussanius — even tried to annihilate the Ethiopian Jews. The chronicles of the Ethiopian kings, who were ardent Christians, describe the persecution of the Ethiopian Jews in great detail, nevertheless expressing admiration for the acts of heroism and the bravery of both men and women, who preferred to die rather than be baptized as Christians.

During the Middle Ages, stories spread through world Jewish communities that descendants of the Ten Lost Tribes were living in Ethiopia. Ethiopian Jews who

Young woman in the "Margam Byet," the hut where women live during menstruation, Wallaka village, Ethiopia.

had been taken as prisoners of war, sold as slaves in the markets of Egypt and ransomed by the Jewish community, told of their brothers in Ethiopia. In the fifteenth century the preacher Eliahu of Ferrara met an Ethiopian Jew in Jerusalem who told him stories of the wars in Ethiopia. Rabbi Ovadia of Bartenora, the famous fifteenth-century mishnaic commentator, met with Ethiopian Jews and tried to determine whether they were Karaites, who rejected rabbinical Judaism and maintained a literal interpretation of the scriptures, or whether they belonged to the mainstream of Jewry. Rabbi David Ben-Zimra — the "Ridzbaz" — the leader of Egyptian Jewry and one of the great sages of the sixteenth century — examined the question of whether the Ethiopian Jews were "rabbinical" Jews or Karaites. His conclusion was that, although the Ethiopian Jews were not acquainted with the Mishna and Talmud and followed only the laws of the Bible, they could not be designated Karaites, because in principle they did not reject the post-biblical tractates. These tractates had simply never reached them because of their isolation from other Jewish communities.

Books written by non-Jews are an interesting source of information on the Ethiopian Jews. The Scottish explorer James Bruce, in the book describing his expedition to discover the sources of the Nile at the end of the eighteenth century, devoted an entire chapter to the Ethiopian Jews. But authoritative and detailed information on the faith and practices of the Ethiopian Jews first reached Europe through the French explorer Antoine D'Abadi in the mid-nineteenth century. This information, along with rumors of extensive activity by Christian missionaries among the Ethiopian Jews, moved the Franco-Jewish association Alliance Israélite Universelle to try and find out the truth in the stories about dark-skinned Jews in Ethiopia. They sent the Orientalist Joseph Halevi on a fact-finding mission. He collected data, acquired manuscripts of their religious literature, and as evidence also brought back with him to France two young men of the Ethiopian Jewish tribe. He maintained that according to his investigations the Ethiopian Jews were Jews in every respect, and that the Jewish community should help them in their distress. But it was only several decades later, in 1905, when Halevi's pupil, Dr. Yaakov Feitelovitch, reached Ethiopia that he succeeded in persuading some communities in Europe and later in the United States to help the Ethiopian Jews. The Ethiopian Jews differed in their practices and religious traditions from the other Jewish communities, and he made great efforts to bring them into the fold of traditional Judaism.

For the most part, the Ethiopian Jews live in villages in sections separated from the other inhabitants. They live in traditional Ethiopian round huts called *tokols*, which are made of branches and grass covered with plaster. Furnishings are meager — beds, mattresses, and a few stools. The cooking utensils are generally made of earthenware, and the cooking is done over a fire or an oven.

The men are employed as shepherds or farmworkers. In general the Ethiopian Jews do not own land, but work as laborers for poor wages. They engage in various trades that are considered menial and which have traditionally been reserved for Ethiopian Jews — weaving, pottery, blacksmithing, and so forth. Very few among them are merchants, since this would require direct contact with the non-Jews, which the Ethiopian Jews avoid at all costs.

Family structure among the Ethiopian Jews is patriarchal, and respect for the old is a most important value. The men have only one wife, and the family framework is considered sacrosanct. The women perform traditional roles in housekeeping and child rearing. The grandfather is usually the head of the family.

Religious life centers around the *Masgid* — the synagogue — which is generally a round wood and plaster hut somewhat larger than the other village huts, but is sometimes a square stone building. The entrance is at the eastern side. The synagogue is generally divided into two parts, separated by a curtain. The inner part, where the priests and their helpers enter, is the "holy of holies" — and contains a table that holds a Bible written in the Gez language on parchment, though not in the form of a scroll but in book form. Before entering the synagogue shoes are removed. The priests traditionally cover their heads, but the other congregants are not required to do so. There is no special place for women in the synagogue, and those who come to pray stand in the back or behind some kind of partition. During prayer they turn towards Jerusalem. Prayers are said with passion to the accompaniment of drums and cymbals, singing, hand movements, and genuflection.

Prayers are recited in Gez and are repeated by rote. Generally only the priests and their assistants know the prayers, and the other worshippers say Amen and join in the singing of some parts. On weekdays only the old and the unoccupied take part in services, but on Sabbaths and festivals all the members of the community come to the synagogue.

Beside the synagogue there is an altar for sacrifices. At the time of Dr. Feitelovitch's visit, the Ethiopian Jews sacrificed on every new moon. Later, because of the decline in their financial situation and also through the influence of Dr. Feitelovitch, who was against the sacrifices, this custom was stopped in almost all the Ethiopian Jewish communities. Only the Passover sacrifice was maintained.

Every Ethiopian Jewish community has priests who care for its religious needs, helped by the *daftars* — cantors, beadles, and teachers. Unlike in other Jewish communities, the priests are not considered descendants of Aaron, nor is the priesthood passed down from father to son. The priests are appointed on the basis of scholarship. In large communities with several priests the most respected of them bears the title of High Priest. The Ethiopian Jews also have hermits who isolate themselves from worldly life and spend their time praying and studying the scriptures. They are regarded as saints. Nowadays very few hermits remain.

The basis of all Ethiopian Jewish religious life is the word of the Bible, tempered with their own traditions that have been handed down from generation to generation. The long years of isolation and hardship, however, somewhat blurred even specific biblical precepts. This led to the disappearance of some observances, such as the fringed garments, phylacteries, *mezuzot,* blowing of the ram's horn on Rosh Hashana, etc.

The Sabbath is observed very strictly by the Ethiopian Jews. They start preparing for it as early as Thursday, when they wash their clothes and bathe. The women prepare the Sabbath meal only after bathing in the river. On Friday, all work stops at midday, when the house is arranged for the Sabbath and festive clothes are donned. Before sunset the oven fires are extinguished although it is the custom to leave a fire burning for light until it goes out by itself on Friday night. This is a special light which was once made from special materials such as wax or grasses, but now gas lamps are used.

The Sabbath service begins at sunset and is attended by all the villagers. On Saturday morning the priests and the elders arise early for morning prayers and are joined by the rest of the villagers later. After the service there is a communal Sabbath meal. Each woman prepares a special dish for her family, as well as a drink somewhat like beer. The dishes are brought to the synagogue and after prayers the priests bless the bread and then all the families eat together, accompanying the meal with songs. Later in the day there are additional prayers and another Sabbath meal.

The Ethiopian Jews are very strict about not working on the Sabbath. All tasks in the household and in the fields are strictly forbidden until the stars come out on Saturday night. Nor do they leave the village or carry anything outside their huts. They wear special robes without belts so that they will not need to tie them as they do on weekdays. Even circumcision, which is performed on the eighth day after birth, is delayed until Sunday if the eighth day falls on a Saturday. They take care not to desecrate the Sabbath even for someone dangerously ill. But in time of war or attack they defend themselves even on the Sabbath.

The Saturdays of the year are divided into groups of seven. The seventh Sabbath of each group is the most sacred, with special prayers and great festivity.

Festivals are celebrated according to a special calendar based on the lunar year. Ethiopian Jews are not familiar with the Hebrew calendar, nor do they have a tradition of counting the years since creation. Even so, the festivals come out on dates close to those observed by other Jewish communities. The names of their months are similar to the Hebrew names, such as "Lissan" for Nissan, "Tomas" for Tammuz, "Lull" for Elul, and so on.

The Ethiopian Jews count the months starting from Nissan, and the first day of the seventh month from Nissan, celebrated throughout Jewry as Rosh Hashana, is celebrated by the Ethiopian Jews, although not as the New Year. They do not blow the *shofar*, which is the main commandment of that day, but instead beat drums and clash cymbals. They call the holiday "the festival of light" and also "the festival of trumpeting," and their prayers mention the blowing of the ram's horn and the binding of Isaac, which took place on this day, according to their tradition. The festival is celebrated for only one day, rather than the two in other communities. On this day all work is forbidden except for tasks connected with the preparation of food, such as gathering fruit, lighting the cooking fire, and so on.

The ten days between "the festival of light" and the Day of Atonement are days of repentance and forgiveness, and the priests and elders fast on these days. The Day of Atonement is called *Ba'al Esterai* — which means the festival of atonement. It takes place on the tenth day of the seventh month, and is a fast day for all from one evening to the next. Children from the age of seven are obliged to fast. As the day begins people ask each other's forgiveness, and most of the day and the night is spent in prayer. The biblical commandment, "Afflict your souls" (Numbers 29:7) is interpreted as an injunction to torture the body, and they therefore try to stay awake all night. Another prevalent practice is to punish their bodies with rhythmic jumping during and between prayers. At the end of the Day of Atonement they scatter seeds for the birds, whom they consider symbols of the dead souls remembered on that day, and also as a sign of their hope that their prayers will be

Kohen Bayene holding a fly whisk in the synagogue of the Wallaka village, Ethiopia.

answered. At the end of the day the women bring food and drink to break the fast in the synagogue. This feast is blessed by the priest and goes on until late at night.

On the fifteenth day of the seventh month, the Ethiopian Jews celebrate the eight-day festival of *Ba'al Metzalat* — meaning the festival of shade or the thatch. They build *sukkot* next to the houses or the synagogue, although in some areas they continue to live in their own huts, since these are constructed in accordance with the laws of making *sukkot.* The tradition of blessing the four different kinds of plants is not practiced. During the holiday, which is a harvest festival, it is their custom to bring some of their produce to the synagogue — corn and peppers ripen at this time — and the priest blesses them. During the eight days of the festival only essential work is permitted and the days are mostly spent spent in festivity and prayer, and also in visiting relatives in other villages. The first and the eighth days are considered more special than the others, but there are no additional prohibitions on work. The festival of Simhat Torah is not known to the Ethiopian Jews. Hanukah is not celebrated at all, and Purim is not a day of rejoicing, as prescribed in the Book of Esther. It is preserved as a day of remembrance of Esther's fast. Many of the priests and elders fast for three days (eating at night) in memory of the occasion.

On the fourteenth day of the month of *Lissan* (Nissan), the Passover sacrifice is slaughtered on the stone altar next to the synagogue. The festival, called *Passiha,* lasts for seven days, and bread and other leavened food is forbidden. Before the festival the house is cleaned and the leavened food is burned. New earthenware dishes are used for Passover. A special unleavened bread called *kita* is baked, similar to the hand-baked *matza* in some communities.

On the first evening of the festival they eat the Passover sacrifice, which has been roasted whole on the fire, and the priests tell the story of the exodus from Egypt.

200

Work is forbidden on all the seven days of Passover. To mark the end of the festival, they prepare bread and beer. First the priests are offered their share and then the family eats the rest.

"*Ba'al Ma'erachi*," the harvest festival, is celebrated on the fiftieth day after the seventh day of Passover, and not as in other communities, which count the fifty days from the first day of Passover. On this day they bring to the synagogue some of the harvest and bread for the priests to bless. Shavuot occurs on the twelfth day of the third month from Nissan, and is regarded as the day when the Law was given.

' In the Ethiopian Jewish tradition there are some special festivals: the first day of each month is a festival when no work is done and special prayers are said. The first day of Nissan is the most festive. On it special bread is baked, a sheep is slaughtered and a special prayer offered. The eighteenth day of the sixth month (Elul), commemorates the death of the forefathers Abraham, Isaac, and Jacob. The twenty-ninth day of the eighth month (Heshvan), the day of *Sigad*, is celebrated publicly. The villagers gather early in the day and in the morning they all go up to the hilltop, stopping many times on the way. The priests stand at the top of the hill holding a Bible. They are separated by a partition and all the congregation stands around them. They read passages from the Bible and also from the books of Ezra and Nehemiah. They say prayers and preach sermons on adhering to the traditional Law. The entire community fasts throughout the day. In the evening they go back to their villages, where they break the fast with meat and tasty dishes, accompanied by singing and dancing.

The Ethiopian Jews are strict about the dietary regulations of the Law. Most of these are similar to the rules followed by other Jewish communities, but some of the details are different. They eat only the meat of animals permitted by the Law. The animals are slaughtered by the priest or someone specially trained for this. During the slaughter the animal's head is turned to face Jerusalem and the priest says a special blessing in which reference is made to the Ten Commandments. They prepare the meat by removing the blood in a special way. After stripping off the skin they remove the arteries, cut the meat into small pieces, which they soak in salted water and rinse thoroughly. The pieces of meat are hung up to dry so that any blood left in the meat will drip out. Another way of removing the blood is by dipping the meat in boiling water several times. They do not cook the meat with milk and generally take care to use separate dishes. The Ethiopian Jews will not eat food that has been touched by non-Jews.

The laws concerning purification and defilement take a central place in the life of the Ethiopian Jews. They bathe and wash their clothes frequently, and therefore they choose to live near rivers. Their Christian neighbors mock them and say that the Ethiopian Jews can be recognized by the smell of water coming from them. Anyone who comes into contact with a non-Jew and anyone who is defiled by contact with the dead is obliged to bathe and purify himself, and only then can he go home and eat with his family. Women who are menstruating leave their homes and live outside the village in a special hut called the "blood hut." The family brings them food on special dishes. A boundary of stones around the hut marks the area into which the pure must not enter. The woman returns to her home after seven days, after washing her clothes and bathing in the river. A woman who is about to

A Jewish woman burning a hole in a pumpkin, Wallak village, Ethiopia.

give birth goes to the blood hut, and here the birth takes place. If the baby is a boy she stays here with it for eight days, and if it is a girl for fourteen days.

On the eighth day the baby boy is circumcised in the blood hut. The people gather round to watch the circumciser perform the ceremony, while the priest stands at a distance, taking care not to approach the hut. The circumcision is not a festive occasion. The circumciser says a blessing recalling Abraham's pact with God and the forefathers and the Ten Commandments. At the same time the priest slaughters a fowl and its blood is put on the cuts, and he too says blessings and prayers. Circumcision is strictly observed, and a person who is not circumcised is considered unclean and defiled and like a non-Jew.

On the day of the circumcision the woman washes her clothes and bathes in water and then moves to a different hut called the childbearer's hut. Here she remains until 40 days after the birth of the child. A woman who gives birth to a daughter goes through the same process of purification on the fourteenth day after the birth, and then goes to the childbearer's hut until 80 days after the birth. At the end of this time she again washes her clothes, washes the baby and bathes in the river. When she returns home the priest reads a prayer and sprinkles pure water over her from a new earthenware dish. He also sprinkles the water over the baby and on the walls and floor of the house, a symbol of purification.

After the ceremony the baby is named and the mother prepares a meal to be eaten in the presence of the village people.

Family life is strictly observed by the Ethiopian Jews. The religious framework and the customs associated with the ceremonies of matchmaking and marriage have been passed down from earlier generations. The marriage arrangements are made by the fathers of the bride and groom when the boy is 18 and the girl is 13. At the matchmaking ceremony the bride's family is given jewels, and they give the groom's family bulls, cows, and so forth.

The wedding ceremony takes place a few years later. Three days before the wedding there are celebrations in the homes of the bride and the groom, each in their separate villages. On the day before the wedding the bride paints her nails and her hands and feet red in a special ceremony accompanied by sacrificing a sheep and feasting.

At the same time the groom's family celebrates the *Keshara* — the tying. The priest blesses the groom and takes two threads or ribbons colored red and white. The white symbolizes the purity of the bridegroom, and the red the purity of the bride. The priest puts the ribbons next to the bridegroom's feet, and moves them upwards past his knees to his heart and finally ties them around his forehead. Then the priests and all the crowd burst into song and dance in honor of the bridegroom. After the tying ceremony the groom is taken on a horse or a mule to the bride's village, while the family bring the presents for the bride.

The bride and her friends wait in a large hut in the village. When the bridegroom's party arrives the wedding ceremony begins. In the presence of the priests and the witnesses the marriage document, the *Ketuba,* is drawn up in three copies, to be given to the bridegroom, the bride, and the priest conducting the marriage. The deed is signed by the bride and groom and by a guarantor chosen by both parties. He accompanies all stages of the ceremony. After the signing of the deed the priest blesses the couple with fertility, the bride's parents take leave of their daughter, and the young couple go to the bridegroom's village.

After a feast accompanied by singing and dancing the young couple go to consummate the marriage in a special house. If the bride is found to be a virgin the crowd cheers and the message is sent to her parents in their village. The marriage celebrations go on for seven days.

If it is found that the bride is not a virgin the bridegroom informs the guarantor and the sponsors and removes the ribbon from his forehead. The marriage deeds are torn up and a divorce document is written. Divorce also occurs if the couple start arguing after being married for some time. In this case the priest, the witnesses, and the guarantor who were present at the wedding meet together with the couple. The priest tears up the wedding documents, and in their place a deed of divorce is drawn up, signed by the husband, the wife, the priest, the witnesses, and the guarantor. The woman is given the divorce document and she is now free to marry anyone.

Ethiopian Jews do not marry blood relations and men do not have more than one wife.

When a person dies they make every effort to bury him on the same day. At the funeral and the burial the priest says prayers of expiation. After the funeral the family returns home and sits on the ground for seven days. Those who come to pay their condolences are received with weeping and mourning and sometimes a special mourning dance is performed. A public sacrifice is offered on the seventh day, which is the day of purification of the soul, and also on the first anniversary of the death.

The cemetery is outside the village and the grave is marked by a heap of stones or by a tree planted over it. There is no gravestone or special sign of a grave. The Ethiopian Jews tend to have a separate cemetery for children. The location of the graves is determined by the importance of the deceased.

During the Middle Ages the community numbered hundreds of thousands and they lived in several regions. Their numbers dwindled as a result of persecution. In the mid-nineteenth century Joseph Halevi estimated that there were 150,000. They lived in several regions around Lake Tanna in northwest Ethiopia. In recent years some of the families and young people have moved to urban areas, particularly to Gundar and also to Addis Abbaba and Asmara. But the majority continue to live in their own small villages, or in separate groups of houses neighboring on the Christian villages. The community is scattered throughout hundreds of small villages in the various regions, with a few families, generally no more than fifteen, in each village. The village is always near a water source such as a river, a spring or a lake, that serves for ritual bathing. The language is that of the surrounding area: Amharic in Amhara, in the Gundar region; Tigrani in Tigri in northeast Ethiopia. The priests and the elders know the prayers and the scriptures written in Gez, which is the ancient language of Ethiopia, and which is also used in the Ethiopian Church.

Since the 1970's groups of Ethiopian Jews began to immigrate to Israel, with the pressure to leave growing as their situation deteriorated. In 1983 the number of Ethiopian Jews was estimated at about 30,000. Since then more than half this number has immigrated to Israel, and today it is estimated that there are less than 10,000 of the House of Israel still remaining in Ethiopia.

Glossary

abaya   burnoose

afikoman   *matza* eaten at conclusion of Passover *Seder* meal

aliya   immigration to Israel

almada'i   beadle (see *shamash*)

brit   circumcision

couscous   North African dish

etrog   citron, used on Sukkot together with *lulav* and two other species

hamin   stew made from meat and potatoes (and/or beans) left simmering overnight

haftara   passage from the Prophets read at the end of the Torah reading in the synagogue

Haggadah   text of Passover story

hakafot   procession inside synagogue during the Simhat Torah services

hamantashen   triangular pastry of poppyseed eaten on Purim

hametz   leavened bread

harosset   a mixture of nuts, apples, cinnamon, and wine, resembling clay, for the *Seder*

havdala   ceremony involving wine, lit candle and spices, marking the termination of the Sabbath

heder   old-fashioned Jewish primary school

hevra kadisha   Burial Society

hupa   wedding canopy

kaddish   mourner's prayer

kadi   Moslem judge

kaparot   "ransom" for sins, during the High Holidays

ketuba   marriage contract with financial guarantees for wife

kiddush   prayer sanctifying wine, usually at beginning of Sabbath or holiday meal

kittel   white robe

kohen   member of the priestly branch of the tribe of Levi

levi   member of the tribe of Levi, with special religious status (but not a *kohen*)

matza   unleavened bread, mandatory for Passover meals

megillah   scroll or book

menora   lamp, candelabrum

mezuza   biblical text (Deut. 6:4-9) hand-printed on parchment, encased in wood or metal and affixed to doorpost

mikve   ritual bath

minha   the afternoon prayer

mishloach manot   a gift of food exchanged on Purim

Mishna   basic commentary on the Bible (the basic codification of the Oral Law)

mitzva   commandment

mohel   performer of circumcision ritual

ne'ila   service concluding Yom Kippur prayers

pita   flat bread (from Arabic)

Seder   Passover meal-service commemorating the Exodus from Egypt

sefira   the counting of the 49 days between Passover and Shavuot

selihot   penitential prayers recited before and during the High Holidays

shamash   beadle; also, candle used to light the eight Hanukah candles
sharif   Moslem ruler
Shema Yisrael   "Hear O Israel" (Deut. 6:4)
shiva   seven (days of mourning)
shofar   ram's horn used as trumpet
shohet   slaughterer of fowl and cattle in accordance with Jewish law
sukka   makeshift hut with roof of foliage constructed for holiday of Sukkot, in commemoration of the Israelites' sojourn in the wilderness
Talmud   compendium of the Oral Law (Mishna and ensuing discussions)
tzaddik   righteous man
yeshiva   Talmudic academy
Zohar   basic Kabbalistic work

BEN-ZVI, YITZHAK. *Journeys Along the Pathways of Israel and Its Neighbors* (Hebrew). Jerusalem, 1965.

_____. *The Exiled of Israel* (Hebrew). Tel Aviv, 1954.

_____. *The Tribes of Israel,* President's Residence, Jerusalem (Hebrew). Tel Aviv, 1959.

Memorial Volume for Yitzhak Ben-Zvi (Hebrew). Jerusalem, 1964.

DINUR, BEN-ZION. *The History of Israel in the Diaspora* (Hebrew). Tel Aviv, 1960.

GOITEIN, S.D. *Jews and the Arabs, Their Contact Through the Ages.* New York, 1953.

LESCHINSKY, JACOB. *The Book of Jewish Dispersion* (Hebrew).

MENDELSSON, SIDNEY. *The Jews of Asia.* New York, 1920.

ROBINSON, NEHEMIA. *The Arab Countries of the Near East and Their Jewish Communities.* New York, 1951.

THON, HANNAH HELENA. *"The Communities of Israel: Chapters in Their Histories and the Tribulations of Their Taking Root in Eretz Israel"* (Hebrew). Jerusalem, 1957.

TRAVELS

Benjamin of Tudela. Edited by A. Asher. London-Berlin, 1840–41.

BENJAMIN, J.J. *Eight Years in Asia and Africa, from 1846 to 1855.* Hanover, 1859.

BRAVER, ABRAHAM JACOB. *The Dusty Road* (Hebrew). Tel Aviv, 1946.

DAINARD, EPHRAIM. *Travels in the Eastern Lands* (Hebrew). Pressburg, 1882.

DAVID D'BET HILLEL. *The Travels of David d'bet Hillel from Jerusalem through Arabia, Kurdistan, Part of Persia and India to Madras.* Madras, 1832.

NEUMARK, EPHRAIM, *Travels in the East* (Hebrew). Edition A. Yaari, Jerusalem, 1947.

SAPHIR, YAACOV. *Sapphire Stone* (Hebrew). Lick, 1866.

Travels of Petachia of Ratisbon. Trans. A. Benisch. London, 1856.

Travel Treasury: Collection of travels of Jewish travelers in Eretz Yisrael, Syria, Egypt and other countries. I.D. Eisenstein, New York, 1927.

YAARI, AVRAHAM. *Travels of a Safad Emissary in Eastern Lands* (Hebrew). Jerusalem, 1942.

PERIODICALS AND ANTHOLOGIES

Mahanayim. Ed. Menahem Hacohen (Hebrew): *The Exiled of Israel,* vol. 93–94. Israel Defence Forces, 1964; *Communities of the East I,* 114, 1967; *Communities of the East, II,* 119, 1968.

Sefunot, Yearbook of Research on Jewish Communities in the East (Hebrew). Vols. 1–4, 1954–1957.

Edot, Folklore and Ethnology Quarterly (Hebrew). Ed. Raphael Patai and Joseph Rivlin. Jerusalem.

East and West (Hebrew).

Echo of the East (Hebrew).

In the Diaspora (Hebrew).

Yeda Am (Hebrew).

NORTH AFRICA

ANSKY, MICHAEL. *Algerian Jewry, from the Cremieux Ordinance to Independence* (Hebrew, translated from the French source, Paris, 1950). Jerusalem, 1963.

ATTAL, ROBERT. *A Bibliography of Publications Concerning Libyan Jerwry.* In the Memorial Volume of Yitzhak Ben-Zvi, *Sefunot* IX. Jerusalem, 1965.

_____. *Comprehensive Bibliographical List on North Africa* (Hebrew). (In *Sefunot,* vol. V).

BEN-NAIM, YOSEF. *Kings of Scholars* (Hebrew). Jerusalem, 1931.

DELACROIX, EUGENE. *Un Mariage Juif au Maroq.* Oeuvres Littéraires I, Etudes Esthétiques.

HIRSCHBERG, H.Z. *A History of the Jews in North Africa.* Jerusalem, 1965.
_____. *Inside Magreb: the Jews in North Africa.* Jerusalem, 1957.
Libyan Jewry. Pub. Committee of Libyan Communities in Israel (Hebrew). Tel Aviv, 1960.
MALKA, ELI. *Essai d'Ethnographie Traditionelle des Mellahs.* Rabbat, 1946.
ROMANILI, SHMUEL. *Aspiration in Arabia* (Hebrew). Warsaw, 1926.
SLOUSCHTZ, NAHUM. *Travels in North Africa.* Philadelphia, 1927.
_____. *The Jews of North Africa.* Philadelphia, 1944.
_____. *My Travels in Libya* (Hebrew). Tel Aviv, 1938–1943.
_____. *The Island of Fali* (Jerba) (Hebrew). Tel Aviv, 1957.
TOLEDANO, YAACOV MOSHE. *Light of the West,* History of Moroccan Jewry (Hebrew). Jerusalem, 1911.

IRAQ
BEN-JACOB, ABRAHAM. *A History of the Jews in Iraq* (Hebrew). Jerusalem, 1959.
_____. *Kurdistan Jewish Communities* (Hebrew). Jerusalem, 1961.
BRAUER, ERICH. *The Jews of Kurdistan, an Ethnological Study* (Hebrew). Jerusalem, 1947.
FISCHEL, WALTER J. *The Jews of Kurdistan. B'nei Brith Magazine,* Cincinnati, 1932.
POLAK, A.N. *Babylonian Jewry* (Hebrew). Israel Defence Forces, 1959.
SASSOON, DAVID SOLOMON. *History of the Jews in Baghdad.* Letchworth, 1949.

PERSIA (IRAN)
ADLER, E.N. *The Persian Jews, Their Books and Ritual. Jewish Quarterly Review,* vol. X, pp. 584. 1898.
FISCHEL, WALTER J. *Israel in Iran: The Jews, Their History, Culture and Religion.* Ed. Louis Finkelstein. Philadelphia, 1949.
MISRACHI, HANINA. *The Jews of Persia* (Hebrew). Tel Aviv, 1959.
Sources of the History of Persian Jewry. Sefunot, vol. II, p. 190. 1958.

BUKHARA
WOLF, JOSEPH. *Narrative of a Mission to Bokhara in the Years 1843–1845.* London, 1846.
YAARI, AVRAHAM. *Sifre Yehudei Bukhara* (Hebrew). Jerusalem, 1942.

CAUCASUS
BEN-ZVI, YITZHAK. *The Exiled of Israel* (Hebrew). Tel Aviv, 1954.
"Caucasus", the Jewish Encyclopedia.
CASDAI, ZVI. *The Kingdom of Ararat* (Hebrew). Odessa, 1912.
CHARNY, JOSEPH YEHUDA. *The Book of Travels in the Caucasus* (Hebrew). St. Petersburg, 1884.
NOY, DOV. *The Mountain Jews — the Tatti* (Hebrew). *Mahanayim,* vols. 93–94, 1964.

INDIA
BAR-GIORA, NAFTALI. *Travels in India* (Hebrew). Israel, 1953.
Bene-Israel: Halachic verdicts and sources for clarification of their case and the question of their origin (Hebrew). Chief Rabbinate of Israel. Jerusalem, 1962.
BENJAMIN J. ISRAEL. *Religious Evolution Among the Bene-Israel of India Since 1750.* Bombay, 1963.
CARMEL, YOSEF. *Travels to Far-flung Brethren* (Hebrew). Tel Aviv, 1957.
EZEKIEL, MOSES. *History and Culture of the Bene-Israel in India.* Nadiad, 1947.
FISCHEL, WALTER J. *The Jews in India, Their Contribution to the Economic and Political Life.* Berkeley, 1960.

KEHIMKAR, HAEEM SAMUEL. *The History of the Bene-Israel of India*. Tel Aviv, 1937.
REUBEN, REBECCA. *The Bene-Israel of Bombay*. Cambridge, 1913.

YEMEN
AKZA, ZECHARIAH BEN-SHLOMO YIHYE. *The Science of Healing in Yemen* (Hebrew). New York, 1959.
BEN-ZE'EV, ISRAEL. *The Jews in Arabia* (Hebrew). Tel Aviv, 1931.
BRAUER, ERICH. *Ethnologie den Jemenitischen Juden*. Heidelberg, 1934.
GOITEIN, S.D. *Travels of Habshush* (Hebrew). Tel Aviv, 1939.
GRIDI, SHIM'ON and I. YESHAYAHU. *From Yemen to Zion* (Hebrew). Tel Aviv, 1938.
HIRSCHBERG, H.Z. *Israel in Arabia* (Hebrew). Tel Aviv, 1946.
KAFIH, JOSEPH. *Jewish Life in San'a* (Hebrew). Jerusalem, 1961.
LEVI, NAHUM YEHUDA. *The Mysteries of Yemenite Jewry* (Hebrew). Tel Aviv, 1962.
NARKIS, M. *The Artcrafts of Yemenite Jewry* (Hebrew). Jerusalem, 1941.
RATHJENS, CARL. *Jewish Domestic Architecture in San'a, Yemen*. Jerusalem, 1957.
RATZABY, YEHUDA. *Yemenite Poems* (Hebrew). Jerusalem, 1968.
SAPIR, JACOB. *Book of Travels in Yemen* (Hebrew). Ed. Avraham Yaari. Jerusalem, 1945.
TABIB, AVRAHAM. *The Yemenite Exile* (Hebrew). Tel Aviv, 1931.
YAVNIELI, SHMUEL. *Travels to Yemen* (Hebrew). Tel Aviv, 1952.
ZADOC, JOSEPH. *Yemenite Storms, the Epic of the Magic Carpet* (Hebrew). Tel Aviv, 1956.
ZADOC, MOSHE. *History and Customs of the Jews in Yemen* (Hebrew). Tel Aviv, 1967.

EGYPT and SYRIA
ASHTOR, ELIYAHU. *History of Egyptian Jewry* (Hebrew). IDF General Staff. Israel, 1957.
BEN-SHIMON, RAPHAEL AHARON. *River of Egypt: Customs and Regulations* (Hebrew). Alexandria, 1905.
FRANKEL, DR. LUDWIG AUGUST. *Travels in Egypt*, trans. Meir Halevi Letteris. Vienna, 1862.
HAZZAN, ELIYAHU. *Neve Shalom: Customs* (Hebrew). Alexandria, 1894.
ISRAEL, YOMTOV. *Customs in Egypt* (Hebrew). Jerusalem, 1865.
LANDAU, JACOB M. *The Jews in Nineteenth Century Egypt* (Hebrew). Israel, 1967.
MANN, JACOB. *The Jews in Egypt and in Palestine Under the Fatimid Caliphs*. Oxford, 1920.
SLOUSCHTZ, NAHUM. *The Jews in Egypt* (Hebrew). Ahiassaf Almanac, 1898.
STRAUSS A. *A History of the Jews in Egypt and Syria Under Mameluke Rule* (Hebrew). Jerusalem, 1944.
TOLEDANO, YAACOV MOSHE. *Otzar Gnazim — Ancient Synagogues* (Hebrew). Jerusalem, 1960.

THE BALKANS
ARDITTI, BENJAMIN. *Bulgarian Jewry Under Nazi Rule 1940–1944* (Hebrew). 1962.
EMANUEL, J.S. *The Great Men of Salonica Down the Generations* (Hebrew). Tel Aviv, 1936.
————. *Monuments of Salonica* (Hebrew). Jerusalem, 1968.
GALANTE, ABRAHAM. *Turcs et Juifs — Etude Historique et Politique*. Istanbul, 1932.
GAON, M.D. *Eastern Jews in Eretz-Israel* (Hebrew). Jerusalem, 1938.
History of the Jews in Turkey and Eastern Lands in Recent Generations (Hebrew). Ed. Yitzhak R. Molho. Jerusalem, 1945.
MOLHO, MICHAEL and NHAMA, JOSEPH. *The Destruction of Greek Jewry, 1941–1944* (Hebrew). Jerusalem, 1965.
NEHAMA, JOSEPH. *Histoire des Israelites de Salonique*. Paris, 1935–6.
ROSANIS, SHLOMO AVRAHAM. *History of Turkish Jewry* (Hebrew). Tel Aviv, 1930.
Salonica, A Center of Jewry (Hebrew). An anthology. Jerusalem, 1967.
Treasury of Spanish Jewry. Ed. Yitzhak R. Molho. Jerusalem, 1959.